COLLE BRITISH STAMPS

A STANLEY GIBBONS CHECKLIST OF
THE STAMPS OF GREAT BRITAIN

1997 (Forty-eighth) Edition

STANLEY GIBBONS LTD

By Appointment to H. M. the Queen
Stanley Gibbons Ltd. London Philatelists.

London and Ringwood

COLLECT BRITISH STAMPS

The 1997 Edition

From the famous Penny Black of 1840 to the absorbing issues of today, the stamps of Great Britain are highly popular with collectors. *Collect British Stamps* has been our message since very early days – but particularly since the First Edition of this checklist in September 1967. This 48th edition includes all the recent issues. Prices have been carefully revised to reflect today's market. Total sales of *Collect British Stamps* are now over 3½ million copies.

Collect British Stamps appears in the autumn of each year. A more detailed Great Britain catalogue, the *Concise*, is published each spring. The *Great Britain Concise* incorporates many additional listings covering watermark varieties, phosphor omitted errors, missing colour errors, stamp booklets and special commemorative First Day Cover postmarks. It is ideally suited for the collector who wishes to discover more about GB stamps.

Listings in this edition of *Collect British Stamps* include all 1996 issues which have appeared up to the publication date.

Scope. *Collect British Stamps* comprises:

- All stamps with different watermark (*wmk*) or perforation (*perf*).
- Visible plate numbers on the Victorian issues.
- Graphite-lined and phosphor issues, including variations in the number of phosphor bands.
- First Day Covers for Definitives from 1952, Regionals and all Special Issues.
- Presentation, Gift and Souvenir Packs.
- Post Office Yearbooks.
- Regional issues and War Occupation stamps of Guernsey and Jersey.
- Postage Due and Official Stamps.
- Post Office Picture Cards (PHQ cards).
- Commemorative gutter pairs and "Traffic Light" gutter pairs listed as mint sets.
- Royal Mail Postage Labels priced as sets and on P.O. First Day Cover.

Stamps of the independent postal administrations of Guernsey, Isle of Man and Jersey are contained in *Collect Channel Islands and Isle of Man Stamps*.

Layout. Stamps are set out chronologically, by date of issue. In the catalogue lists the first numeral is the Stanley Gibbons catalogue number; the black (boldface) numeral alongside is the type number referring to the respective illustration. A blank in this column implies that the number immediately above is repeated. The denomination and colour of the stamp are then shown. Before February 1971 British currency was:

£1 = 20s   One pound = twenty shillings *and*
1s = 12d   One shilling = twelve pence.

Upon decimalisation this became:

£1 = 100p   One pound = one hundred (new) pence.

The catalogue list then shows two price columns. The left-hand is for unused stamps and the right-hand for used. Corresponding small boxes are provided in which collectors may wish to check off the items in their collection.

Our method of indicating prices is:
Numerals for pence, e.g. 10 denotes 10p (10 pence). Numerals for pounds and pence, e.g. 4·25 denotes £4·25 (4 pounds and 25 pence). For £100 and above, prices are in whole pounds and so include the £ sign and omit the zeros for pence.

Colour illustrations. The colour illustrations of stamps are intended as a guide only; they may differ in shade from the originals.

Size of illustrations. To comply with Post Office regulations stamp illustrations are three-quarters linear size. Separate illustrations of surcharges, overprints and watermarks are actual size.

Prices. Prices quoted in this catalogue are our selling prices at the time the book went to press. They are for stamps in fine condition; in issues where condition varies we may ask more for the superb and less for the sub-standard. The unused prices for stamps of Queen Victoria to King Edward VIII are for lightly hinged examples. Unused prices for King George VI and Queen Elizabeth II are for unmounted mint (though when not available unmounted, mounted stamps are often supplied at a lower price). Prices for used stamps refer to postally used copies. All prices are subject to change without prior notice and we give no guarantee to supply all stamps priced, since it is not possible to keep every catalogued item in stock. Individual low value stamps sold at 399, Strand are liable to an additional handling charge. Commemorative issues may, at times, only be available in complete sets.

In the price columns:

† = Does not exist.

(—) or blank = Exists, or may exist, but price cannot be quoted.

* = Not normally issued (the so-called 'Abnormals' of 1862–80).

Perforations. The 'perforation' is the number of holes in a length of 2 cm, as measured by the Gibbons *Instanta* gauge. The stamp is viewed against a dark background with the transparent gauge put on top of it. Perforations are quoted to the nearest half. Stamps without perforation are termed 'imperforate'.

From 1992 certain stamps occur with a large elliptical (oval) hole inserted in each line of vertical perforations. The £10 definitive, No. 1658, is unique in having two such holes in the horizontal perforations.

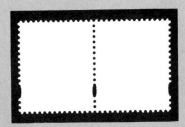

Elliptical perforations

Se-tenant combinations. *Se-tenant* means 'joined together'. Some sets include stamps of different design arranged *se-tenant* as blocks or strips and these are often collected unsevered as issued. Where such combinations exist the stamps are priced both mint and used, as singles or complete combinations. The set price for mint refers to the unsevered combination plus singles of any other values in the set. The used set price is for single stamps of all values.

First day covers. Prices for first day covers are for complete sets used on plain covers (1924, 1925, 1929) or on special covers (1935 onwards), the stamps of which are cancelled with ordinary operational postmarks (1924–1962) or by the *standard* "First Day of Issue" postmarks (1963 onwards). The British Post Office did not provide "First Day" treatment for every definitive issued after 1963. Where the stamps in a set were issued on different days, prices are for a cover from each day.

Presentation Packs. Special packs comprising slip-in cards with printed information inside a protective covering, were introduced for the 1964 Shakespeare issue. Collectors packs, containing commemoratives from the preceding twelve months, were issued from 1967. Some packs with text in German from 1968–69 exist as does a Japanese version of the pack for Nos. 916/17. Yearbooks, hardbound and illustrated in colour within a slip cover, joined the product range in 1984.

PHQ cards. Since 1973 the Post Office has produced a series of picture cards, which can be sent through the post as postcards. Each card shows an enlarged colour reproduction of a current British stamp, either of one or more values from a set or of all values. Cards are priced here in fine mint condition for sets complete as issued. The Post Office gives each card a 'PHQ' serial number, hence the term. The cards are usually on sale shortly before the date of issue of the stamps, but there is no officially designated 'first day'.

Used prices are for cards franked with the stamp depicted, on the obverse or reverse; the stamp being cancelled with an official postmark for first day of issue.

Gutter pairs. All modern Great Britain commemoratives are produced in sheets containing two panes of stamps separated by a blank horizontal or vertical margin known as a gutter. This feature first made its appearance on some supplies of the 1972 Royal Silver Wedding 3p, and marked the introduction of Harrison & Sons' new "Jumelle" stamp-printing press. There are advantages for both the printer and the Post Office in such a layout which has now been used for all commemorative issues since 1974.

The term "gutter pair" is used for a pair of stamps separated by part of the blank gutter margin.

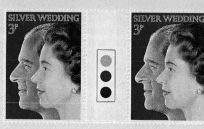

Traffic light gutter pair

Gutter pair

Most printers include some form of colour check device on the sheet margins, in addition to the cylinder or plate numbers. Harrison & Sons use round "dabs", or spots of colour, resembling traffic lights. For the period from the 1972 Royal Silver Wedding until the end of 1979 these colour dabs appeared in the gutter margin. Gutter pairs showing these "traffic lights" are worth considerably more than the normal version.

Catalogue numbers used. The checklist us the same catalogue numbers as the Stan Gibbons *British Commonwealth* Catalog (Part 1), 1997 edition.

Latest issue date for stamps recorded in t edition is 28 October 1996.

STANLEY GIBBONS LTD

Head Office: 399 Strand, London WC2R 0L Auction Room and Specialist Stamp D partments—Open Monday-Friday 9.30 a. to 5 p.m.
Shop—Open Monday to Friday 8.30 a.m. 6 p.m. and Saturday 10.00 a.m. to 4 p.m.

Telephone 0171-836 8444 for a departments

Stanley Gibbons Publications:
5, Parkside, Christchurch Road, Ringwood, Hants BH24 3SH.
Telephone 01425 472363
Publications Mail Order
FREEPHONE 0800 611622
Trade Desk 0145 478776

ISBN: 0-85259-418-6
© Stanley Gibbons Ltd 1996

Printed in Great Britain by Century Litho, Cornwall

Capture tomorrow's history with beautiful British stamps

Whether it's First Day Covers, Presentation Packs or the Mint Stamps themselves, British stamps can be sent direct to your home from the British Philatelic Bureau.

For further information, or to place an order, call our UK Telephone Order Line on 0345 641 641, 9.00 am to 5.00 pm Monday to Friday.

British Philatelic Bureau

A Royal Mail Service

QUEEN VICTORIA

837 (20 June)–1901 (22 Jan.)

IDENTIFICATION. In this checklist Victorian stamps are classified firstly according to which printing method was used line-engraving, embossing or surface-printing.

Corner letters. Numerous stamps also have letters in all our, or just the lower, corners. These were an anti-forgery evice and the letters differ from stamp to stamp. If present in all our corners the upper pair are the reverse of the lower. Note the mportance of these corner letters in the way the checklist is ranged.

Watermarks. Further classification depends on water-arks: these are illustrated in normal position, with stamps riced accordingly.

Line-engraved Issues

1a

2

a White lines added above and below head

3 Small Crown watermark

4 Large Crown watermark

Letters in lower corners

840 *Wmk Small Crown Type* **3** *Imperforate*

Cat. No.	Type		Unused	Used		
2	**1**	1d black	£3000	£150	☐	☐
5	**2**	2d blue	£5500	£300	☐	☐

841

| 8 | **1a** | 1d red-brown .. | £130 | 4·00 | ☐ | ☐ |
| 4 | **2a** | 2d blue .. .. | £1000 | 40·00 | ☐ | ☐ |

1854–57 (*i*) *Wmk Small Crown Type* **3** *Perf* 16

| 17 | **1a** | 1d red-brown .. .. | £140 | 5·00 | ☐ | ☐ |
| 19 | **2a** | 2d blue .. .. .. | £1500 | 40·00 | ☐ | ☐ |

(*ii*) *Wmk Small Crown Type* **3** *Perf* 14

| 24 | **1a** | 1d red-brown .. .. | £275 | 18·00 | ☐ | ☐ |
| 23 | **2a** | 2d blue .. .. .. | £2000 | £125 | ☐ | ☐ |

(*iii*) *Wmk Large Crown Type* **4** *Perf* 16

| 26 | **1a** | 1d red .. .. | £550 | 40·00 | ☐ | ☐ |
| 27 | **2a** | 2d blue .. .. | £2500 | £150 | ☐ | ☐ |

(*iv*) *Wmk Large Crown Type* **4** *Perf* 14

| 40 | **1a** | 1d red .. .. | 25·00 | 2·00 | ☐ | ☐ |
| 34 | **2a** | 2d blue .. .. | £1200 | 30·00 | ☐ | ☐ |

5

6 Watermark extending over three stamps

7

8

9

Letters in all four corners

Plate numbers. Stamps included a 'plate number' in their design and this affects valuation. The cheapest plates are priced here; see complete list of plate numbers overleaf.

1858–70 (*i*) *Wmk Type* **6** *Perf* 14

| 48 | **5** | ½d red .. .. .. | 45·00 | 8·00 | ☐ | ☐ |

(*ii*) *Wmk Large Crown Type* **4** *Perf* 14

43	**7**	1d red	4·50	1·00	☐	☐
51	**8**	1½d red	£200	22·00	☐	☐
45	**9**	2d blue	£150	5·00	☐	☐

PLATE NUMBERS
on stamps of 1858–70 having letters in all four corners

Shows
Plate 9 (½d)

Shows
Plate 170 (1d 2d)

Shows
Plate 3 (1½d)

HALFPENNY VALUE (S.G. 48)

Plate	Un.	Used		Plate	Un.	Used	
1	£100	45·00	□ □	11	45·00	8·00	□ □
3	60·00	15·00	□ □	12	45·00	8·00	□ □
4	75·00	10·00	□ □	13	45·00	8·00	□ □
5	55·00	8·00	□ □	14	45·00	8·00	□ □
6	45·00	8·00	□ □	15	60·00	12·00	□ □
8	90·00	45·00	□ □	19	95·00	25·00	□ □
9	£2250	£325	□ □	20	£100	35·00	□ □
10	75·00	8·00	□ □				

Plates 2, 7, 16, 17 and 18 were not completed, while Plates 21 and 22, though made, were not used. Plate 9 was a reserve plate, not greatly used

PENNY VALUE (S.G. 43)

Plate	Un	Used		Plate	Un	Used		Plate	Un	Used		Plate	Un	Used	
71	12·00	2·00	□ □	112	30·00	1·50	□ □	154	7·50	1·00	□ □	190	7·00	3·50	□ □
72	18·00	2·50	□ □	113	8·00	7·50	□ □	155	8·00	1·50	□ □	191	5·00	4·00	□ □
73	12·00	2·00	□ □	114	£175	8·00	□ □	156	7·50	1·00	□ □	192	13·00	1·00	□ □
74	10·00	1·00	□ □	115	50·00	1·50	□ □	157	7·50	1·00	□ □	193	5·00	1·00	□ □
76	20·00	1·00	□ □	116	38·00	6·00	□ □	158	5·00	1·00	□ □	194	7·50	5·00	□ □
77	—	—	□ □	117	8·00	1·00	□ □	159	5·00	1·00	□ □	195	7·50	5·00	□ □
78	50·00	1·00	□ □	118	12·00	1·00	□ □	160	5·00	1·00	□ □	196	5·00	3·00	□ □
79	15·00	1·00	□ □	119	5·00	1·00	□ □	161	15·00	4·00	□ □	197	8·00	6·00	□ □
80	10·00	1·00	□ □	120	5·00	1·00	□ □	162	8·00	4·00	□ □	198	4·50	3·50	□ □
81	30·00	1·50	□ □	121	20·00	6·00	□ □	163	7·50	2·00	□ □	199	10·00	3·50	□ □
82	60·00	2·50	□ □	122	5·00	1·00	□ □	164	7·50	2·00	□ □	200	10·00	1·00	□ □
83	70·00	4·00	□ □	123	6·00	1·00	□ □	165	10·00	1·00	□ □	201	5·00	3·00	□ □
84	30·00	1·50	□ □	124	6·00	1·00	□ □	166	7·50	3·50	□ □	202	7·50	5·00	□ □
85	12·00	1·50	□ □	125	8·00	1·50	□ □	167	5·00	1·00	□ □	203	5·00	10·00	□ □
86	15·00	2·50	□ □	127	17·00	1·50	□ □	168	6·00	5·50	□ □	204	6·00	1·50	□ □
87	4·50	1·00	□ □	129	6·00	5·00	□ □	169	15·00	4·00	□ □	205	6·00	2·00	□ □
88	80·00	5·50	□ □	130	9·00	1·50	□ □	170	6·00	1·00	□ □	206	6·00	6·00	□ □
89	20·00	1·00	□ □	131	38·00	11·00	□ □	171	5·00	1·00	□ □	207	6·00	6·00	□ □
90	14·00	1·00	□ □	132	50·00	16·00	□ □	172	5·00	1·00	□ □	208	6·00	10·00	□ □
91	20·00	3·50	□ □	133	45·00	6·00	□ □	173	25·00	6·00	□ □	209	7·50	6·00	□ □
92	7·00	1·00	□ □	134	5·00	1·00	□ □	174	5·00	1·00	□ □	210	10·00	8·00	□ □
93	20·00	1·00	□ □	135	50·00	20·00	□ □	175	18·00	2·00	□ □	211	22·00	15·00	□ □
94	20·00	3·00	□ □	136	50·00	15·00	□ □	176	13·00	1·50	□ □	212	7·50	7·50	□ □
95	12·00	1·00	□ □	137	8·00	1·50	□ □	177	5·00	1·00	□ □	213	7·50	7·50	□ □
96	14·00	1·00	□ □	138	6·00	1·00	□ □	178	7·50	2·00	□ □	214	13·00	13·00	□ □
97	8·00	2·00	□ □	139	16·00	11·00	□ □	179	8·00	1·50	□ □	215	13·00	13·00	□ □
98	8·00	3·50	□ □	140	6·00	1·00	□ □	180	8·00	3·00	□ □	216	13·00	13·00	□ □
99	12·00	3·00	□ □	141	75·00	6·00	□ □	181	7·50	1·00	□ □	217	10·00	4·00	□ □
100	18·00	1·50	□ □	142	25·00	18·00	□ □	182	50·00	3·00	□ □	218	6·00	5·00	□ □
101	25·00	6·00	□ □	143	15·00	10·00	□ □	183	13·00	2·00	□ □	219	30·00	50·00	□ □
102	10·00	1·00	□ □	144	50·00	15·00	□ □	184	5·00	1·50	□ □	220	5·00	4·00	□ □
103	10·00	2·00	□ □	145	5·00	1·50	□ □	185	7·50	2·00	□ □	221	15·00	10·00	□ □
104	14·00	3·00	□ □	146	5·00	3·50	□ □	186	15·00	1·50	□ □	222	25·00	25·00	□ □
105	35·00	4·00	□ □	147	9·00	2·00	□ □	187	6·00	1·00	□ □	223	30·00	40·00	□ □
106	15·00	1·00	□ □	148	10·00	2·00	□ □	188	10·00	7·00	□ □	224	35·00	35·00	□ □
107	20·00	3·75	□ □	149	7·50	3·50	□ □	189	18·00	4·00	□ □	225	£1100	£350	□ □
108	15·00	1·50	□ □	150	5·00	1·00	□ □								
109	38·00	2·00	□ □	151	13·00	6·00	□ □								
110	10·00	6·00	□ □	152	9·00	3·25	□ □								
111	18·00	1·50	□ □	153	35·00	6·00	□ □								

Plates 69, 70, 75, 77, 126 and 128 were prepared but rejected. No stamps therefore exist, except for a very few from Plate 77 which somehow reached the public. Plate 177 stamps, by accident or design, are sometimes passed off as the rare Plate 77

THREE-HALFPENNY VALUE (S.G. 51)

Plate	Un.	Used		Plate	Un.	Used	
(1)	£400	35·00	□ □	3	£200	22·00	□ □

Plate 1 did not have the plate number in the design. Plate 2 was not completed and no stamps exist

TWOPENNY VALUE (S.G. 45)

Plate	Un	Used		Plate	Un	Used	
7	£400	20·00	□ □	13	£180	10·00	□ □
8	£450	15·00	□ □	14	£200	12·00	□ □
9	£150	5·00	□ □	15	£160	10·00	□ □
12	£750	45·00	□ □				

Plates 10 and 11 were prepared but rejected

Embossed Issues

...ices are for stamps cut square and with average to fine ...mbossing. Stamps with exceptionally clear embossing are ...orth more.

 **11**

 **12**

 13

347–54 *Wmk* **13** (6d), *no wmk* (*others*)   *Imperforate*

9	10	6d lilac	..	.. ..	£3000	£450	☐ ☐
7	11	10d brown	..	.. ..	£2750	£625	☐ ☐
4	12	1s green ..	..	.. ..	£3250	£400	☐ ☐

Surface-printed Issues

IDENTIFICATION. Check first whether the design includes ...orner letters or not, as mentioned for 'Line-engraved ...sues'. The checklist is divided up according to whether any ...tters are small or large, also whether they are white ...ncoloured) or printed in the colour of the stamp. Further ...entification then depends on watermark.

PERFORATION. Except for Nos. 126/9 all the following ...sues of Queen Victoria are perf 14.

 14

5 **Small Garter**   **16** Medium Garter   **17** Large Garter

---

 18   **19**   **20** Emblems

No corner letters

1855–57 (*i*) *Wmk Small Garter Type* **15**

62	**14**	4d red	..	.. ..	£2500	£190	☐ ☐

(*ii*) *Wmk Medium Garter Type* **16**

64	**14**	4d red	..	.. ..	£2000	£160	☐ ☐

(*iii*) *Wmk Large Garter Type* **17**

66a	**14**	4d red	..	.. ..	£650	32·00	☐ ☐

(*iv*) *Wmk Emblems Type* **20**

70	**18**	6d lilac	..	..	£525	40·00	☐ ☐
72	**19**	1s green	..	..	£675	£150	☐ ☐

Plate numbers. Stamps Nos. 90/163 should be checked for the 'plate numbers' indicated, as this affects valuation (the cheapest plates are priced here). The mark '*Pl.*' shows that several numbers exist, priced in a separate list overleaf.

Plate numbers are the small numerals appearing in duplicate in some part of the frame design or adjacent to the lower corner letters (in the 5s value a single numeral above the lower inscription).

 21   **22**   **23**

24   **25**

Small white corner letters

1862–64 *Wmk Emblems Type* **20**, except 4d (*Large Garter Type* **17**)

77	**21**	3d red	..	..	..	£750	£100	☐ ☐
80	**22**	4d red	..	..	..	£550	35·00	☐ ☐
84	**23**	6d lilac	..	..	..	£675	30·00	☐ ☐
87	**24**	9d bistre	..	..	..	£1400	£140	☐ ☐
90	**25**	1s green *Pl.*	..	..	£800	70·00	☐ ☐

26

27

28 (hyphen in SIX·PENCE)

32

33 Spray of Rose

34

29

30

31

Large white corner letters

1865–67 *Wmk Emblems Type* **20**, *except 4d (Large Garter Type* **17***)*

92	**26**	3d red (Plate 4) ..	£450	50·00	☐ ☐
94	**27**	4d vermilion *Pl.* ..	£250	18·00	☐ ☐
97	**28**	6d lilac *Pl.*	£375	30·00	☐ ☐
98	**29**	9d straw *Pl.*	£800	£200	☐ ☐
99	**30**	10d brown (Plate 1)		†£12000	☐
101	**31**	1s green (Plate 4)	£725	80·00	☐ ☐

1867–80 *Wmk Spray of Rose Type* **33**

103	**26**	3d red *Pl.*	£200	14·00	☐ ☐
105	**28**	6d lilac (with hyphen) (Plate 6)	£600	35·00	☐ ☐
109		6d mauve (without hyphen) *Pl.*	£275	25·00	☐ ☐
111	**29**	9d straw (Plate 4)	£675	£120	☐ ☐
112	**30**	10d brown *Pl.*	£1000	£160	☐ ☐
117	**31**	1s green *Pl.*	£350	12·00	☐ ☐
119	**32**	2s blue *Pl.*	£1000	65·00	☐ ☐
121		2s brown (Plate 1)	£7000	£1400	☐ ☐

1872–73 *Wmk Spray of Rose Type* **33**

122*a*	**34**	6d brown *Pl.*	£350	20·00	☐ ☐
125		6d grey (Plate 12)	£750	£100	☐ ☐

PLATE NUMBERS
on stamps
of 1862–83

Cat No		Plate No	Un	Used	

Small White Corner Letters (1862–64)

90	1s green	2	£800	70·00	☐ ☐
		3	£11000		☐ ☐

Plate 2 is actually numbered as '1' and Plate 3 as '2' on the stamps.

Large White Corner Letters (1865–83)

103	3d red	4	£300	60·00	☐ ☐
		5	£200	16·00	☐ ☐
		6	£225	14·00	☐ ☐
		7	£300	17·00	☐ ☐
		8	£250	16·00	☐ ☐
		9	£250	22·00	☐ ☐
		10	£300	50·00	☐ ☐
94	4d verm	7	£325	22·00	☐ ☐
		8	£325	22·00	☐ ☐
		9	£275	18·00	☐ ☐
		10	£325	35·00	☐ ☐
		11	£275	18·00	☐ ☐
		12	£250	18·00	☐ ☐
		13	£275	19·00	☐ ☐
		14	£325	40·00	☐ ☐
97	6d lilac	5	£375	30·00	☐ ☐
		6	£1100	60·00	☐ ☐
109	6d mauve	8	£275	25·00	☐ ☐
		9	£275	25·00	☐ ☐
		10	*	£12000	☐ ☐
122*a*	6d brown	11	£350	20·00	☐ ☐
		12	£800	70·00	☐ ☐
98	9d straw	4	£800	£200	☐ ☐
		5	£10000		☐ ☐
112	10d brown	1	£1000	£160	☐ ☐
		2	£12000	£2500	☐ ☐
117	1s green	4	£350	17·00	☐ ☐
		5	£400	14·00	☐ ☐
		6	£550	12·00	☐ ☐
		7	£550	35·00	☐ ☐
119	2s blue	1	£1000	65·00	☐ ☐
		3	*	£3000	☐ ☐
126	5s red	1	£2750	£300	☐ ☐
		2	£3750	£375	☐ ☐

Large Coloured Corner Letters (1873–83)

139	2½d mauve	1	£275	35·00	☐ ☐
		2	£275	35·00	☐ ☐
		3	£450	40·00	☐ ☐
141	2½d mauve	3	£550	35·00	☐ ☐
		4	£225	14·00	☐ ☐
		5	£225	18·00	☐ ☐
		6	£225	14·00	☐ ☐
		7	£225	14·00	☐ ☐
		8	£225	18·00	☐ ☐
		9	£225	14·00	☐ ☐
		10	£275	25·00	☐ ☐
		11	£225	14·00	☐ ☐
		12	£225	18·00	☐ ☐
		13	£225	18·00	☐ ☐
		14	£225	14·00	☐ ☐
		15	£225	14·00	☐ ☐
		16	£225	14·00	☐ ☐
		17	£600	£100	☐ ☐
142	2½d blue	17	£200	25·00	☐ ☐
		18	£225	16·00	☐ ☐
		19	£200	14·00	☐ ☐
		20	£200	14·00	☐ ☐
157	2½d blue	21	£225	11·00	☐ ☐
		22	£180	10·00	☐ ☐
		23	£180	8·00	☐ ☐
143	3d red	11	£200	13·00	☐ ☐
		12	£225	15·00	☐ ☐
		14	£250	16·00	☐ ☐
		15	£200	15·00	☐ ☐
		16	£200	15·00	☐ ☐
		17	£225	15·00	☐ ☐
		18	£225	15·00	☐ ☐
		19	£200	15·00	☐ ☐
		20	£200	32·00	☐ ☐
158	3d red	20	£275	50·00	☐ ☐
		21	£225	35·00	☐ ☐
152	4d verm	15	£700	£150	☐ ☐
		16	*	£10000	☐ ☐
153	4d green	15	£500	£120	☐ ☐
		16	£450	£110	☐ ☐
		17	*	£6000	☐ ☐
160	4d brown	17	£180	25·00	☐ ☐
		18	£180	25·00	☐ ☐
147	6d grey	13	£225	22·00	☐ ☐
		14	£225	22·00	☐ ☐
		15	£225	20·00	☐ ☐
		16	£225	20·00	☐ ☐
		17	£325	45·00	☐ ☐
161	6d grey	17	£190	28·00	☐ ☐
		18	£175	28·00	☐ ☐
150	1s green	8	£350	45·00	☐ ☐
		9	£350	45·00	☐ ☐
		10	£325	45·00	☐ ☐
		11	£325	45·00	☐ ☐
		12	£275	32·00	☐ ☐
		13	£275	32·00	☐ ☐
		14	*	£10000	☐ ☐
163	1s brown	13	£325	50·00	☐ ☐
		14	£275	50·00	☐ ☐

36

37

44

45

46

38

9 Maltese Cross   **40** Large Anchor

47 Small Anchor   **48** Orb

Large coloured corner letters

1873–80 (*i*) *Wmk Small Anchor Type* **47**

139	**41**	2½d mauve *Pl.*	£275	35·00	☐	☐

(*ii*) *Wmk Orb Type* **48**

141	**41**	2½d mauve *Pl.*	£225	14·00	☐	☐
142		2½d blue *Pl.*	£200	14·00	☐	☐

(*iii*) *Wmk Spray of Rose Type* **33**

143	**42**	3d red *Pl.*	£200	13·00	☐	☐
145	**43**	6d pale buff			☐	☐
		(Plate 13)		£4500	☐	☐
147		6d grey *Pl.*	£225	20·00	☐	☐
150	**44**	1s green *Pl.*	£275	32·00	☐	☐
151		1s brown (Plate 13)	£1300	£225	☐	☐

(*iv*) *Wmk Large Garter Type* **17**

152	**45**	4d vermilion *Pl.*	£700	£150	☐	☐
153		4d green *Pl.*	£450	£110	☐	☐
154		4d brown (Plate 17)	£650	£175	☐	☐
156	**46**	8d orange (Plate 1)	£550	£140	☐	☐

3d   **6d**

49 Imperial Crown   **(50)** Surcharges in red **(51)**

1880–83 *Wmk Imperial Crown Type* **49**

157	**41**	2½d blue *Pl.*	£180	8·00	☐	☐
158	**42**	3d red *Pl.*	£225	35·00	☐	☐
159		3d on 3d lilac				
		(surch Type **50**)	£250	80·00	☐	☐
160	**45**	4d brown *Pl.*	£180	25·00	☐	☐
161	**43**	6d grey *Pl.*	£175	28·00	☐	☐
162		6d on 6d lilac				
		(surch Type **51**)	£225	75·00	☐	☐
163	**44**	1s brown *Pl.*	£275	50·00	☐	☐

1867–83 (*i*) *Wmk Maltese Cross Type* **39**   *Perf* 15½ × 15

26	**35**	5s red *Pl.*	£2750	£300	☐	☐
28	**36**	10s grey (Plate 1)	£20000	£900	☐	☐
29	**37**	£1 brown (Plate 1)	£25000	£1400	☐	☐

(*ii*) *Wmk Large Anchor Type* **40**   *Perf* 14

34	**35**	5s red (Plate 4)	£5000	£1000	☐	☐
31	**36**	10s grey (Plate 1)	£23000	£1500	☐	☐
32	**37**	£1 brown (Plate 1)	£30000	£2500	☐	☐
37	**38**	£5 orange (Plate 1)	£4500	£1400	☐	☐

1

42

43

52   53   54

55   56

1880–81 *Wmk Imperial Crown Type* **49**

164	52	½d green		18·00	4·00	□ □
166	53	1d brown		6·00	3·00	□ □
167	54	1½d brown		85·00	18·00	□ □
168	55	2d red		£100	38·00	□ □
169	56	5d indigo		£350	50·00	□ □

57   Die I   Die II

1881 *Wmk Imperial Crown Type* **49**
   (*a*) 14 *dots in each corner, Die* I

171	57	1d lilac		75·00	12·00	□ □

   (*b*) 16 *dots in each corner, Die* II

173	57	1d lilac		1·00	50	□ □

58   59

60

Coloured letters in the corners

1883-84 *Wmk Anchor Type* **40**

179	58	2s 6d deep lilac		£225	65·00	□ □
181	59	5s red		£425	80·00	□ □
183	60	10s blue		£800	£250	□ □

61

1884 *Wmk 3 Imperial Crowns Type* **49**

185	61	£1 brown		£12000	£1000	□ □

1888 *Wmk 3 Orbs Type* **48**

186	61	£1 brown		£18000	£1500	□ □

1891 *Wmk 3 Imperial Crowns Type* **49**

212	61	£1 green		£2000	£375	□ □

62   63   64

65   66

1883–84 *Wmk Imperial Crown Type* **49** (*sideways on horiz designs*)

187	52	½d blue		10·00	2·00	□ □
188	62	1½d lilac		55·00	18·00	□ □
189	63	2d lilac		80·00	35·00	□ □
190	64	2½d lilac		40·00	5·00	□ □
191	65	3d lilac		£100	50·00	□ □
192	66	4d dull green		£300	£100	□ □
193	62	5d dull green		£300	£100	□ □
194	63	6d dull green		£325	£110	□ □
195	64	9d dull green		£600	£275	□ □
196	65	1s dull green		£400	£140	□ □

The above prices are for stamps in the true dull green colour. Stamps which have been soaked, causing the colour to run, are virtually worthless.

7

68

69

79

80

81

KING EDWARD VII
1901 (22 Jan.)–1910 (6 May)

0

71

72

82

83

84

3

74

75

85

86

87

76

77

78

88

89

'Jubilee' issue

1887–1900 *The bicoloured stamps have the value tablets, or the frames including the value tablets, in the second colour.*
Wmk Imperial Crown Type 49

197	67	½d vermilion ..	1·00	50	☐	☐
213		½d green*	1·00	70	☐	☐
198	68	1½d purple and green	12·00	4·50	☐	☐
200	69	2d green and red ..	18·00	8·50	☐	☐
201	70	2½d purple on blue	12·00	1·50	☐	☐
203	71	3d purple on yellow	16·00	2·00	☐	☐
205	72	4d green and brown	18·00	8·50	☐	☐
206	73	4½d green and red ..	6·00	25·00	☐	☐
207a	74	5d purple and blue	20·00	7·50	☐	☐
208	75	6d purple on red ..	18·00	7·50	☐	☐
209	76	9d purple and blue	45·00	28·00	☐	☐
210	77	10d purple and red	35·00	28·00	☐	☐
211	78	1s green	£150	40·00	☐	☐
214		1s green and red ..	45·00	90·00	☐	☐
	Set of 14	.. ..	£350	£220	☐	☐

*The ½d. No. 213 in blue is a colour changeling

90

91

92

93

7

1902–13 *Wmks Imperial Crown Type* **49** ($\frac{1}{2}d$ *to* 1s). *Anchor Type* **40** (2s 6d *to* 10s). *Three Crowns Type* **49** (£1)

(a) *Perf* 14

215	79	$\frac{1}{2}d$ blue-green	.. ..	75	30	□ □
217		$\frac{1}{2}d$ yellow-green	.. ..	75	30	□ □
219		1d red	.. ..	75	30	□ □
222	80	$1\frac{1}{2}d$ purple and green	..	14·00	4·75	□ □
291	81	2d green and red	..	13·00	7·00	□ □
231	82	$2\frac{1}{2}d$ blue	.. ..	6·00	3·00	□ □
232	83	3d purple on yellow	..	19·00	3·00	□ □
236a	84	4d green and brown	..	20·00	7·00	□ □
240		4d orange	..	9·00	7·50	□ □
294	85	5d purple and blue	..	14·00	7·00	□ □
246	79	6d purple	.. ..	17·00	6·00	□ □
249	86	7d grey	.. ..	5·00	7·00	□ □
307	87	9d purple and blue	..	32·00	27·00	□ □
311	88	10d purple and red	..	35·00	27·00	□ □
314	89	1s green and red	..	30·00	12·00	□ □
260	90	2s 6d lilac	..	£110	50·00	□ □
263	91	5s red	..	£120	60·00	□ □
265	92	10s blue	..	£325	£200	□ □
266	93	£1 green	..	£800	£325	□ □
		Set of 15 (*to* 1s)	..	£190	£110	

(b) *Perf* 15 × 14

279	79	$\frac{1}{2}d$ green	..	22·00	27·00	□ □
281		1d red	..	8·50	7·00	□ □
283	82	$2\frac{1}{2}d$ blue	..	13·00	5·00	□ □
285	83	3d purple on yellow	..	20·00	5·00	□ □
286	84	4d orange	..	14·00	6·50	□ □
		Set of 5	.. ..	70·00	45·00	

KING GEORGE V
1910 (6 May)–1936 (20 Jan.)

PERFORATION. All the following issues are Perf 15 × 14 except vertical commemorative stamps which are 14 × 15, unless otherwise stated.

94 (Hair dark)   **95** (Lion unshaded)   **96**

1911–12 *Wmk Imperial Crown Type* **49**

322	94	$\frac{1}{2}d$ green	.. ..	3·00	1·50	□ □
327	95	1d red	.. ..	3·00	1·50	□ □

1912 *Wmk Royal Cypher* (*'Simple'*) *Type* **96**

335	94	$\frac{1}{2}d$ green	..	28·00	30·00	□ □
336	95	1d red	.. ..	18·00	18·00	□ □

97 (Hair light)   **98** (Lion shaded)   **99**

1912 *Wmk Imperial Crown Type* **49**

339	97	$\frac{1}{2}d$ green	.. ..	3·50	75	□
341	98	1d red	..	2·25	1·00	□

1912 *Wmk Royal Cypher* (*'Simple'*) *Type* **96**

344	97	$\frac{1}{2}d$ green	..	3·50	1·00	□
345	98	1d red	..	4·50	1·00	□

1912 *Wmk Royal Cypher* (*'Multiple'*) *Type* **99**

348	97	$\frac{1}{2}d$ green	..	6·50	4·00	□
350	98	1d red	..	5·50	5·50	□

100   **101**   **102**

103   **104**

1912–24 *Wmk Royal Cypher Type* **96**

351	101	$\frac{1}{2}d$ green	..	50	35	□
357	100	1d red	.. ..	50	25	□
362	101	$1\frac{1}{2}d$ brown	..	1·75	40	□
368	102	2d orange	..	1·50	60	□
371	100	$2\frac{1}{2}d$ blue	..	5·00	1·25	□
375	102	3d violet	..	2·25	1·25	□
379		4d grey-green	..	4·50	1·00	□
381	103	5d brown	..	4·50	3·25	□
385		6d purple	..	6·50	2·50	□
		a. *Perf* 14		65·00	£100	□
387		7d olive-green	..	10·00	5·00	□
390		8d black on yellow	..	20·00	8·50	□
392	104	9d black	..	10·00	3·25	□
393a		9d olive-green	..	70·00	20·00	□
394		10d blue	..	10·00	14·00	□
395		1s brown	..	10·00	1·25	□
		Set of 15		£140	55·00	

1913 *Wmk Royal Cypher ('Multiple')* Type **99**

97	**101**	½d green	£100	£140 ☐ ☐
398	**100**	1d red	£175	£175 ☐ ☐

See also Nos. 418/29.

108

109

105

106

British Empire Exhibition

1924–25 *Wmk* **107** *Perf* 14

(*a*) 23.4.24. *Dated '1924'*

430	**108**	1d red	5·00	8·00 ☐ ☐
431	**109**	1½d brown	8·00	12·00 ☐ ☐
		First Day Cover		£350 ☐

(*b*) 9.5.25. *Dated '1925'*

432	**108**	1d red	10·00	19·00 ☐ ☐
433	**109**	1½d brown	30·00	50·00 ☐ ☐
		First Day Cover		£1200 ☐

T 105. *Background around portrait consists of horizontal lines*

1913–18 *Wmk Single Cypher Type* **106** *Perf* 11 · 12

413a	**105**	2s 6d brown	60·00	30·00 ☐ ☐
416		5s red	£150	45·00 ☐ ☐
417		10s blue	£225	85·00 ☐ ☐
403		£1 green	£1100	£600 ☐ ☐
		Set of 4	£1400	£700 ☐ ☐

See also Nos. 450/2.

110   111   112

107

1924–26 *Wmk Block Cypher Type* **107**

418	**101**	½d green	40	25 ☐ ☐
419	**100**	1d red	40	25 ☐ ☐
420	**101**	1½d brown	40	25 ☐ ☐
421	**102**	2d orange	1·25	1·00 ☐ ☐
422	**100**	2½d blue	3·00	1·25 ☐ ☐
423	**102**	3d violet	5·00	1·25 ☐ ☐
424		4d grey-green	6·50	1·00 ☐ ☐
425	**103**	5d brown	10·00	1·75 ☐ ☐
426a		6d purple	1·75	50 ☐ ☐
427	**104**	9d olive-green	6·00	2·25 ☐ ☐
428		10d blue	20·00	20·00 ☐ ☐
429		1s brown	12·00	1·50 ☐ ☐
		Set of 12	60·00	28·00 ☐ ☐

113 St George and the Dragon

114

For full information on all future British issues, collectors should write to the British Post Office Philatelic Bureau, 20 Brandon Street, Edinburgh EH3 5TT

Ninth Universal Postal Union Congress

1929 (10 MAY) (*a*) *Wmk* **107**

434	110	½d green.		1·75	1·75	□ □
435	111	1d red		1·75	1·75	□ □
436		1½d brown		1·50	1·25	□ □
437	112	2½d blue		9·00	9·00	□ □

(*b*) *Wmk* **114** *Perf* 12

438	113	£1 black		£550	£400	□ □
434/7	*Set of 4*			12·50	12·00	□ □
434/7	*First Day Cover* (4 vals.)				£500	□
434/8	*First Day Cover* (5 vals.)				£3000	□

115

116

117

118 119

1934–36 *Wmk* **107**

439	115	½d green		10	25	□ □
440	116	1d red		15	25	□ □
441	115	1½d brown		10	25	□ □
442	117	2d orange		30	40	□ □
443	116	2½d blue		1·00	1·00	□ □
444	117	3d violet		1·00	60	□ □
445		4d grey-green		1·50	65	□ □
446	118	5d brown		5·00	2·00	□ □
447	119	9d olive-green		11·00	1·60	□ □
448		10d blue		14·00	9·00	□ □
449		1s brown		14·00	75	□ □
	Set of 11			42·00	15·00	□ □

**T 105 (re-engraved). Background around portrait
consists of horizontal and diagonal lines**

1934 *Wmk* **106** *Perf* 11 × 12

450	105	2s 6d brown		50·00	20·00	□ □
451		5s red		£100	65·00	□ □
452		10s blue		£250	55·00	□ □
	Set of 3			£350	£120	□ □

120 121

122 123

Silver Jubilee

1935 (7 MAY) *Wmk* **107**

453	120	½d green		40	30	□ □
454	121	1d red		1·25	1·50	□ □
455	122	1½d brown		40	30	□ □
456	123	2½d blue		4·50	5·50	□ □
	Set of 4			5·75	6·75	□ □
	First Day Cover				£500	□

KING EDWARD VIII
1936 (20 Jan.–10 Dec.)

124

125

1936 *Wmk* **125**

457	124	½d green		20	20	□ □
458		1d red		50	25	□ □
459		1½d brown		25	20	□ □
460		2½d blue		25	75	□ □
	Set of 4			1·00	1·25	□ □

126 King George VI
and Queen Elizabeth

127

Coronation

1937 (13 MAY) Wmk 127

461	126	1½d brown	... ...	40	30	□ □
		First Day Cover	... ...		28·00	□

128

129

130

King George VI and National Emblems

1937–47 Wmk 127

462	128	½d green	...	10	15	□ □
463		1d scarlet	...	10	15	□ □
464		1½d brown	...	20	15	□ □
465		2d orange	...	75	45	□ □
466		2½d blue	...	25	15	□ □
467		3d violet	...	3·25	80	□ □
468	129	4d green	...	35	40	□ □
469		5d brown	...	2·00	50	□ □
470		6d purple	...	1·00	40	□ □
471	130	7d green	...	3·25	50	□ □
472		8d red	... ...	3·50	50	□ □
473		9d deep green	...	5·25	60	□ □
474		10d blue	...	4·75	60	□ □
474a		11d plum	...	2·00	1·50	□ □
475		1s brown	...	5·75	50	□ □
		Set of 15	...	29·00	6·50	□ □

For later printings of the lower values in apparently lighter
shades and different colours, see Nos. 485/90 and 503/8.

For full information on all future British issues, collectors
should write to the British Post Office Philatelic Bureau, 20
Brandon Street, Edinburgh EH3 5TT

131 King George VI

131a

132

132a

133

1939–48 Wmk 133 Perf 14

476	131	2s 6d brown	38·00	6·00	□ □
476a		2s 6d green	7·00	1·00	□ □
477	131a	5s red	14·00	1·50	□ □
478	132	10s dark blue	£170	18·00	□ □
478a		10s bright blue	35·00	5·00	□ □
478b	132a	£1 brown	10·00	20·00	□ □
		Set of 6	£250	45·00	□ □

134 Queen Victoria and King George VI

Centenary of First Adhesive Postage Stamps

1940 (6 MAY) Wmk 127 Perf 14½ × 14

479	134	½d green	...	30	20	□ □
480		1d red	...	1·00	40	□ □
481		1½d brown	...	30	30	□ □
482		2d orange	...	50	40	□ □
483		2½d blue	...	2·25	80	□ □
484		3d violet	...	3·00	3·50	□ □
		Set of 6	...	6·50	5·00	□ □
		First Day Cover	...		42·00	□

Head as Nos. 462-7, but lighter background

1941–42 Wmk **127**

485	**128**	½d pale green	15	10	☐	☐
486		1d pale red	15	10	☐	☐
487		1½d pale brown	75	45	☐	☐
488		2d pale orange	50	40	☐	☐
489		2½d light blue	15	10	☐	☐
490		3d pale violet	1·50	50	☐	☐
	Set of 6		2·75	1·50	☐	☐

135 Symbols of Peace and Reconstruction

136 Symbols of Peace and Reconstruction

Victory

1946 (11 JUNE) Wmk **127**

491	**135**	2½d blue	25	15	☐	☐
492	**136**	3d violet	25	15	☐	☐
	First Day Cover			55·00		☐

137 King George VI and Queen Elizabeth

138 King George VI and Queen Elizabeth

Royal Silver Wedding

1948 (26 APR.) Wmk **127**

493	**137**	2½d blue	30	30	☐	☐
494	**138**	£1 blue	35·00	32·00	☐	☐
	First Day Cover			£350		☐

1948 (10 MAY)

Stamps of 1d and 2½d showing seaweed-gathering were on sale at eight Head Post Offices elsewhere in Great Britain, but were primarily for use in the Channel Islands and are listed there (see after Regional Issues).

139 Globe and Laurel Wreath

140 'Speed'

141 Olympic Symbol

142 Winged Victory

Olympic Games

1948 (29 JULY) Wmk **127**

495	**139**	2½d blue	10	10	☐	
496	**140**	3d violet	30	30	☐	
497	**141**	6d purple	60	30	☐	
498	**142**	1s brown	1·25	1·50	☐	
	Set of 4		2·00	2·00	☐	
	First Day Cover			35·00		

143 Two Hemispheres

144 U.P.U. Monument, Berne

145 Goddess Concordia, Globe and Points of Compass

146 Posthorn and Globe

75th Anniversary of Universal Postal Union

1949 (10 OCT.) Wmk **127**

499	**143**	2½d blue	10	10	☐	☐
500	**144**	3d violet	30	40	☐	☐
501	**145**	6d purple	60	75	☐	☐
502	**146**	1s brown	1·25	1·50	☐	☐
	Set of 4		2·00	2·75	☐	☐
	First Day Cover			50·00		☐

d as No. 468 and others as Nos. 485/9, but colours
hanged

1950–51 *Wmk* **127**

03	**128**	½d pale orange	..	20	30	☐	☐
04		1d light blue	..	20	30	☐	☐
05		1½d pale green	..	30	40	☐	☐
06		2d pale brown	..	30	30	☐	☐
07		2½d pale red	..	30	30	☐	☐
08	**129**	4d light blue	..	2·00	1·25	☐	☐
	Set of 6			3·00	2·50	☐	☐

153 Tudor Crown

154

47 HMS *Victory*

148 White Cliffs of Dover

155

156

157

49 St George and the Dragon

150 Royal Coat of Arms

158

159

160

951 (3 MAY) *Wmk* **133**   *Perf* 11 × 12

09	**147**	2s 6d green	..	5·00	75	☐	☐
10	**148**	5s red	..	28·00	1·50	☐	☐
11	**149**	10s blue	..	18·00	8·00	☐	☐
12	**150**	£1 brown	..	30·00	16·00	☐	☐
	Set of 4			70·00	22·00	☐	☐

151 Commerce and Prosperity

152 Festival Symbol

Festival of Britain

1951 (3 MAY) *Wmk* **127**

513	**151**	2½d red	..	..	25	15	☐ ☐
514	**152**	4d blue	..	..	50	45	☐ ☐
	First Day Cover	..	..		28·00		☐

1952–54 *Wmk* **153**

515	**154**	½d orange	..	10	15	☐	☐
516		1d blue		20	20	☐	☐
517		1½d green	..	10	15	☐	☐
518		2d brown	..	20	15	☐	☐
519	**155**	2½d red	..	10	15	☐	☐
520		3d lilac	..	1·00	50	☐	☐
521	**156**	4d blue	..	3·00	1·00	☐	☐
		4½d (*See Nos.* 577, 594 609 *and* 616b)					
522	**157**	5d brown	..	90	2·50	☐	☐
523		6d purple	..	3·00	80	☐	☐
524		7d green	..	9·00	4·25	☐	☐
525	**158**	8d magenta	..	1·00	75	☐	☐
526		9d bronze-green		22·00	3·50	☐	☐
527		10d blue	..	18·00	3·50	☐	☐
528		11d plum	..	30·00	18·00	☐	☐
529	**159**	1s bistre	..	1·25	50	☐	☐
530	**160**	1s 3d green		4·50	2·50	☐	☐
531	**159**	1s 6d indigo	..	11·00	3·00	☐	☐
	Set of 17			95·00	35·00	☐	☐

First Day Covers

5 Dec. 1952	Nos. 517, 519	.. .. ..	8·00	☐
6 July 1953	Nos. 522, 525, 529	.. ..	40·00	☐
31 Aug. 1953	Nos. 515/16, 518	.. .. ..	40·00	☐
2 Nov. 1953	Nos. 521, 530/1	.. .. ..	£140	☐
18 Jan. 1954	Nos. 520, 523/4	.. .. ..	85·00	☐
8 Feb. 1954	Nos. 526/8	.. .. ..	£170	☐

See also Nos. 540/56, 561/6, 570/94 and 599/618a.

161

162

163

164

Coronation

1953 (3 June) *Wmk* **153**

532	**161**	2½d red	..	..	10	50	☐ ☐
533	**162**	4d blue			40	1·50	☐ ☐
534	**163**	1s 3d green			3·50	2·75	☐ ☐
535	**164**	1s 6d blue		..	7·00	3·50	☐ ☐
	Set of 4		..	..	10·00	7·50	☐ ☐
	First Day Cover					38·00	☐

165 St Edward's Crown

166 Carrickfergus Castle

167 Caernarvon Castle

168 Edinburgh Castle

169 Windsor Castle

1955 (1–23 Sept.) *Wmk* **165** *Perf* 11 × 12

536	**166**	2s 6d brown	..	..	10·00	2·00	☐ ☐
537	**167**	5s red ..	..	..	30·00	3·50	☐ ☐
538	**168**	10s blue	..	..	80·00	12·00	☐ ☐

539	**169**	£1 black	..	..	£130	35·00	☐ ☐
	Set of 4	..	..	..	£225	48·00	☐ ☐
	First Day Cover (*Nos.* 538/9)						
	(1 Sept.)					£500	☐
	First Day Cover (*Nos.* 536/7)						
	(23 Sept.)					£325	☐

See also Nos 595*a*/8*a* and 759/62.

1955–58 *Wmk* **165**

540	**154**	½d orange		10	15	☐ ☐
541		1d blue	..	25	15	☐ ☐
542		1½d green	..	25	25	☐ ☐
543		2d red-brown		20	25	☐ ☐
543*b*		2d light red-brown		20	25	☐ ☐
544	**155**	2½d red		20	25	☐ ☐
545		3d lilac		20	25	☐ ☐
546	**156**	4d blue	..	1·40	50	☐ ☐
547	**157**	5d brown	..	5·50	4·50	☐ ☐
548*a*		6d purple		3·50	1·00	☐ ☐
549		7d green		50·00	8·50	☐ ☐
550	**158**	8d magenta	..	6·00	1·00	☐ ☐
551		9d bronze-green		23·00	2·25	☐ ☐
552		10d blue		19·00	2·25	☐ ☐
553		11d plum		50	1·50	☐ ☐
554	**159**	1s bistre		19·00	50	☐ ☐
555	**160**	1s 3d green		27·00	1·50	☐ ☐
556	**159**	1s 6d indigo		19·00	1·25	☐ ☐
	Set of 18			£150	23·00	☐ ☐

170 Scout Badge and 'Rolling Hitch'

171 'Scouts coming to Britain'

172 Globe within a Compass

173

World Scout Jubilee Jamboree

1957 (1 Aug.) *Wmk* **165**

557	**170**	2½d red	..		15	25	☐ ☐
558	**171**	4d blue	..		50	1·25	☐ ☐
559	**172**	1s 3d green		..	5·00	4·75	☐ ☐
	Set of 3		..	..	5·00	5·50	☐ ☐
	First Day Cover		..	..		17·00	☐

46th Inter Parliamentary Union Conference

1957 (12 Sept.) *Wmk* **165**

560	**173**	4d blue		..	1·00	1·25	☐ ☐
	First Day Cover		..	..		85·00	☐

Graphite-lined and Phosphor Issues

These are used in connection with automatic sorting machinery, originally experimentally at Southampton but now also operating elsewhere. In such areas these stamps were the normal issue, but from mid 1967 *all* low-value stamps bear phosphor markings.

The graphite lines were printed in black on the back, beneath the gum; two lines per stamp except for the 2d (*see below*).

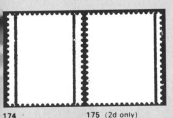

174   175 (2d only)

(Stamps viewed from back)

In November 1959, phosphor bands, printed on the front, replaced the graphite. They are wider than the graphite, not easy to see, but show as broad vertical bands at certain angles to the light.

Values representing the rate for printed papers (and second class mail from 1968) have one band and others have two, three or four bands according to size and format. From 1972 onwards some commemorative stamps were printed with 'all-over' phosphor.

In the small stamps the bands are on each side with the single band at left (except where otherwise stated). In the large-size commemorative stamps the single band may be at left, centre or right varying in different issues. The bands are vertical on both horizontal and vertical designs except where otherwise stated.

See also notes on page 36.

Graphite-lined issue

1957 (19 Nov.) *Two graphite lines on the back, except 2d value, which has one line. Wmk* **165**

561	**154**	½d orange	20	30	☐ ☐
562		1d blue	20	50	☐ ☐
563		1½d green	30	1·75	☐ ☐
564		2d light red-brown	2·50	2·00	☐ ☐
565	**155**	2½d red	7·00	6·25	☐ ☐
566		3d lilac	30	50	☐ ☐
	Set of 6		9·50	10·00	☐ ☐
	First Day Cover			70·00	☐

See also Nos. 587/94.

176 Welsh Dragon

177 Flag and Games Emblem

178 Welsh Dragon

Sixth British Empire and Commonwealth Games, Cardiff

1958 (18 July) *Wmk* **165**

567	**176**	3d lilac	.. ..	15	10	☐ ☐
568	**177**	6d mauve	.. ..	25	45	☐ ☐
569	**178**	1s 3d green	.. ..	2·50	2·50	☐ ☐
	Set of 3		.. ..	2·50	2·50	☐ ☐
	First Day Cover		.. ..		55·00	☐

179 Multiple Crowns

WATERMARK. All the following issues to No. 755 are Watermark **179** (sideways on the vertical commemorative stamps) unless otherwise stated.

1958–65 *Wmk* **179**

570	**154**	½d orange	.. ..	10	10	☐ ☐
571		1d blue	.. ..	10	10	☐ ☐
572		1½d green	.. ..	10	15	☐ ☐
573		2d light red-brown		10	10	☐ ☐
574	**155**	2½d red	.. ..	10	10	☐ ☐
575		3d lilac	.. ..	10	20	☐ ☐
576*a*	**156**	4d blue	.. ..	15	10	☐ ☐
577		4½d brown	.. ..	10	30	☐ ☐
578	**157**	5d brown	.. ..	25	40	☐ ☐
579		6d purple	.. ..	25	30	☐ ☐
580		7d green	.. ..	40	50	☐ ☐
581	**158**	8d magenta	.. ..	40	30	☐ ☐
582		9d bronze-green	..	40	40	☐ ☐
583		10d blue	.. ..	1·00	40	☐ ☐
584	**159**	1s bistre	.. ..	50	30	☐ ☐
585	**160**	1s 3d green	.. ..	25	30	☐ ☐
586	**159**	1s 6d indigo	.. ..	4·00	40	☐ ☐
	Set of 17		.. ..	8·00	4·00	☐ ☐
	First Day Cover (*No.* 577) (9 Feb. 1959)		.. ..		£150	☐

For full information on all future British issues, collectors should write to the British Post Office Philatelic Bureau, 20 Brandon Street, Edinburgh EH3 5TT

Graphite-lined issue

1958–59 Two graphite lines on the back, except 2d value, which has one line. Wmk **179**

587	**154**	½d orange	.. ..	1·25	2·25	☐	☐
588		1d blue	.. ..	1·00	1·50	☐	☐
589		1½d green	.. ..	40·00	40·00	☐	☐
590		2d light red-brown		6·00	3·25	☐	☐
591	**155**	2½d red	.. ..	8·00	10·00	☐	☐
592		3d lilac	.. ..	50	50	☐	☐
593	**156**	4d blue	.. ..	3·50	4·50	☐	☐
594		4½d brown	.. ..	5·00	4·00	☐	☐
	Set of 8		..	60·00	60·00	☐	☐

The prices quoted for Nos. 587 and 589 are for examples with inverted watermark. Stamps with upright watermark are priced at: ½d. £7 mint or used and 1½d £95 mint, £60 used.

1959–63 Wmk **179** Perf 11 × 12

595a	**166**	2s 6d brown	..	50	30	☐	☐
596a	**167**	5s red	..	1·00	60	☐	☐
597a	**168**	10s blue	.. ..	3·00	3·50	☐	☐
598a	**169**	£1 black	..	8·00	5·00	☐	☐
	Set of 4		..	11·00	8·50	☐	☐

Phosphor-Graphite issue

1959 (18 Nov.) Two phosphor bands on front and two graphite lines on back, except 2d value, which has one band on front and one line on back

(a) Wmk **165**

599	**154**	½d orange	.. ..	4·00	6·00	☐	☐
600		1d blue	.. ..	8·00	6·50	☐	☐
601		1½d green	.. ..	2·00	6·00	☐	☐

(b) Wmk **179**

605	**154**	2d light red-brown (1 band)	..	4·50	4·00	☐	☐
606	**155**	2½d red	.. ..	20·00	12·00	☐	☐
607		3d lilac	.. ..	9·00	8·00	☐	☐
608	**156**	4d blue	.. ..	12·00	25·00	☐	☐
609		4½d brown	.. ..	35·00	15·00	☐	☐
	Set of 8		..	80·00	70·00	☐	☐

Phosphor issue

1960–67 Two phosphor bands on front, except where otherwise stated. Wmk **179**

610	**154**	½d orange	..	10	15	☐	☐
611		1d blue	..	10	10	☐	☐
612		1½d green	..	10	20	☐	☐
613		2d light red-brown (1 band)	..	16·00	20·00	☐	☐
613a		2d light red-brown (2 bands)		10	10	☐	☐
614	**155**	2½d red (2 bands)	..	10	40	☐	☐
614a		2½d red (1 band)	..	40	90	☐	☐
615		3d lilac (2 bands)	..	60	60	☐	☐
615c		3d lilac (1 side band)	..	50	75	☐	☐
615e		3d lilac (1 centre band)	.. ..	25	40	☐	☐

616a	**156**	4d blue	.. ..	15	15	☐	☐
616b		4½d brown	.. ..	15	25	☐	☐
616c	**157**	5d brown	.. ..	20	50	☐	☐
617		6d purple	.. ..	40	20	☐	☐
617a		7d green	.. ..	60	25	☐	☐
617b	**158**	8d magenta	.. ..	20	25	☐	☐
617c		9d bronze-green	..	60	25	☐	☐
617d		10d blue	.. ..	80	35	☐	☐
617e	**159**	1s bistre	.. ..	40	40	☐	☐
618	**160**	1s 3d green	..	1·75	2·75	☐	☐
618a	**159**	1s 6d indigo	..	2·00	1·25	☐	☐
	Set of 17 (one of each value)			7·00	6·50	☐	☐

No. 615c exists with the phosphor band at the left or right of the stamp.

180 Postboy of 1660   **181** Posthorn of 1660

Tercentenary of Establishment of 'General Letter Office'

1960 (7 July)

619	**180**	3d lilac	.. ..	20	10	☐	☐
620	**181**	1s 3d green	..	3·50	3·50	☐	☐
	Set of 2		.. ..	3·50	3·50	☐	☐
	First Day Cover	..	..		48·00		

182 Conference Emblem

First Anniversary of European Postal and Telecommunications Conference

1960 (19 Sept.)

621	**182**	6d green and purple	..	40	60	☐	☐
622		1s 6d brown and blue		6·00	4·50	☐	☐
	Set of 2		.. ..	6·25	4·50	☐	☐
	First Day Cover	..	..		38·00		

183 Thrift Plant   **184** 'Growth of Savings'

185 Thrift Plant

Centenary of Post Office Savings Bank

1961 (28 Aug.)

₵23	183	2½d black and red		10	10	☐	☐
₵24	184	3d orange-brown and violet	..	10	10	☐	☐
₵25	185	1s 6d red and blue	..	2·50	2·25	☐	☐
	Set of 3	.. .. ..	..	2·50	2·25	☐	☐
	First Day Cover	.. ..			60·00		☐

186 C E P T Emblem

187 Doves and Emblem

188 Doves and Emblem

European Postal and Telecommunications (C.E.P.T.) Conference, Torquay

1961 (18 Sept.)

₵26	186	2d orange, pink and brown	..	10	10	☐	☐
₵27	187	4d buff, mauve and ultramarine	..	20	10	☐	☐
₵28	188	10d turquoise, green and blue	.. ..	40	45	☐	☐
	Set of 3	.. .. ..		60	60	☐	☐
	First Day Cover	.. .. ..			5·00		☐

189 Hammer Beam Roof, Westminster Hall

190 Palace of Westminster

Seventh Commonwealth Parliamentary Conference

1961 (25 Sept.)

629	**189**	6d purple and gold	25	25	☐	☐
630	**190**	1s 3d green and blue	2·50	2·25	☐	☐
	Set of 2	.. ..	2·50	2·25	☐	☐
	First Day Cover ..			26·00		☐

191 'Units of Productivity'

192 'National Productivity'

193 'Unified Productivity'

National Productivity Year

1962 (14 Nov.) *Wmk* **179** *(inverted on 2½d and 3d)*

631	**191**	2½d green and red ..	20	10	☐	☐
		p. Phosphor ..	1·00	50	☐	☐
632	**192**	3d blue and violet	25	10	☐	☐
		p. Phosphor ..	1·00	50	☐	☐
633	**193**	1s 3d red, blue and green ..	1·75	2·00	☐	☐
		p. Phosphor	29·00	20·00	☐	☐
	Set of 3 (Ordinary)		2·00	2·00	☐	☐
	Set of 3 (Phosphor) ..		29·00	20·00	☐	☐
	First Day Cover (Ordinary)			35·00		☐
	First Day Cover (Phosphor)			85·00		☐

194 Campaign Emblem and Family

195 Children of Three Races

Freedom from Hunger

1963 (21 Mar.) *Wmk* **179** *(inverted)*

634	**194**	2½d crimson and pink	10	10	☐	☐
		p. Phosphor ..	1·00	1·25	☐	☐
635	**195**	1s 3d brown and yellow	2·00	2·00	☐	☐
		p. Phosphor ..	29·00	20·00	☐	☐
	Set of 2 (Ordinary)	..	2·00	2·00	☐	☐
	Set of 2 (Phosphor) ..		29·00	20·00	☐	☐
	First Day Cover (Ordinary) ..			27·00		☐
	First Day Cover (Phosphor)..			30·00		☐

196 Paris Conference

Paris Postal Conference Centenary

1963 (7 MAY) *Wmk* **179** *(inverted)*

636	**196**	6d green and mauve	50	50	☐	☐
		p Phosphor	6·50	6·00	☐	☐
		First Day Cover (Ordinary)		12·00	☐	
		First Day Cover (Phosphor)		20·00	☐	

197 Posy of Flowers

198 Woodland Life

National Nature Week

1963 (16 MAY)

637	**197**	3d multicoloured	25	20	☐	☐
		p. Phosphor	50	60	☐	☐
638	**198**	4½d multicoloured	40	50	☐	☐
		p. Phosphor	2·50	2·50	☐	☐
		Set of 2 (Ordinary)	60	70	☐	☐
		Set of 2 (Phosphor)	3·00	3·00	☐	☐
		First Day Cover (Ordinary)		19·00	☐	
		First Day Cover (Phosphor)		27·00	☐	

199 Rescue at Sea   200 19th-century Lifeboat

201 Lifeboatmen

Ninth International Lifeboat Conference, Edinburgh

1963 (31 MAY)

639	**199**	2½d blue, black and red	10	10	☐	☐
		p. Phosphor	40	50	☐	☐
640	**200**	4d multicoloured	40	30	☐	☐
		p. Phosphor	20	50	☐	☐
641	**201**	1s 6d sepia, yellow and blue	2·50	2·75	☐	☐
		p. Phosphor	40·00	27·00	☐	·
		Set of 3 (Ordinary)	2·75	2·75	☐	☐
		Set of 3 (Phosphor)	40·00	27·00	☐	☐
		First Day Cover (Ordinary)		26·00	☐	
		First Day Cover (Phosphor)		32·00	☐	

202 Red Cross   203

204   205 Commonwealth Cable

Red Cross Centenary Congress

1963 (15 AUG.)

642	**202**	3d red and lilac	10	10	☐	☐
		p. Phosphor	60	60	☐	☐
643	**203**	1s 3d red, blue and grey	3·25	2·75	☐	☐
		p. Phosphor	40·00	35·00	☐	☐
644	**204**	1s 6d red, blue and bistre	3·00	2·75	☐	☐
		p. Phosphor	35·00	27·00	☐	☐
		Set of 3 (Ordinary)	6·00	5·00	☐	☐
		Set of 3 (Phosphor)	70·00	55·00	☐	☐
		First Day Cover (Ordinary)		30·00	☐	
		First Day Cover (Phosphor)		60·00	☐	

Opening of COMPAC (Trans-Pacific Telephone Cable)

1963 (3 DEC.)

645	**205**	1s 6d blue and black	2·25	2·25	☐	☐
		p. Phosphor	17·00	17·00	☐	☐
		First Day Cover (Ordinary)		22·00	☐	
		First Day Cover (Phosphor)		28·00	☐	

6 Puck and Bottom
(*A Midsummer Night's Dream*)

207 Feste (*Twelfth Night*)

8 Balcony Scene
(*Romeo and Juliet*)

209 Eve of Agincourt
(*Henry V*)

210 Hamlet contemplating
Yorick's skull (*Hamlet*)
and Queen Elizabeth II

hakespeare Festival

964 (23 APR.) Perf 11 · 12 (2s 6d) or 15 · 14 (others)

46	206	3d bis, blk & vio-bl	10	10	☐	☐
		p Phosphor	20	30	☐	☐
47	207	6d multicoloured	20	30	☐	☐
		p Phosphor	60	90	☐	☐
48	208	1s 3d multicoloured	90	1·00	☐	☐
		p Phosphor	5·75	6·00	☐	☐
49	209	1s 6d multicoloured	1·25	1·00	☐	☐
		p Phosphor	10·00	6·25	☐	☐
50	210	2s 6d deep slate-purple	2·00	2·25	☐	☐
		Set of 5 (*Ordinary*)	4·00	4·25	☐	☐
		Set of 4 (*Phosphor*)	14·00	12·00	☐	☐
		First Day Cover (*Ordinary*)		8·50		☐
		First Day Cover (*Phosphor*)		12·00		☐
		Presentation Pack (*Ordinary*)	10·00			☐

RESENTATION PACKS were first introduced by the P.O. for the Shakespeare Festival issue. The packs include ne set of stamps and details of the designs, the designer nd the stamp printer. They were issued for almost all later efinitive and special issues

11 Flats near Richmond Park
('Urban Development')

212 Shipbuilding Yards, Belfast
('Industrial Activity')

213 Beddgelert Forest Park,
Snowdonia (Forestry)

214 Nuclear Reactor, Dounreay
(Technological Development)

20th International Geographical Congress, London

1964 (1 JULY)

651	211	2½d multicoloured	10	10	☐	☐
		p Phosphor	50	40	☐	☐
652	212	4d multicoloured	25	25	☐	☐
		p Phosphor	75	70	☐	☐
653	213	8d multicoloured	60	50	☐	☐
		p Phosphor	1·75	1·50	☐	☐
654	214	1s 6d multicoloured	3·25	3·25	☐	☐
		p Phosphor	25·00	20·00	☐	☐
		Set of 4 (*Ordinary*)	4·00	4·00	☐	☐
		Set of 4 (*Phosphor*)	25·00	20·00	☐	☐
		First Day Cover (*Ordinary*)		19·00		☐
		First Day Cover (*Phosphor*)		29·00		☐
		Presentation Pack (*Ordinary*)	95·00			☐

215 Spring Gentian

216 Dog Rose

217 Honeysuckle

218 Fringed Water Lily

Tenth International Botanical Congress, Edinburgh

1964 (5 AUG.)

655	215	3d vio. blue & green	10	10	☐	☐
		p Phosphor	20	30	☐	☐
656	216	6d multicoloured	20	20	☐	☐
		p Phosphor	2·00	1·50	☐	☐
657	217	9d multicoloured	1·60	2·50	☐	☐
		p Phosphor	4·50	3·00	☐	☐
658	218	1s 3d multicoloured	2·50	1·90	☐	☐
		p Phosphor	22·00	19·00	☐	☐
		Set of 4 (*Ordinary*)	4·00	4·00	☐	☐
		Set of 4 (*Phosphor*)	26·00	21·00	☐	☐
		First Day Cover (*Ordinary*)		22·00		☐
		First Day Cover (*Phosphor*)		32·00		☐
		Presentation Pack (*Ordinary*)	90·00			☐

219 Forth Road Bridge

220 Forth Road and Railway Bridges

Opening of Forth Road Bridge

1964 (4 SEPT.)

659	**219**	3d black, blue and violet	15	10	☐	☐
		p Phosphor	50	50	☐	☐
660	**220**	6d black, blue and red	45	40	☐	☐
		p Phosphor	4·50	4·50	☐	☐
		Set of 2 (Ordinary)	60	50	☐	☐
		Set of 2 (Phosphor)	5·00	5·00	☐	☐
		First Day Cover (Ordinary)		6·50	☐	
		First Day Cover (Phosphor)		10·00	☐	
		Presentation Pack (Ordinary)	£225		☐	

221 Sir Winston Churchill

222 Sir Winston Churchill

Churchill Commemoration

1965 (8 JULY)

661	**221**	4d black and drab	15	10	☐	☐
		p Phosphor	30	30	☐	☐
662	**222**	1s 3d black and grey	45	40	☐	☐
		p Phosphor	3·50	3·50	☐	☐
		Set of 2 (Ordinary)	60	50	☐	☐
		Set of 2 (Phosphor)	3·50	3·50	☐	☐
		First Day Cover (Ordinary)		4·00	☐	
		First Day Cover (Phosphor)		6·50	☐	
		Presentation Pack (Ordinary)	15·00		☐	

223 Simon de Montfort's Seal

224 Parliament Buildings
(after engraving by Hollar 1647)

700th Anniversary of Simon de Montfort's Parliament

1965 (19 JULY)

663	**223**	6d green	10	10	☐	
		p Phosphor	70	80	☐	
664	**224**	2s 6d black, grey and drab	1·25	1·25	☐	
		Set of 2 (Ordinary)	1·25	1·25	☐	
		First Day Cover (Ordinary)		10·00		
		First Day Cover (Phosphor)		15·00		
		Presentation Pack (Ordinary)	35·00		☐	

225 Bandsmen and Banner

226 Three Salvationists

Salvation Army Centenary

1965 (9 AUG.)

665	**225**	3d multicoloured	10	10	☐	☐
		p Phosphor	50	40	☐	☐
666	**226**	1s 6d multicoloured	1·00	1·00	☐	☐
		p Phosphor	3·00	3·25	☐	☐
		Set of 2 (Ordinary)	1·10	1·10	☐	☐
		Set of 2 (Phosphor)	3·50	3·50	☐	☐
		First Day Cover (Ordinary)		20·00		
		First Day Cover (Phosphor)		27·00		

227 Lister's Carbolic Spray

228 Lister and Chemical Symbols

Centenary of Joseph Lister's Discovery of Antiseptic Surgery

1965 (1 SEPT.)

667	**227**	4d indigo, chestnut and grey	10	10	☐	☐
		p Phosphor	15	20	☐	☐
668	**228**	1s black, purple and blue	1·00	1·50	☐	☐
		p Phosphor	2·40	2·40	☐	☐
		Set of 2 (Ordinary)	1·10	1·50	☐	☐
		Set of 2 (Phosphor)	2·50	2·50	☐	☐
		First Day Cover (Ordinary)		11·00		
		First Day Cover (Phosphor)		13·00		

9 Trinidad Carnival Dancers   **230** Canadian Folk dancers

Commonwealth Arts Festival

1965 (1 Sept.)

9	**229**	6d black and orange	10	10	☐	☐
		p *Phosphor*	30	30	☐	☐
0	**230**	1s 6d black and violet	1·25	1·50	☐	☐
		p *Phosphor*	2·25	2·25	☐	☐
		Set of 2 (Ordinary)	1·25	1·50	☐	☐
		Set of 2 (Phosphor)	2·50	2·50	☐	☐
		First Day Cover (Ordinary)		14·00		☐
		First Day Cover (Phosphor)		20·00		☐

1 Flight of Supermarine Spitfires

232 Pilot in Hawker Hurricane Mk I

3 Wing-tips of Supermarine Spitfire and Messerschmitt Bf 109

234 Supermarine Spitfires attacking Heinkel HE 111H Bomber

5 Supermarine Spitfire attacking Junkers Ju 87B "Stuka" Dive-bomber

236 Hawker Hurricanes Mk I over Wreck of Dornier Do-17Z Bomber

he above were issued together *se-tenant* in blocks of six (3 × 2) within he sheet.

37 Anti-aircraft Artillery in Action   **238** Air battle over St Paul's Cathedral

25th Anniversary of Battle of Britain

1965 (13 Sept.)

671	**231**	4d olive and black	30	35	☐	☐
	a	*Block of 6*				
		Nos 671/6	5·50	7·50	☐	☐
	p	*Phosphor*	40	50	☐	☐
	pa	*Block of 6*				
		Nos 671p/6p	10·50	12·00	☐	☐
672	**232**	4d olive, blackish olive and black	30	35	☐	☐
		p *Phosphor*	40	50	☐	☐
673	**233**	4d multicoloured	30	35	☐	☐
		p *Phosphor*	40	50	☐	☐
674	**234**	4d olive and black	30	35	☐	☐
		p *Phosphor*	40	50	☐	☐
675	**235**	4d olive and black	30	35	☐	☐
		p *Phosphor*	40	50	☐	☐
676	**236**	4d multicoloured	30	35	☐	☐
		p *Phosphor*	40	50	☐	☐
677	**237**	9d violet, orange and purple	1·25	1·25	☐	☐
		p *Phosphor*	1·25	80	☐	☐
678	**238**	1s 3d multicoloured	1·25	1·25	☐	☐
		p *Phosphor*	1·25	80	☐	☐
		Set of 8 (Ordinary)	7·25	4·25	☐	☐
		Set of 8 (Phosphor)	12·00	4·25	☐	☐
		First Day Cover (Ordinary)		22·00		☐
		First Day Cover (Phosphor)		22·00		☐
		Presentation Pack (Ordinary)	45·00		☐	

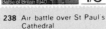 

239 Tower and Georgian Buildings   **240** Tower and Nash Terrace. Regent's Park

Opening of Post Office Tower

1965 (8 Oct.)

679	**239**	3d yellow, blue and green	10	10	☐	☐
		p *Phosphor*	10	10	☐	☐
680	**240**	1s 3d green and blue	65	75	☐	☐
		p *Phosphor*	50	50	☐	☐
		Set of 2 (Ordinary)	75	85	☐	☐
		Set of 2 (Phosphor)	60	60	☐	☐
		First Day Cover (Ordinary)		6·00		☐
		First Day Cover (Phosphor)		8·00		☐
		Presentation Pack (Ordinary)	3·00		☐	
		Presentation Pack (Phosphor)	3·00		☐	

241 U N Emblem   **242** I C Y Emblem

20th Anniversary of UNO and International Co-operation Year

1965 (25 Oct.)

681	**241**	3d	blk, orge & bl	15	20	☐	☐
		p.	Phosphor	25	40	☐	☐
682	**242**	1s 6d	blk, pur & bl	1·10	1·10	☐	☐
		p.	Phosphor	2·75	3·00	☐	☐
	Set of 2 (Ordinary)			1·25	1·10	☐	☐
	Set of 2 (Phosphor)			2·75	3·25	☐	☐
	First Day Cover (Ordinary)				10·50		☐
	First Day Cover (Phosphor)				12·50		☐

243 Telecommunications Network   **244** Radio Waves and Switchboard

I.T.U. Centenary

1965 (15 Nov.)

683	**243**	9d	multicoloured	20	25	☐	☐
		p.	Phosphor	60	50	☐	☐
684	**244**	1s 6d	multicoloured	1·60	1·50	☐	☐
		p.	Phosphor	5·25	5·25	☐	☐
	Set of 2 (Ordinary)			1·50	1·25	☐	☐
	Set of 2 (Phosphor)			5·00	5·00	☐	☐
	First Day Cover (Ordinary)				13·00		☐
	First Day Cover (Phosphor)				17·00		☐

245 Robert Burns (after Skirving chalk drawing)   **246** Robert Burns (after Nasmyth portrait)

Burns Commemoration

1966 (25 Jan.)

685	**245**	4d	blk, indigo & bl	15	15	☐	☐
		p.	Phosphor	25	25	☐	☐
686	**246**	1s 3d	blk, bl & orge	70	70	☐	☐
		p.	Phosphor	2·00	2·00	☐	☐
	Set of 2 (Ordinary)			85	85	☐	☐
	Set of 2 (Phosphor)			2·50	2·50	☐	☐
	First Day Cover (Ordinary)				3·00		☐
	First Day Cover (Phosphor)				3·75		☐
	Presentation Pack (Ordinary)			38·00			☐

247 Westminster Abbey   **248** Fan Vaulting, Henry VII Chapel

900th Anniversary of Westminster Abbey

1966 (28 Feb.)   Perf 15 × 14 (3d) or 11 × 12 (2s 6d)

687	**247**	3d	black, brown and blue	15	20	☐	☐
		p.	Phosphor	30	30	☐	☐
688	**248**	2s 6d	black	85	1·10	☐	☐
	Set of 2			1·00	1·25	☐	☐
	First Day Cover (Ordinary)				6·00		☐
	First Day Cover (Phosphor)				10·00		☐
	Presentation Pack (Ordinary)			15·00			☐

249 View near Hassocks, Sussex   **250** Antrim, Northern Ireland

251 Harlech Castle, Wales   **252** Cairngorm Mountains, Scotland

Landscapes

1966 (2 May)

689	**249**	4d	black, yellow-green and blue	15	15	☐	☐
		p.	Phosphor	15	15	☐	☐
690	**250**	6d	black, green and blue	15	15	☐	☐
		p.	Phosphor	25	25	☐	☐
691	**251**	1s 3d	black, yellow and blue	35	35	☐	☐
		p.	Phosphor	35	35	☐	☐
692	**252**	1s 6d	black, orange and blue	50	50	☐	☐
		p.	Phosphor	50	50	☐	☐
	Set of 4 (Ordinary)			1·00	1·00	☐	☐
	Set of 4 (Phosphor)			1·00	1·00	☐	☐
	First Day Cover (Ordinary)				8·50		☐
	First Day Cover (Phosphor)				8·50		☐

53 Players with Ball

260 Cup Winners

254 Goalmouth Mêlée

255 Goalkeeper saving Goal

World Cup Football Competition

1966 (1 June)

693	**253**	4d multicoloured		15	10	☐	☐
		p Phosphor		15	10	☐	☐
694	**254**	6d multicoloured		20	20	☐	☐
		p Phosphor		20	20	☐	☐
695	**255**	1s 3d multicoloured		50	65	☐	☐
		p Phosphor		50	65	☐	☐
		Set of 3 (Ordinary)		75	90	☐	☐
		Set of 3 (Phosphor)		75	90	☐	☐
		First Day Cover (Ordinary)			9·50		☐
		First Day Cover (Phosphor)			10·00		☐
		Presentation Pack (Ordinary)	14·00			☐	

256 Black-headed Gull

257 Blue Tit

258 Robin

259 Blackbird

The above were issued *se-tenant* in blocks of four within the sheet.

British Birds

1966 (8 Aug.)

696	**256**	4d multicoloured		10	15	☐	☐
	a	Block of 4					
		Nos. 696/9		1·00	1·25	☐	☐
	p	Phosphor		10	15	☐	☐
	pa	Block of 4					
		Nos. 696p/9p		1·00	1·00	☐	☐
697	**257**	4d multicoloured		10	15	☐	☐
		p Phosphor		10	15	☐	☐
698	**258**	4d multicoloured		10	15	☐	☐
		p Phosphor		10	15	☐	☐
699	**259**	4d multicoloured		10	15	☐	☐
		p Phosphor		10	15	☐	☐
		Set of 4 (Ordinary)		1·00	50	☐	☐
		Set of 4 (Phosphor)		1·00	50	☐	☐
		First Day Cover (Ordinary)			10·00		☐
		First Day Cover (Phosphor)			10·00		☐
		Presentation Pack (Ordinary)	8·00			☐	

England's World Cup Football Victory

1966 (18 Aug.)

700	**260**	4d multicoloured		20	20	☐	☐
		First Day Cover			4·50		☐

261 Jodrell Bank Radio Telescope

262 British Motor-cars

263 SR N6 Hovercraft

264 Windscale Reactor

British Technology

1966 (19 Sept.)

701	**261**	4d black and lemon		15	15	☐	☐
		p Phosphor		15	15	☐	☐
702	**262**	6d red, blue and orange		15	15	☐	☐
		p Phosphor		15	15	☐	☐
703	**263**	1s 3d multicoloured		30	40	☐	☐
		p Phosphor		45	50	☐	☐
704	**264**	1s 6d multicoloured		50	45	☐	☐
		p Phosphor		65	60	☐	☐
		Set of 4 (Ordinary)		1·00	1·00	☐	☐
		Set of 4 (Phosphor)		1·25	1·25	☐	☐
		First Day Cover (Ordinary)			5·50		☐
		First Day Cover (Phosphor)			6·00		☐
		Presentation Pack (Ordinary)	8·00			☐	

265　　　　　266

267　　　　　268

269　　　　　270

The above show battle scenes, they were issued together *se-tenant* in horizontal strips of six within the sheet.

271　Norman Ship

272　Norman Horsemen attacking Harold's Troops

900th Anniversary of Battle of Hastings

1966 (14 Oct.) *Designs show scenes from Bayeux Tapestry.* Wmk **179** (*sideways on 1s 3d*)

705	**265**	4d	multicoloured	..	10	15	☐ ☐
		a.	Strip of 6				
			Nos. 705/10		2·25	3·00	☐ ☐
		p.	Phosphor		10	25	☐ ☐
		pa	Strip of 6				
			Nos. 705p/10p		2·25	3·00	☐ ☐
706	**266**	4d	multicoloured	..	10	15	☐ ☐
		p.	Phosphor	..	10	25	☐ ☐
707	**267**	4d	multicoloured	..	10	15	☐ ☐
		p.	Phosphor		10	25	☐ ☐
708	**268**	4d	multicoloured	..	10	15	☐
		p.	Phosphor		10	25	☐
709	**269**	4d	multicoloured		10	15	☐
		p.	Phosphor		10	25	☐
710	**270**	4d	multicoloured		10	15	☐
		p.	Phosphor		10	25	☐
711	**271**	6d	multicoloured	..	10	10	☐
		p.	Phosphor		10	10	☐
712	**272**	1s 3d	multicoloured		20	20	☐
		p.	Phosphor		20	20	☐
	Set of 8 (Ordinary)			..	2·25	1·50	☐
	Set of 8 (Phosphor)			..	2·25	1·90	☐
	First Day Cover (Ordinary)					4·00	
	First Day Cover (Phosphor)					4·00	
	Presentation Pack (Ordinary)				9·00		☐

273　King of the Orient　　　274　Snowman

Christmas

1966 (1 Dec.) Wmk **179** (*upright on 1s 6d*)

713	**273**	3d	multicoloured	..	10	10	☐
		p.	Phosphor	..	10	10	☐
714	**274**	1s 6d	multicoloured		40	40	☐
		p.	Phosphor	..	40	40	☐
	Set of 2 (Ordinary)			..	50	·50	☐
	Set of 2 (Phosphor)			..	50	50	☐
	First Day Cover (Ordinary)					3·00	
	First Day Cover (Phosphor)					3·00	
	Presentation Pack (Ordinary)				9·00		

275　Sea Freight　　　276　Air Freight

European Free Trade Association (EFTA)

1967 (20 Feb.)

715	**275**	9d	multicoloured		15	15	☐ ☐
		p.	Phosphor	..	15	15	☐ ☐
716	**276**	1s 6d	multicoloured	..	30	30	☐ ☐
		p.	Phosphor	..	30	30	☐ ☐
	Set of 2 (Ordinary)			..	40	40	☐ ☐
	Set of 2 (Phosphor)			..	40	40	☐ ☐
	First Day Cover (Ordinary)					3·00	
	First Day Cover (Phosphor)					3·25	
	Presentation Pack (Ordinary)				3·00		☐

277 Hawthorn and Bramble   **278** Larger Bindweed and Viper's Bugloss

279 Ox-eye Daisy, Coltsfoot and Buttercup   **280** Bluebell, Red Campion and Wood Anemone

The above were issued together *se-tenant* in blocks of four within the sheet.

281 Dog Violet   **282** Primroses

British Wild Flowers

1967 (24 APR.)

717	277	4d multicoloured ..	15	10	☐	☐
	a.	Block of 4				
		Nos. 717/20 ..	1·25	2·00	☐	☐
	p.	Phosphor ..	10	10	☐	☐
	pa.	Block of 4				
		Nos. 717p/20p	1·00	1·75		☐
718	278	4d multicoloured ..	15	10	☐	☐
	p.	Phosphor	10	10	☐	☐
719	279	4d multicoloured ..	15	10	☐	☐
	p.	Phosphor	10	10	☐	☐
720	280	4d multicoloured ..	15	10	☐	☐
	p.	Phosphor	10	10	☐	☐
721	281	9d multicoloured ..	15	10	☐	☐
	p.	Phosphor	10	10	☐	☐
722	282	1s 9d multicoloured ..	20	20	☐	☐
	p.	Phosphor	30	20	☐	☐
		Set of 6 (Ordinary)	1·40	65	☐	☐
		Set of 6 (Phosphor)	1·25	65	☐	☐
		First Day Cover (Ordinary)		4·50		☐
		First Day Cover (Phosphor)		5·00		☐
		Presentation Pack (Ordinary)	4·25			☐
		Presentation Pack (Phosphor)	4·25			☐

283 (value at left)   **284** (value at right)

Two types of the 2d.
I. Value spaced away from left side of stamp.
II. Value close to left side from new multi-positive. This results in the portrait appearing in the centre, thus conforming with the other values.

1967–69 *Two phosphor bands, except where otherwise stated. No wmk*

723	283	½d orange-brown	10	20	☐	☐
724		1d olive (2 bands)	10	10	☐	☐
725		1d olive (1 centre band)	25	30	☐	☐
726		2d lake-brown (Type I) (2 bands)	10	15	☐	☐
727		2d lake-brown (Type II) (2 bands)	15	15	☐	☐
728		2d lake-brown (Type II) (1 centre band) ..	50	75	☐	☐
729		3d violet (1 centre band)	10	10	☐	☐
730		3d violet (2 bands)	30	30	☐	☐
731		4d sepia (2 bands)	10	10	☐	☐
732		4d olive-brown (1 centre band) ..	10	10	☐	☐
733		4d vermilion (1 centre band) ..	10	10	☐	☐
734		4d vermilion (1 side band) ..	1·40	1·75	☐	☐
735		5d blue	10	10	☐	☐
736		6d purple	20	20	☐	☐
737	284	7d emerald	40	30	☐	☐
738		8d vermilion ..	15	30	☐	☐
739		8d turquoise-blue ..	55	60	☐	☐
740		9d green	50	30	☐	☐
741	283	10d drab	45	50	☐	☐
742		1s violet	40	30	☐	☐
743		1s 6d blue and dp blue	50	30	☐	☐
		c. Phosphorised paper	85	90	☐	☐
744		1s 9d orange and black	40	30	☐	☐
		Set of 16 (one of each value and colour)	3·00	3·25	☐	☐
		Presentation Pack (one of each value)	6·00			☐
		Presentation Pack (German)	35·00			☐

First Day Covers

5 June 1967	Nos. 731, 742, 744	1·00	☐
8 Aug. 1967	Nos. 729, 740, 743	1·00	☐
5 Feb. 1968	Nos. 723/4, 726, 736	1·00	☐
1 July 1968	Nos. 735, 737/8, 741	1·00	☐

No. 734 exists with phosphor band at the left or right.

285 'Master Lambton'
(Sir Thomas Lawrence)

286 'Mares and Foals in a
Landscape' (George Stubbs)

287 Children Coming Out
of School (L. S. Lowry)

288 Gipsy Moth IV

British Paintings

1967 (10 JULY) *Two phosphor bands. No wmk*

748	**285**	4d multicoloured		10	10	☐	☐
749	**286**	9d multicoloured		20	20	☐	☐
750	**287**	1s 6d multicoloured		35	25	☐	☐
		Set of 3		50	50	☐	☐
		First Day Cover			3·50		☐
		Presentation Pack		7·50		☐	

Sir Francis Chichester's World Voyage

1967 (24 JULY) *Three phosphor bands. No wmk*

751	**288**	1s 9d multicoloured		25	25	☐	☐
		First Day Cover			2·00		☐

289 Radar Screen

290 *Penicillium notatum*

291 Vickers VC-10 Jet Engines

292 Television Equipment

British Discovery and Invention

1967 (19 SEPT.) *Two phosphor bands (except 4d, thre
bands). Wmk 179 (sideways on 1s 9d)*

752	**289**	4d yell, blk & verm		10	10	☐
753	**290**	1s multicoloured		10	10	☐
754	**291**	1s 6d multicoloured		25	15	☐
755	**292**	1s 9d multicoloured		30	20	☐
		Set of 4		60	50	☐
		First Day Cover			2·25	
		Presentation Pack		2·75		☐

NO WATERMARK. All the following issues are on ur
watermarked paper unless stated.

293 'The Adoration of
the Shepherds'
(School of Seville)

294 'Madonna and
Child' (Murillo)

295 'The Adoration of the Shepher
(Louis Le Nain)

Christmas

1967 *Two phosphor bands (except 3d, one phosphor band*

756	**293**	3d multicoloured (27 Nov.)		10	10	☐
757	**294**	4d multicoloured (18 Oct.)		10	10	☐
758	**295**	1s 6d multicoloured (27 Nov.)		35	35	☐
		Set of 3		50	50	☐
		First Day Covers (2)			4·00	

Gift Pack 1967

1967 (27 NOV.) *Comprises Nos. 715p/22p and 748/58*

	Gift Pack		2·50	☐

1967–68 *No wmk   Perf 11×12*

759	**166**	2s 6d brown		40	50	☐
760	**167**	5s red		1·00	1·00	☐
761	**168**	10s blue		5·00	6·00	☐
762	**169**	£1 black		4·00	5·00	☐
		Set of 4		9·00	11·00	☐

296 Tarr Steps, Exmoor

297 Aberfeldy Bridge

298 Menai Bridge

299 M4 Viaduct

British Bridges

1968 (29 APR.) *Two phosphor bands*

763	296	4d multicoloured ..	10	10	☐	☐
764	297	9d multicoloured ..	10	10	☐	☐
765	298	1s 6d multicoloured ..	20	15	☐	☐
766	299	1s 9d multicoloured ..	25	30	☐	☐
		Set of 4	60	60	☐	☐
		First Day Cover		2·75		☐
		Presentation Pack	2·25		☐	

300 'TUC' and Trades Unionists

301 Mrs Emmeline Pankhurst (statue)

302 Sopwith Camel and English
Electric Lightning Fighters

303 Captain Cook's *Endeavour* and
Signature

British Anniversaries. Events described on stamps

1968 (29 MAY) *Two phosphor bands*

767	300	4d multicoloured ..	10	10	☐	☐
768	301	9d violet, grey and black	10	10	☐	☐
769	302	1s multicoloured ..	20	20	☐	☐
770	303	1s 9d ochre and brown	25	25	☐	☐
		Set of 4	60	60	☐	☐
		First Day Cover		5·00		☐
		Presentation Pack	3·50		☐	

304 'Queen Elizabeth I'
(Unknown Artist)

305 'Pinkie' (Lawrence)

306 'Ruins of St Mary
Le Port' (Piper)

307 'The Hay Wain' (Constable)

British Paintings

1968 (12 AUG.) *Two phosphor bands*

771	304	4d multicoloured ..	10	10	☐	☐
772	305	1s multicoloured ..	15	15	☐	☐
773	306	1s 6d multicoloured ..	20	20	☐	☐
774	307	1s 9d multicoloured ..	25	25	☐	☐
		Set of 4	60	60	☐	☐
		First Day Cover		2·50		☐
		Presentation Pack	2·00		☐	
		Presentation Pack (German)	5·00		☐	

Gift Pack 1968

1968 (16 SEPT.) *Comprises Nos.* 763/74

Gift Pack	8·00	☐
Gift Pack (German)	18·00	☐

Collectors Pack 1968

1968 (16 SEPT.) *Comprises Nos.* 752/8 *and* 763/74

Collectors Pack	8·00	☐

308 Girl and Boy
with Rocking Horse

309 Girl with Doll's House   **310** Boy with Train Set

Christmas

1968 (25 Nov.) *Two phosphor bands (except 4d, one centre phosphor band)*

775	**308**	4d multicoloured		10	10	☐ ☐
776	**309**	9d multicoloured		15	15	☐ ☐
777	**310**	1s 6d multicoloured		25	25	☐ ☐
	Set of 3			40	40	☐ ☐
	First Day Cover				2·00	☐
	Presentation Pack		3·50			☐
	Presentation Pack (German)		4·00			☐

311 *Queen Elizabeth 2*

312 Elizabethan Galleon

313 East Indiaman

314 *Cutty Sark*

315 *Great Britain*

The 9d and 1s values were arranged in horizontal strips of three and pairs respectively throughout the sheet.

RMS Mauretania   **316** *Mauretania I*

British Ships

1969 (15 Jan.) *Two phosphor bands (except 5d, one horiz phosphor band, 1s, two vert phosphor bands at right)*

778	**311**	5d multicoloured		10	10	☐ ☐
779	**312**	9d multicoloured		10	15	☐ ☐
		a. Strip. Nos. 779/81		1·00	1·50	☐ ☐
780	**313**	9d multicoloured		10	15	☐ ☐
781	**314**	9d multicoloured		10	15	☐ ☐
782	**315**	1s multicoloured		25	25	☐ ☐
		a. Pair. Nos. 782/3		90	1·25	☐ ☐
783	**316**	1s multicoloured		25	25	☐ ☐
	Set of 6			1·75	90	☐ ☐
	First Day Cover				5·00	☐
	Presentation Pack			3·50		☐
	Presentation Pack (German)			19·00		☐

317 Concorde in Flight

318 Plan and Elevation Views

319 Concorde's Nose and Tail

320 (See also Type **359a**)

First Flight of Concorde

1969 (3 Mar.) *Two phosphor bands*

784	**317**	4d multicoloured		10	10	☐ ☐
785	**318**	9d multicoloured		20	20	☐ ☐
786	**319**	1s 6d deep blue, grey and light blue		30	30	☐ ☐
	Set of 3			50	50	☐ ☐
	First Day Cover				2·75	☐
	Presentation Pack			3·50		☐
	Presentation Pack (German)			15·00		☐

1969 (5 Mar.) *P 12*

787	**320**	2s 6d brown		50	30	☐ ☐
788		5s lake		2·25	60	☐ ☐
789		10s ultramarine		7·00	6·00	☐ ☐
790		£1 black		3·00	1·60	☐ ☐
	Set of 4			11·50	7·50	☐ ☐
	First Day Cover				7·50	☐
	Presentation Pack			18·00		☐
	Presentation Pack (German)			38·00		☐

321 Page from the *Daily Mail,* and Vickers FB-27 Vimy Aircraft

322 Europa and C.E.P.T. Emblems

323 I.L.O. Emblem

324 Flags of N.A.T.O. Countries

325 Vickers FB-27 Vimy Aircraft and Globe showing Flight

Anniversaries. Events described on stamps

1969 (2 APR.) *Two phosphor bands*

791	321	5d multicoloured ..	10	10	☐	☐
792	322	9d multicoloured ..	20	20	☐	☐
793	323	1s claret, red and blue	20	20	☐	☐
794	324	1s 6d multicoloured ..	20	20	☐	☐
795	325	1s 9d olive, yellow and turquoise-green	25	25	☐	☐
		Set of 5	85	85	☐	☐
		First Day Cover		3·50		☐
		Presentation Pack	2·75			☐
		Presentation Pack (German)	35·00			☐

326 Durham Cathedral

327 York Minster

328 St Giles' Cathedral. Edinburgh

329 Canterbury Cathedral

The above were issued together *se-tenant* in blocks of four within the sheet.

330 St Paul's Cathedral

331 Liverpool Metropolitan Cathedral

British Architecture (Cathedrals)

1969 (28 MAY) *Two phosphor bands*

796	326	5d multicoloured ..	10	10	☐	☐
	a	Block of 4				
		Nos. 796/9	85	1·50	☐	☐
797	327	5d multicoloured ..	10	10	☐	☐
798	328	5d multicoloured ..	10	10	☐	☐
799	329	5d multicoloured ..	10	10	☐	☐
800	330	9d multicoloured ..	15	15	☐	☐
801	331	1s 6d multicoloured ..	15	15	☐	☐
		Set of 6	1·00	55	☐	☐
		First Day Cover		3·00		☐
		Presentation Pack	4·00			☐
		Presentation Pack (German)	16·00			☐

332 The King's Gate. Caernarvon Castle

333 The Eagle Tower. Caernarvon Castle

334 Queen Eleanor's Gate. Caernarvon Castle

335 Celtic Cross. Margam Abbey

The 5d values were printed *se-tenant* in strips of three throughout the sheet.

336 Prince Charles

337 Mahatma Gandhi

Investiture of H.R.H. The Prince of Wales

1969 (1 July) *Two phosphor bands*

802	**332**	5d multicoloured	10	10	☐	☐
		a. Strip of 3				
		Nos. 802/4	70	1·25		☐
803	**333**	5d multicoloured	10	10	☐	☐
804	**334**	5d multicoloured	10	10	☐	☐
805	**335**	9d multicoloured	20	10	☐	☐
806	**336**	1s black and gold	20	10	☐	☐
		Set of 5	1·00	45	☐	☐
		First Day Cover		1·50		☐
		Presentation Pack	1·60			☐
		Presentation Pack (German)	16·00			☐

Gandhi Centenary Year

1969 (13 Aug.) *Two phosphor bands*

807	**337**	1s 6d multicoloured	30	30	☐	☐
		First Day Cover		2·00		☐

Collectors Pack 1969

1969 (15 Sept.) *Comprises Nos. 775/86 and 791/807*

	Collectors Pack	20·00	☐

338 National Giro

339 Telecommunications

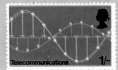

340 Telecommunications

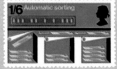

341 Automatic Sorting

British Post Office Technology

1969 (1 Oct.) *Two phosphor bands*   Perf 13½ × 14

808	**338**	5d multicoloured	10	10	☐	☐
809	**339**	9d green, bl & blk	15	15	☐	☐
810	**340**	1s green, lav & blk	15	15	☐	☐
811	**341**	1s 6d multicoloured	40	40	☐	☐
		Set of 4	70	70	☐	☐
		First Day Cover		2·25		☐
		Presentation Pack	3·00			☐

342 Herald Angel

343 The Three Shepherds

344 The Three Kings

Christmas

1969 (26 Nov.) *Two phosphor bands (5d, 1s 6d) or one centre band (4d)*

812	**342**	4d multicoloured	10	10	☐	☐
813	**343**	5d multicoloured	10	10	☐	☐
814	**344**	1s 6d multicoloured	30	30	☐	☐
		Set of 3	45	45	☐	☐
		First Day Cover		2·50		☐
		Presentation Pack	2·50			☐

345 Fife Harling

346 Cotswold Limestone

347 Welsh Stucco

348 Ulster Thatch

British Rural Architecture

1970 (11 Feb.) *Two phosphor bands*

815	**345**	5d multicoloured	10	10	☐	☐
816	**346**	9d multicoloured	20	20	☐	☐
817	**347**	1s multicoloured	20	20	☐	☐
818	**348**	1s 6d multicoloured	35	35	☐	☐
		Set of 4	75	75	☐	☐
		First Day Cover		1·50		☐
		Presentation Pack	3·25			☐

349 Signing the Declaration of Arbroath

350 Florence Nightingale attending Patients

351 Signing of International Co-operative Alliance

352 Pilgrims and *Mayflower*

353 Sir William Herschel, Francis Baily, Sir John Herschel and Telescope

Anniversaries. Events described on stamps

1970 (1 Apr.) *Two phosphor bands*

819	**349**	5d	multicoloured	10	10	□	□
820	**350**	9d	multicoloured	15	15	□	□
821	**351**	1s	multicoloured	25	25	□	□
822	**352**	1s 6d	multicoloured	30	30	□	□
823	**353**	1s 9d	multicoloured	30	30	□	□
		Set of 5		1·00	1·00	□	□
		First Day Cover			3·50		□
		Presentation Pack		3·25		□	

354 'Mr Pickwick and Sam' (*Pickwick Papers*)

355 'Mr and Mrs Micawber' (*David Copperfield*)

356 'David Copperfield and Betsy Trotwood' (*David Copperfield*)

357 'Oliver asking for more' (*Oliver Twist*)

358 'Grasmere' (from engraving by J Farrington, R.A.)

The 5d values were issued together *se-tenant* in blocks of four within the sheet.

Literary Anniversaries. Events described on stamps

1970 (3 June) *Two phosphor bands*

824	**354**	5d	multicoloured	10	10	□	□
	a	Block of 4 Nos. 824/7		90	1·50	□	□
825	**355**	5d	multicoloured	10	10	□	□
826	**356**	5d	multicoloured	10	10	□	□
827	**357**	5d	multicoloured	10	10	□	□
828	**358**	1s 6d	multicoloured	20	20	□	□
		Set of 5		1·00	55	□	□
		First Day Cover			3·50		□
		Presentation Pack		3·25		□	

359

359a (Value redrawn)

Decimal Currency

1970 (17 June)–**72** *10p and some printings of the 50p were issued on phosphor paper* Perf 12

829	**359**	10p	cerise	1·00	75	□	□
830		20p	olive-green	70	15	□	□
831		50p	ultramarine	1·50	40	□	□
831*b*	**359a**	£1	black	3·50	75	□	□
		Set of 4		6·00	1·75	□	□
829/31	First Day Cover				2·00		□
831*b*	First Day Cover (6 Dec. 1972)				2·75		□
829/31	Presentation Pack			7·50		□	
790 (or 831*b*), 830/1							
	Presentation Pack			8·00		□	

360 Runners

361 Swimmers

362 Cyclists

Ninth British Commonwealth Games

1970 (15 JULY) *Two phosphor bands*   *Perf* $13\frac{1}{2} \times 14$

832	**360**	5d pink, emerald, greenish yellow & yellow-green	10	10	☐	☐
833	**361**	1s 6d greenish blue, lilac, brown and Prussian blue	50	50	☐	☐
834	**362**	1s 9d yellow-orange, lilac, salmon and red-brown	50	50	☐	☐
		Set of 3	1·00	1·00	☐	☐
		First Day Cover		2·00		☐
		·Presentation Pack	2·75		☐	

Collectors Pack 1970

1970 (14 SEPT.) *Comprises Nos. 808/28 and 832/4*

Collectors Pack	22·00	☐

363 1d Black   **364** 1s Green   **365** 4d Carmine
(1840)   (1847)   (1855)

'Philympia 70' Stamp Exhibition

1970 (18 SEPT.) *Two phosphor bands*   *Perf* $14 \times 14\frac{1}{2}$

835	**363**	5d multicoloured	10	10	☐	☐
836	**364**	9d multicoloured	35	35	☐	☐
837	**365**	1s 6d multicoloured	40	50	☐	☐
		Set of 3	75	90	☐	☐
		First Day Cover		1·50		☐
		Presentation Pack	2·75		☐	

366 Shepherds and   **367** Mary, Joseph, and
Apparition of the Angel   Christ in the Manger

368 The Wise Men bearing Gifts

Christmas

1970 (25 NOV.) *Two phosphor bands* (5d, 1s 6d) *or one centre phosphor band* (4d)

838	**366**	4d multicoloured	10	10	☐	☐
839	**367**	5d multicoloured	10	10	☐	☐
840	**368**	1s 6d multicoloured	35	35	☐	☐
		Set of 3	50	50	☐	☐
		First Day Cover		1·00		☐
		Presentation Pack	3·25		☐	

369   **369**a

Decimal Currency

1971-96. Type 369

(a) *Printed in photogravure by Harrison & Sons (except for some ptgs of Nos. X879 and X913 which were produced by Enschedé) with phosphor bands. Perf* 15×14.

X841		$\frac{1}{2}$p turq-bl (2 bands)	10	10	☐	☐
X842		$\frac{1}{2}$p turq-bl (1 side band)	70·00	35·00	☐	☐
X843		$\frac{1}{2}$p turquoise-blue (1 centre band)	30	20	☐	☐
X844		1p crimson (2 bands)	10	10	☐	☐
X845		1p crim (1 centre band)	20	20	☐	☐
X846		1p crimson ('all-over' phosphor)	20	20	☐	☐
X847		1p crimson (1 side band)	1·00	1·25	☐	☐
X848		$1\frac{1}{2}$p black (2 bands)	20	15	☐	☐
X849		2p myr-grn (face value as in T **369**) (2 bands)	20	10	☐	☐
X850		2p myr-grn (face value as in T **369**) 'all-over' phosphor	20	15	☐	☐
X851		$2\frac{1}{2}$p mag (1 centre band)	15	10	☐	☐
X852		$2\frac{1}{2}$p magenta (1 side band)	1·25	1·75	☐	☐
X853		$2\frac{1}{2}$p magenta (2 bands)	30	75	☐	☐
X854		$2\frac{1}{2}$p rose-red (2 bands)	50	75	☐	☐
X855		3p ultramarine (2 bands)	20	10	☐	☐
X856		3p ultram (1 centre band)	20	25	☐	☐
X857		3p bright magenta (2 bands)	30	25	☐	☐
X858		$3\frac{1}{2}$p olive-grey (2 bands)	30	30	☐	☐
X859		$3\frac{1}{2}$p ol-grey (1 centre band)	30	15	☐	☐

X860	3½p	purple-brown (1 centre band)	1·25	1·50	□	□
X861	4p	ochre-brown (2 bands)	20	20	□	□
X862	4p	greenish bl (2 bands)	1·50	1·50	□	□
X863	4p	greenish blue (1 centre band)	1·00	1·00	□	□
X864	4p	greenish blue (1 side band)	1·50	2·00	□	□
X865	4½p	grey-blue (2 bands)	20	25	□	□
X866	5p	pale violet (2 bands)	20	10	□	□
X867	5p	claret (1 centre band)	1·50	1·50	□	□
X868	5½p	violet (2 bands)	25	25	□	□
X869	5½p	violet (1 centre band)	20	20	□	□
X870	6p	light emerald (2 bands)	30	15	□	□
X871	6½p	greenish bl (2 bands)	45	45	□	□
X872	6½p	greenish blue (1 centre band)	30	15	□	□
X873	6½p	greenish blue (1 side band)	60	55	□	□
X874	7p	purple-brn (2 bands)	35	25	□	□
X875	7p	purple-brown (1 centre band)	35	20	□	□
X876	7p	purple-brown (1 side band)	60	75	□	□
X877	7½p	chestnut (2 bands)	30	25	□	□
X878	8p	rosine (2 bands)	25	20	□	□
X879	8p	rosine (1 centre band)	25	15	□	□
X880	8p	rosine (1 side band)	70	70	□	□
X881	8½p	yellowish green (2 bands)	35	20	□	□
X882	9p	yellow-orange and black (2 bands)	60	30	□	□
X883	9p	deep violet (2 bands)	45	25	□	□
X884	9½p	purple (2 bands)	45	30	□	□
X885	10p	orange-brown and chestnut (2 bands)	40	30	□	□
X886	10p	orange-brn (2 bands)	40	20	□	□
X887	10p	orange-brown ('all-over' phosphor)	30	45	□	□
X888	10p	orange-brown (1 centre band)	30	20	□	□
X889	10p	orange-brown (1 side band)	75	90	□	□
X890	10½p	yellow (2 bands)	40	30	□	□
X891	10½p	blue (2 bands)	60	45	□	□
X892	11p	brown-red (2 bands)	60	25	□	□
X893	11½p	drab (1 centre band)	45	30	□	□
X894	11½p	drab (1 side band)	60	75	□	□
X895	12p	yellowish green (2 bands)	60	40	□	□
X896	12p	bright emerald (1 centre band)	60	40	□	□
X897	12p	bright emerald (1 side band)	75	90	□	□
X898	12½p	light emerald (1 centre band)	45	25	□	□
X899	12½p	light emerald (1 side band)	60	60	□	□
X900	13p	pale chestnut (1 centre band)	45	35	□	□
X901	13p	pale chestnut (1 side band)	60	60	□	□
X902	14p	grey-blue (2 bands)	1·00	45	□	□
X903	14p	dp bl (1 centre band)	60	40	□	□
X904	14p	dp blue (1 side band)	1·75	2·00	□	□
X905	15p	brt bl (1 centre band)	25	20	□	□
X906	15p	brt blue (1 side band)	1·75	2·25	□	□
X907	15½p	pale violet (2 bands)	45	45	□	□
X908	16p	olive-drab (2 bands)	1·25	1·25	□	□
X909	17p	grey-blue (2 bands)	75	75	□	□
X910	17p	dp bl (1 centre band)	50	50	□	□
X911	17p	dp bl (1 side band)	1·00	1·25	□	□
X912	18p	dp ol-grey (2 bands)	75	75	□	□
X913	18p	bright green (1 centre band)	45	35	□	□
X914	19p	bright orange-red (2 bands)	1·25	1·25	□	□
X915	20p	dull purple (2 bands)	90	40	□	□
X916	20p	brownish black (2 bands)	1·50	1·75	□	□
X917	22p	bright orange-red (2 bands)	1·25	1·25	□	□
X917a	25p	rose-red (2 bands)	50	50	□	□
X918	26p	rosine (2 bands)	7·00	7·50	□	□
X919	31p	purple (2 bands)	10·00	10·00	□	□
X920	34p	ochre-brown (2 bands)	7·00	7·50	□	□
X921	50p	ochre-brown (2 bands)	2·00	50	□	□
X922	50p	ochre (2 bands)	3·00	3·50	□	□

(b) Printed in photogravure by Harrison and Sons on phosphorised paper. Perf 15 × 14

X924	½p	turquoise-blue	10	10	□	□
X925	1p	crimson	10	10	□	□
X926	2p	myrtle-green (face value as in T **369**)	10	10	□	□
X927	2p	deep green (smaller value as in T **369a**)	10	10	□	□
X928	2p	myr-grn (smaller value as in T **369a**)	1·00	1·00	□	□
X929	2½p	rose-red	20	20	□	□
X930	3p	bright magenta	20	20	□	□
X931	3½p	purple-brown	45	45	□	□
X932	4p	greenish blue	40	20	□	□
X933	4p	new blue	10	10	□	□
X934	5p	pale violet	30	25	□	□
X935	5p	dull red-brown	10	10	□	□
X936	6p	olive-yellow	10	15	□	□
X937	7p	brownish red	1·75	1·75	□	□
X938	8½p	yellowish green	30	55	□	□
X939	10p	orange-brown	30	20	□	□
X940	10p	dull orange	15	15	□	□
X941	11p	brown-red	75	75	□	□
X942	11½p	ochre-brown	50	45	□	□
X943	12p	yellowish green	45	40	□	□
X944	13p	olive-grey	60	45	□	□
X945	13½p	purple-brown	65	60	□	□
X946	14p	grey-blue	50	40	□	□
X947	15p	ultramarine	50	40	□	□
X948	15½p	pale violet	50	40	□	□
X949	16p	olive-drab	60	30	□	□
X950	16½p	pale chestnut	85	75	□	□
X951	17p	light emerald	70	40	□	□
X952	17p	grey-blue	50	40	□	□
X953	17½p	pale chestnut	80	80	□	□
X954	18p	deep violet	70	75	□	□
X955	18p	deep olive-grey	70	60	□	□

X956	19p bright orange-red ..	70	50	□ □
X957	19½p olive-grey	1·50	1·50	□ □
X958	20p dull purple ..	90	30	□ □
X959	20p turquoise-green ..	80	60	□ □
X960	20p brownish black	70	40	□ □
X961	20½p ultramarine ..	1·25	1·00	□ □
X962	22p blue	60	45	□ □
X963	22p yellow-green .	60	55	□ □
X964	22p bright orange-red ..	60	50	□ □
X965	23p brown-red	1·00	60	□ □
X966	23p bright green	1·00	60	□ □
X967	24p violet ..	1·10	1·00	□ □
X968	24p Indian red ..	1·40	1·00	□ □
X969	24p chestnut ..	60	45	□ □
X970	25p purple	90	90	□ □
X971	26p rosine	90	30	□ □
X972	26p drab ..	80	80	□ □
X973	27p chestnut	1·00	1·00	□ □
X974	27p violet	1·00	75	□ □
X975	28p deep violet	1·00	90	□ □
X976	28p ochre	1·00	90	□ □
X977	28p deep bluish grey	1·00	90	□ □
X978	29p ochre-brown	1·50	1·00	□ □
X979	29p deep mauve	1·50	1·00	□ □
X980	30p deep olive-grey	1·00	80	□ □
X981	31p purple	1·00	1·25	□ □
X982	31p ultramarine	1·00	1·00	□ □
X983	32p greenish blue	1·00	1·00	□ □
X984	33p light emerald	1·00	90	□ □
X985	34p ochre-brown	1·25	90	□ □
X986	34p deep bluish grey	1·00	90	□ □
X987	34p deep mauve	1·00	80	□ □
X988	35p sepia	1·25	1·00	□ □
X989	35p yellow	1·25	1·00	□ □
X990	37p rosine	1·25	1·25	□ □
X991	39p bright mauve	1·00	85	□ □

(c) Printed in photogravure by Harrison and Sons on ordinary paper. Perf 15 × 14

| X992 | 50p ochre-brown .. .. | 1·75 | 80 | □ □ |
| X993 | 75p grey-black (smaller values as T 369a) .. | 2·25 | 2·25 | □ □ |

(d) Printed in photogravure by Harrison and Sons on ordinary paper or phosphorised paper. Perf 15 × 14

| X994 | 50p ochre .. .. .. | 1·50 | 60 | □ □ |

(e) Printed in lithography by John Waddington. Perf 14.

X996	4p greenish blue (2 bands)	20	25	□ □
X997	4p greenish blue (phosphorised paper)	35	20	□ □
X998	20p dull purple (2 bands)	1·00	40	□ □
X999	20p dull purple (phosphorised paper)	1·25	40	□ □

(f) Printed in lithography by Questa. Perf 14 (Nos X1000, X1003/4 and X1023) or 15 × 14 (others)

| X1000 | 2p emerald-green (face value as in T 369) (phosphorised paper) | 20 | 20 | □ □ |
| | a Perf 15 × 14 .. | 30 | 20 | □ □ |

X1001	2p bright grn and dp grn (smaller value as in T 369a) (phosphorised paper)	1·00	60	□ □
X1002	4p greenish blue (phosphorised paper)	50	50	□ □
X1003	5p light violet (phosphorised paper)	40	20	□ □
X1004	5p claret (phosphorised paper)	50	20	□ □
	a Perf 15 × 14	50	25	□ □
X1005	13p pale chest (1 centre band)	70	70	□ □
X1006	13p pale chest (1 side band)	1·00	1·00	□ □
X1007	14p dp bl (1 centre band) ..	1·50	1·25	□ □
X1008	17p dp bl (1 centre band)	75	75	□ □
X1009	18p deep olive-grey (phosphorised paper)	75	75	□ □
X1010	18p dp ol-grey (2 bands)	5·00	5·00	□ □
X1011	18p bright green (1 centre band)	1·00	1·25	□ □
X1012	18p bright green (1 side band)	1·25	1·25	□ □
X1013	19p bright orange-red (phosphorised paper)	1·75	1·75	□ □
X1014	20p dull purple (phosphorised paper)	1·25	1·25	□ □
X1015	22p yell-grn (2 bands)	8·00	8·00	□ □
X1016	22p bright.orange-red (phosphorised paper)	1·00	1·00	□ □
X1017	24p chestnut (phosphorised paper)	90	70	□ □
X1018	24p chestnut (2 bands)	1·10	1·10	□ □
X1019	33p light emerald (phosphorised paper)	1·50	1·50	□ □
X1020	33p light emer (2 bands)	1·25	1·25	□ □
X1021	34p ochre-brn (2 bands)	6·00	6·00	□ □
X1022	39p brt mauve (2 bands)	1·75	1·75	□ □
X1023	75p black (face value as T 369) (ordinary paper)	3·00	1·75	□ □
	a Perf 15 × 14	3·50	3·50	□ □
X1024	75p brownish grey and black (smaller value as T 369a) (ordinary paper)	10·00	9·00	□ □

(g) Printed in lithography by Walsall. Perf 14

X1050	2p deep green (phosphorised paper)	80	90	□ □
X1051	14p deep blue (1 side band)	3·00	3·00	□ □
X1052	19p bright orange-red (2 bands)	1·50	1·75	□ ⊔
X1053	24p chestnut (phosphorised paper)	90	90	□ □
X1054	29p deep mauve (2 bands)	4·50	5·00	□ □
X1055	29p deep mauve (phosphorised paper)	5·50	6·00	□ □
X1056	31p ultramarine (phosphorised paper)	1·50	1·75	□ □
X1057	33p light emerald (phosphorised paper)	1·00	1·25	□ □
X1058	39p bright mauve (phosphorised paper)	1·00	1·25	□ □

Presentation Pack (contains ½p (X841), 1p (X844), 1½p (X848), 2p (X849), 2½p (X851), 3p (X855), 3½p (X858), 4p (X861), 5p (X866), 6p (X870), 7½p (X877), 9p (X882)) 5·00 □

Presentation Pack ('Scandinavia 71') (contents as above) .. .. .. 35·00 □

Presentation Pack (contains ½p (X841), 1p (X844), 1½p (X848), 2p (X849), 2½p (X851), 3p (X855 *or* X856), 3½p (X858 *or* X859), 4p (X861), 4½p (X865), 5p (X866), 5½p (X868 *or* X869), 6p (X870), 6½p (X871 *or* X872), 7p (X874), 7½p (X877), 8p (X878), 9p (X882), 10p (X885)) .. .. 5·00 □

Presentation Pack (contains ½p (X841), 1p (X844), 1½p (X848), 2p (X849), 2½p (X851), 3p (X856), 5p (X866), 6½p (X872), 7p (X874 *or* X875), 7½p (X877), 8p (X878), 8½p (X881), 9p (X883), 9½p (X884) 10p (X886), 10½p (X890), 11p (X892) 20p (X915), 50p (X921)) .. .. 5·00 □

Presentation Pack (contains 2½p (X929), 3p (X930), 4p (X996), 10½p (X891), 11½p (X893), 11½p (X942), 12p (X943), 13p (X944), 13½p (X945), 14p (X946), 15p (X947), 15½p (X948), 17p (X951), 17½p (X953), 18p (X954), 22p (X962), 25p (X970), 75p (X1023)) 16·00 □

Presentation Pack (Contains ½p (X924), 1p (X925), 2p (X1000), 3p (X930), 3½p (X931), 4p (X997), 5p (X1004), 10p (X888), 12½p (X898), 16p (X949), 16½p (X950), 17p (X952), 20p (X999), 20½p (X961), 23p (X965), 26p (X971), 28p (X975), 31p (X981), 50p (X992), 75p (X1023)) .. .. .. 22·00 □

Presentation Pack (contains ½p (X924), 1p (X925), 2p (X1000*a*), 3p (X930), 4p (X997), 5p (X1004*a*), 10p (X939), 13p (X900), 16p (X949), 17p (X952), 18p (X955), 20p (X999), 22p (X963), 24p (X967), 26p (X971), 28p (X975), 31p (X981), 34p (X985), 50p (X992), 75p (X1023*a*)) .. .. 22·00 □

Presentation Pack (contains 1p (X925), 2p (X1000*a*), 3p (X930), 4p (X997), 5p (X1004*a*), 7p (X937), 10p (X939), 12p (X896), 13p (X900), 17p (X952), 18p (X955), 20p (X999), 22p (X963), 24p (X967), 26p (X971), 28p (X975), 31p (X981), 34p (X985), 50p (X992), 75p (X1023*a*)) .. .. 18·00 □

Presentation Pack (contains 14p (X903), 19p (X956), 20p (X959), 23p (X966), 27p (X973), 28p (X976), 32p (X983), 35p (X988)) 10·00 □

Presentation Pack (contains 15p (X905), 20p (X960), 24p (X968), 29p (X979), 30p (X980), 34p (X986), 37p (X990) .. .. .. 8·00 □

Presentation Pack (contains 10p (X940), 17p (X910), 22p (X964), 26p (X972), 27p (X974), 31p (X982), 33p (X984) .. .. .. 7·00 □

Presentation Pack (contains 1p (X925), 2p (X927), 3p (X930), 4p (X933), 5p (X935), 10p (X940), 17p (X910), 20p (X959), 22p (X964), 26p (X972), 27p (X974), 30p (X980), 31p (X982), 32p (X983), 33p (X984), 37p (X990), 50p (X994), 75p (X993)) .. .. 13·00 □

Presentation Pack (contains 6p (X936), 18p (X913), 24p (X969), 28p (X977), 34p (X987), 35p (X989), 39p (X991)) .. .. .. 5·00 □

First Day Covers

15 Feb. 1971	*½p, 1p, 1½p, 2p, 2½p, 3p, 3½p, 4p, 5p, 6p, 7½p, 9p (Nos.* X841, X844, X848/9, X851, X855, X858, X861, X866, X870, X877, X882) *(Covers carry* "POSTING DELAYED BY THE POST OFFICE STRIKE 1971" *cachet)* ..	3·00	□
11 Aug. 1971	10*p* (*No.* X885)	1·00	□
24 Oct. 1973	4½*p*, 5½*p*, 8*p* (*Nos.* X865 X868, X878)	1·00	□
4 Sept. 1974	6½*p* (*No.* X871)	1·00	□
15 Jan. 1975	7*p* (*No.* X874)	1·00	□
24 Sept. 1975	8½*p* (*No.* X881)	1·00	□
25 Feb. 1976	9*p*, 9½*p*, 10*p*, 10½*p*, 11*p*, 20*p* (*Nos.* X883/4, X886, X890, X892, X915)	2·00	□
2 Feb. 1977	50*p* (*No.* X921)	1·00	□
26 April. 1978	10½*p* (*No.* X891)	1·00	□
15 Aug. 1979	11½*p*, 13*p*, 15*p* (*Nos.* X942, X944, X947)	1·00	□
30 Jan. 1980	4*p*, 12*p*, 13½*p*, 17*p*, 17½*p*, 75*p* (*Nos.* X996, X943, X945, X951, X953, X1023)	2·00	□
22 Oct. 1980	3*p*, 22*p*, (*Nos.* X930, X962)	1·00	□

14 Jan. 1981	$2\frac{1}{2}p$, $11\frac{1}{2}p$, 14p, $15\frac{1}{2}p$, 18p, 25p (Nos. X929, X893, X946, X948, X954, X970)	1·00	☐
27 Jan. 1982	5p, $12\frac{1}{2}p$, $16\frac{1}{2}p$, $19\frac{1}{2}p$, 26p, 29p (Nos. X1004, X898, X950, X957, X971, X978) ..	2·00	☐
30 March 1983	$3\frac{1}{2}p$, 16p, 17p, $20\frac{1}{2}p$, 23p, 28p, 31p (Nos. X931, X949, X952, X961, X965, X975, X981)	3·00	☐
28 Aug. 1984	13p,. 18p, 22p, 24p, 34p (Nos. X900, X955, X963, X967, X985)	3·00	☐
29 Oct. 1985	7p, 12p (Nos. X937, X896)	2·00	☐
23 Aug. 1988	14p, 19p, 20p, 23p, 27p, 28p, 32p, 35p (Nos. X903, X956, X959, X966, X973, X976, X983, X988)	3·75	☐
26 Sept. 1989	15p, 20p, 24p, 29p, 30p, 34p, 37p (Nos. X905, X960, X968, X979/80, X986, X990) ..	4·50	☐
4 Sept. 1990	10p, 17p, 22p, 26p, 27p, 31p, 33p (Nos. X940, X910, X964, X972, X974, X982, X984)	4·50	☐
10 Sept. 1991	6p, 18p, 24p, 28p, 34p, 35p, 39p (Nos. X936, X913, X969, X977, X987, X989, X991) ..	4·00	☐

PHOSPHOR BANDS See notes on page 15.
Phosphor bands are applied to the stamps, after the design has been printed, by a separate cylinder. On issues with "all-over" phosphor the "band" covers the entire stamp. Parts of the stamp covered by phosphor bands, or the entire surface for "all-over" phosphor versions, appear matt.
Nos. X847, X852, X864, X873, X876, X880, X889, X894, X897, X899, X901, X906, X911, X1006 and X1012 exist with the phosphor band at the left or right of the stamp.

PHOSPHORISED PAPER. First introduced as an experiment for a limited printing of the 1s 6d value (No. 743c) in 1969 this paper has the phosphor, to activate the automatic sorting machinery, added to the paper coating before the stamps were printed. Issues on this paper have a completely shiny surface. Although not adopted after this first trial further experiments on the $8\frac{1}{2}$p in 1976 led to this paper being used for new printings of current values.

For similar stamps, but with elliptical perforations see Nos. Y1667/1759 in 1993.

370 'A Mountain Road' (T P Flanagan)

371 'Deer's Meadow' (Tom Carr)

372 'Slieve na brock' (Colin Middleton)

'Ulster '71' Paintings

1971 (16 JUNE) *Two phosphor bands*

881	**370**	3p multicoloured	..	10	10	☐	☐
882	**371**	7½p multicoloured	..	50	50	☐	☐
883	**372**	9p multicoloured	..	50	50	☐	☐
	Set of 3		.. ..	1·00	1·00	☐	☐
	First Day Cover		.. ..		2·25		☐
	Presentation Pack		.. ..	5·00		☐	

373 John Keats (150th Death Anniv)

374 Thomas Gray (Death Bicentenary)

375 Sir Walter Scott (Birth Bicentenary)

Literary Anniversaries. Events described above

1971 (28 JULY) *Two phosphor bands*

884	**373**	3p black, gold & bl ..		10	10	☐	☐
885	**374**	5p blk, gold & olive		50	50	☐	☐
886	**375**	7½p black, gold & brn		50	50	☐	☐
	Set of 3		.. ..	1·00	1·00	☐	☐
	First Day Cover		.. ..		4·00		☐
	Presentation Pack		..	5·00		☐	

376 Servicemen and Nurse of 1921

377 Roman Centurion

378 Rugby Football, 1871

British Anniversaries. Events described on stamps

1971 (25 AUG.) *Two phosphor bands*

887	**376**	3p multicoloured	..	10	10	☐	☐
888	**377**	7½p multicoloured	..	50	50	☐	☐
889	**378**	9p multicoloured	..	50	50	☐	☐
	Set of 3		.. ..	1·00	1·00	☐	☐
	First Day Cover		.. ..		2·75		☐
	Presentation Pack		..	5·00		☐	

379 Physical Sciences Building, University College of Wales, Aberystwyth

380 Faraday Building, Southampton University

381 Engineering Department, Leicester University

382 Hexágon Restaurant, Essex University

British Architecture (Modern University Buildings)

1971 (22 Sept.) *Two phosphor bands*

890	**379**	3p multicoloured	10	10	□	□
891	**380**	5p multicoloured	20	20	□	□
892	**381**	7½p ochre, black and purple-brown	50	50	□	□
893	**382**	9p multicoloured	90	90	□	□
		Set of 4	1·50	1·50	□	□
		First Day Cover		3·50	□	
		Presentation Pack	5·50		□	

Collectors Pack 1971

1971 (29 Sept.) *Comprises Nos. 835/40 and 881/93*

	Collectors Pack	25·00	□

383 Dream of the Wise Men

384 Adoration of the Magi

385 Ride of the Magi

Christmas

1971 (13 Oct.) *Two phosphor bands (3p, 7½p) or one centre phosphor band (2½p)*

894	**383**	2½p multicoloured	10	10	□	□
895	**384**	3p multicoloured	10	10	□	□
896	**385**	7½p multicoloured	90	90	□	□
		Set of 3	1·00	1·00	□	□
		First Day Cover		3·50	□	
		Presentation Pack	4·50		□	

386 Sir James Clark Ross

387 Sir Martin Frobisher

388 Henry Hudson

389 Capt. Robert F. Scott

British Polar Explorers

1972 (16 Feb.) *Two phosphor bands*

897	**386**	3p multicoloured	10	10	□	□
898	**387**	5p multicoloured	20	20	□	□
899	**388**	7½p multicoloured	50	50	□	□
900	**389**	9p multicoloured	90	90	□	□
		Set of 4	1·50	1·50	□	□
		First Day Cover		4·50	□	
		Presentation Pack	5·00		□	

390 Statuette of Tutankhamun

391 19th-century Coastguard

392 Ralph Vaughan Williams and Score

Anniversaries. Events described on stamps

1972 (26 Apr.) *Two phosphor bands*

901	**390**	3p multicoloured	10	10	□	□
902	**391**	7½p multicoloured	50	50	□	□
903	**392**	9p multicoloured	50	50	□	□
		Set of 3	1·00	1·00	□	□
		First Day Cover		2·75	□	
		Presentation Pack	4·50		□	

393 St Andrew's, Greensted-
juxta-Ongar, Essex.

394 All Saints, Earls
Barton, Northants

395 St Andrew's,
Letheringsett, Norfolk

396 St Andrew's,
Helpringham, Lincs

397 St Mary the Virgin, Huish
Episcopi, Somerset

British Architecture (Village Churches)

1972 (21 June) *Two phosphor bands*

904	**393**	3p multicoloured	10	10	☐	☐
905	**394**	4p multicoloured	20	20	☐	☐
906	**395**	5p multicoloured	20	25	☐	☐
907	**396**	7½p multicoloured	70	80	☐	☐
908	**397**	9p multicoloured	75	90	☐	☐
	Set of 5		1·75	2·00	☐	☐
	First Day Cover			4·50		☐
	Presentation Pack		5·50		☐	

'Belgica '72' Souvenir Pack

1972 (24 June) *Comprises Nos.* 894/6 *and* 904/8

	Souvenir Pack	6·00	☐

398 Microphones, 1924–69

399 Horn Loudspeaker

400 TV Camera, 1972

401 Oscillator and Spark
Transmitter, 1897

Broadcasting Anniversaries. Events described on stamp

1972 (13 Sept.) *Two phosphor bands*

909	**398**	3p multicoloured	10	10	☐
910	**399**	5p multicoloured	15	20	☐
911	**400**	7½p multicoloured	60	60	☐
912	**401**	9p multicoloured	60	60	☐
	Set of 4		1·25	1·25	☐
	First Day Cover			3·50	
	Presentation Pack		3·50		☐

402 Angel holding Trumpet

403 Angel playing Lute

404 Angel playing Harp

Christmas

1972 (18 Oct.) *Two phosphor bands (3p, 7½p) or one centre phosphor band (2½p)*

913	**402**	2½p multicoloured	10	15	☐	☐
914	**403**	3p multicoloured	10	15	☐	☐
915	**404**	7½p multicoloured	90	80	☐	☐
		Set of 3	1·00	1·00	☐	☐
		First Day Cover		2·25	☐	
		Presentation Pack	2·75		☐	

405 Queen Elizabeth II and Prince Philip

406 Europe

Royal Silver Wedding

1972 (20 Nov.) *3p 'all-over' phosphor, 20p without phosphor*

916	**405**	3p brownish black, deep blue and silver	20	20	☐	☐
917		20p brownish black, reddish purple and silver	80	80	☐	☐
		Set of 2	1·00	1·00	☐	☐
		First Day Cover		1·50	☐	
		Presentation Pack	2·25		☐	
		Presentation Pack (Japanese)	3·50		☐	
		Souvenir Book	3·00		☐	
		Gutter Pair (3p)	1·00		☐	
		Traffic Light Gutter Pair (3p)	20·00		☐	

Collectors Pack 1972

1972 (20 Nov.) *Comprises Nos. 897/917*

		Collectors Pack	25·00	☐

Nos. 920/1 were issued horizontally *se-tenant* throughout the sheet.

Britain's Entry into European Communities

1973 (3 Jan.) *Two phosphor bands*

919	**406**	3p multicoloured	10	10	☐	☐
920		5p multicoloured (blue jigsaw)	25	35	☐	☐
	a.	Pair. Nos. 920/1	1·25	1·40	☐	☐
921		5p multicoloured (green jigsaw)	25	35	☐	☐
		Set of 3	1·25	70	☐	☐
		First Day Cover		2·50	☐	
		Presentation Pack	2·25		☐	

Oak Quercus robur

407 Oak Tree

British Trees (1st issue)

1973 (28 Feb.) *Two phosphor bands*

922	**407**	9p multicoloured	50	50	☐	☐
		First Day Cover		1·75	☐	
		Presentation Pack	2·25		☐	

See also No. 949.

408 David Livingstone

409 H M Stanley

The above were issued horizontally *se-tenant* throughout the sheet.

410 Sir Francis Drake

411 Sir Walter Raleigh

412 Charles Sturt

British Explorers

1973 (18 Apr.) 'All-over' phosphor

923	**408**	3p multicoloured	25	20	☐	☐
		a. Pair. Nos. 923/4	1·00	1·25	☐	☐
924	**409**	3p multicoloured ..	25	20	☐	☐
925	**410**	5p multicoloured ..	20	30	☐	☐
926	**411**	7½p multicoloured ..	20	30	☐	☐
927	**412**	9p multicoloured ..	25	40	☐	☐
		Set of 5	1·50	2·00	☐	☐
		First Day Cover		3·50		☐
		Presentation Pack	3·50		☐	

413   **414**

415

County Cricket 1873–1973

1973 (16 May) Designs show sketches of W. G. Grace by Harry Furniss. Queen's head in gold 'All-over' phosphor

928	**413**	3p black and brown	10	10	☐	☐
929	**414**	7½p black and green	80	70	☐	☐
930	**415**	9p black and blue	1·00	90	☐	☐
		Set of 3	1·75	1·50	☐	☐
		First Day Cover		3·00		☐
		Presentation Pack	3·50		☐	
		Souvenir Book	6·25		☐	
		PHQ Card (No. 928)	48·00	£120	☐	

The PHQ Card did not become available until mid-July. The used price quoted is for an example used in July or August 1973.

416 'Self-portrait' (Sir Joshua Reynolds)   **417** 'Self-portrait' (Sir Henry Raeburn)

418 'Nelly O'Brien' (Sir Joshua Reynolds)   **419** 'Rev R. Walker (The Skater)' (Sir Henry Raeburn)

Artistic Anniversaries. Events described on stamps

1973 (4 July) 'All-over' phosphor

931	**416**	3p multicoloured ..	10	10	☐	☐
932	**417**	5p multicoloured ..	20	25	☐	☐
933	**418**	7½p multicoloured ..	55	40	☐	☐
934	**419**	9p multicoloured ..	60	50	☐	☐
		Set of 4	1·25	1·10	☐	☐
		First Day Cover		2·25		☐
		Presentation Pack	2·75		☐	

420 Court Masque Costumes   **421** St Paul's Church, Covent Garden

422 Prince's Lodging, Newmarket   **423** Court Masque Stage Scene

42

The 3p and 5p values were printed horizontally *se-tenant* within the sheet.

400th Anniversary of the Birth of Inigo Jones

1973 (15 Aug.) *'All-over' phosphor*

935	420	3p deep mauve, black and gold	10	15	☐	☐
		a. Pair. Nos. 935/6	35	40	☐	☐
936	421	3p deep brown, black and gold	10	15	☐	☐
937	422	5p blue, black and gold	40	45	☐	☐
		a. Pair. Nos. 937/8	1·50	1·50	☐	☐
938	423	5p grey-olive, black and gold	40	45	☐	☐
		Set of 4	1·60	1·10	☐	☐
		First Day Cover		2·25		☐
		Presentation Pack	3·75		☐	
		PHQ Card (No. 936)	£120	95·00	☐	☐

424 Palace of Westminster seen from Whitehall

425 Palace of Westminster seen from Millbank

19th Commonwealth Parliamentary Conference

1973 (12 Sept.) *'All-over' phosphor*

939	424	8p black, grey and pale buff	50	60	☐	☐
940	425	10p gold and black	50	40	☐	☐
		Set of 2	1·00	1·00	☐	☐
		First Day Cover		2·00		☐
		Presentation Pack	2·50		☐	
		Souvenir Book	5·00		☐	
		PHQ Card (No. 939)	40·00	90·00	☐	☐

426 Princess Anne and Captain Mark Phillips

Royal Wedding

1973 (14 Nov.) *'All-over' phosphor*

941	426	3½p violet and silver	10	10	☐	☐
942		20p brown and silver	90	90	☐	☐
		Set of 2	1·00	1·00	☐	☐
		First Day Cover		1·50		☐
		Presentation Pack	2·50		☐	
		PHQ Card (No. 941)	7·50	20·00	☐	☐
		Set of 2 Gutter Pairs	4·00		☐	
		Set of 2 Traffic Light Gutter Pairs	95·00		☐	

427

428

429

430

431

432 'Good King Wenceslas, the Page and Peasant'

The 3p values depict the carol 'Good King Wenceslas' and were printed horizontally *se-tenant* within the sheet.

Christmas

1973 (28 Nov.) *One phosphor band (3p) or 'all-over' phosphor (3½p)*

943	427	3p multicoloured	15	15	☐	☐
		a. Strip of 5. Nos. 943/7	2·75	3·00	☐	☐
944	428	3p multicoloured	15	15	☐	☐
945	429	3p multicoloured	15	15	☐	☐
946	430	3p multicoloured	15	15	☐	☐
947	431	3p multicoloured	15	15	☐	☐
948	432	3½p multicoloured	15	15	☐	☐
		Set of 6	2·75	80	☐	☐
		First Day Cover		3·00		☐
		Presentation Pack	3·25		☐	

Collectors Pack 1973

1973 (28 Nov.) *Comprises Nos. 919/48*

	Collectors Pack	23·00	☐

433 Horse Chestnut

British Trees (2nd issue)

1974 (27 Feb.) 'All-over' phosphor

949	**433**	10p multicoloured	50	50	☐	☐
		First Day Cover		2·00		☐
		Presentation Pack	2·25		☐	
		PHQ Card	£110	70·00	☐	☐
		Gutter Pair	3·00		☐	
		Traffic Light Gutter Pair	60·00		☐	

434 First Motor Fire-engine, 1904

435 Prize-winning Fire-engine, 1863

436 Steam Fire-engine, 1830

437 Fire-engine, 1766

200th Anniversary of Public Fire Services

1974 (24 Apr.) 'All-over' phosphor

950	**434**	3½p multicoloured	10	10	☐	☐
951	**435**	5½p multicoloured	25	25	☐	☐
952	**436**	8p multicoloured	35	35	☐	☐
953	**437**	10p multicoloured	40	40	☐	☐
		Set of 4	1·00	1·00	☐	☐
		First Day Cover		3·00		☐
		Presentation Pack	3·00		☐	
		PHQ Card (No. 950)	£120	70·00	☐	☐
		Set of 4 Gutter Pairs	4·00		☐	
		Set of 4 Traffic Light Gutter Pairs	60·00		☐	

438 P & O Packet Peninsular, 1888

439 Farman H.F. III Biplane, 1911

440 Airmail-blue Van and Postbox, 1930

441 Imperial Airways Short S.21 Flying Boat Maia, 1937

Centenary of Universal Postal Union

1974 (12 June) 'All-over' phosphor

954	**438**	3½p multicoloured	10	10	☐	☐
955	**439**	5½p multicoloured	20	25	☐	☐
956	**440**	8p multicoloured	30	35	☐	☐
957	**441**	10p multicoloured	50	40	☐	☐
		Set of 4	1·00	1·00	☐	☐
		First Day Cover		1·50		☐
		Presentation Pack	2·00		☐	
		Set of 4 Gutter Pairs	4·00		☐	
		Set of 4 Traffic Light Gutter Pairs	45·00		☐	

442 Robert the Bruce

443 Owain Glyndŵr

444 Henry the Fifth

445 The Black Prince

Medieval Warriors

1974 (10 July) 'All-over' phosphor

958	**442**	4½p multicoloured	10	10	☐	☐
959	**443**	5½p multicoloured	20	20	☐	☐
960	**444**	8p multicoloured	50	40	☐	☐
961	**445**	10p multicoloured	55	40	☐	☐
		Set of 4	1·25	1·00	☐	☐
		First Day Cover		2·25		☐
		Presentation Pack	4·00		☐	
		PHQ Cards (set of 4)	30·00	22·00	☐	☐
		Set of 4 Gutter Pairs	6·00		☐	
		Set of 4 Traffic Light Gutter Pairs	65·00		☐	

446 Churchill in Royal Yacht Squadron Uniform

447 Prime Minister, 1940

448 Secretary for War and Air 1919

449 War Correspondent, South Africa, 1899

Birth Centenary of Sir Winston Churchill

1974 (9 Oct.) *Queen's head and inscription in silver. 'All-over' phosphor*

962	**446**	4½p green and blue	15	15	□	□
963	**447**	5½p grey and black	20	25	□	□
964	**448**	8p rose and lake	50	50	□	□
965	**449**	10p stone and brown	55	50	□	□
		Set of 4	1·25	1·25	□	□
		First Day Cover		1·40		□
		Presentation Pack	1·75		□	
		Souvenir Book	2·50		□	
		PHQ Card (No. 963)	6·00	12·00	□	□
		Set of 4 Gutter Pairs	4·00		□	
		Set of 4 Traffic Light Gutter Pairs	40·00		□	

450 Adoration of the Magi (York Minster, c. 1355)

451 The Nativity (St Helen's Church, Norwich, c. 1480)

452 Virgin and Child (Ottery St Mary Church, c. 1350)

453 Virgin and Child (Worcester Cathedral, c. 1224)

Christmas

1974 (27 Nov.) *Designs show church roof bosses. One phosphor band (3½p) or 'all-over' phosphor (others)*

966	**450**	3½p multicoloured	10	10	□	□
967	**451**	4½p multicoloured	10	10	□	□
968	**452**	8p multicoloured	45	45	□	□
969	**453**	10p multicoloured	50	50	□	□
		Set of 4	1·00	1·00	□	□
		First Day Cover		1·50		□
		Presentation Pack	1·75		□	
		Set of 4 Gutter Pairs	4·00		□	
		Set of 4 Traffic Light Gutter Pairs	40·00		□	

Collectors Pack 1974

1974 (27 Nov.) *Comprises Nos. 949-69*

	Collectors Pack	8·50	□

454 Invalid in Wheelchair

Health and Handicap Funds

1975 (22 Jan.) *'All-over' phosphor*

970	**454**	4½p + 1½p azure and blue	25	25	□	□
		First Day Cover		75		□
		Gutter Pair	50		□	
		Traffic Light Gutter Pair	1·00		□	

455 'Peace - Burial at Sea'

456 'Snowstorm - Steamer off a Harbour's Mouth'

457 The Arsenal, Venice

458 St Laurent

Birth Bicentenary of J. M. W. Turner

1975 (19 Feb.) *'All-over' phosphor*

971	**455**	4½p multicoloured	10	10	□	□
972	**456**	5½p multicoloured	15	15	□	□
973	**457**	8p multicoloured	40	40	□	□
974	**458**	10p multicoloured	45	45	□	□
		Set of 4	1·00	1·00	□	□
		First Day Cover		1·25		□
		Presentation Pack	2·50		□	
		PHQ Card (No. 972)	35·00	11·00	□	□
		Set of 4 Gutter Pairs	2·50		□	
		Set of 4 Traffic Light Gutter Pairs	7·00		□	

459 Charlotte Square,
Edinburgh

460 The Rows, Chester

The above were printed horizontally *se-tenant* throughout the sheet.

461 Royal Observatory,
Greenwich

462 St George's
Chapel, Windsor

463 National Theatre, London

European Architectural Heritage Year
1975 (23 APR.) *'All-over' phosphor*

975	**459**	7p multicoloured ..	30	30	□	□
	a. Pair. Nos. 975/6		80	90	□	□
976	**460**	7p multicoloured ..	30	30	□	□
977	**461**	8p multicoloured ..	20	25	□	□
978	**462**	10p multicoloured ..	20	25	□	□
979	**463**	12p multicoloured ..	20	35	□	□
	Set of 5		1·25	1·25	□	□
	First Day Cover			1·25		□
	Presentation Pack		3·50		□	
	PHQ Cards (Nos. 975/7) ..		8·00	11·00	□	□
	Set of 5 Gutter Pairs		4·00		□	
	Set of 5 Traffic Light					
	Gutter Pairs		16·00		□	

464 Sailing Dinghies

465 Racing Keel Boats

466 Cruising Yachts

467 Multihulls

Sailing
1975 (11 JUNE) *'All-over' phosphor*

980	**464**	7p multicoloured ..	20	20	□	□
981	**465**	8p multicoloured ..	30	30	□	□
982	**466**	10p multicoloured ..	30	30	□	□
983	**467**	12p multicoloured ..	35	35	□	□
	Set of 4		1·00	1·00	□	□
	First Day Cover			1·25		□
	Presentation Pack ..		1·50		□	
	PHQ Card (No. 981) ..		4·50	10·00	□	□
	Set of 4 Gutter Pairs ..		2·50		□	
	Set of 4 Traffic Light					
	Gutter Pairs		24·00		□	

468 Stephenson's
Locomotion, 1825

469 *Abbotsford,*
1876

470 *Caerphilly Castle,* 1923

471 High Speed Train, 1975

150th Anniversary of Public Railways
1975 (13 AUG.) *'All-over' phosphor*

984	**468**	7p multicoloured ..	20	20	□	□
985	**469**	8p multicoloured ..	35	25	□	□
986	**470**	10p multicoloured ..	40	30	□	□
987	**471**	12p multicoloured ..	45	35	□	□
	Set of 4		1·25	1·00	□	□
	First Day Cover			2·50		□
	Presentation Pack		2·75		□	
	Souvenir Book		3·00		□	
	PHQ Cards (set of 4)		55·00	22·00	□	□
	Set of 4 Gutter Pairs		3·00		□	
	Set of 4 Traffic Light					
	Gutter Pairs		11·00		□	

472 Palace of Westminster

62nd Inter-Parliamentary Union Conference

1975 (3 SEPT) *All-over phosphor*

988	472	12p multicoloured	50	50	☐	☐
		First Day Cover		75		☐
		Presentation Pack	1·25		☐	
		Gutter Pair	1·00		☐	
		Traffic Light Gutter Pair	3·00		☐	

473 Emma and Mr
Woodhouse
(*Emma*)

474 Catherine Morland
(*Northanger Abbey*)

475 Mr Darcy
(*Pride and Prejudice*)

476 Mary and Henry
Crawford (*Mansfield Park*)

Birth Bicentenary of Jane Austen (Novelist)

1975 (22 OCT) *All-over phosphor*

989	473	8½p multicoloured	20	20	☐	☐
990	474	10p multicoloured	25	25	☐	☐
991	475	11p multicoloured	30	30	☐	☐
992	476	13p multicoloured	35	35	☐	☐
		Set of 4	1·00	1·00	☐	☐
		First Day Cover		1·25		☐
		Presentation Pack	2·25		☐	
		PHQ Cards (set of 4)	20·00	16·00	☐	☐
		Set of 4 Gutter Pairs	2·50		☐	
		Set of 4 Traffic Light Gutter Pairs	7·00		☐	

477 Angels with
Harp and Lute

478 Angel with
Mandolin

479 Angel with Horn

480 Angel with
Trumpet

Christmas

1975 (26 NOV) *One phosphor band (6½p) phosphor-inked (8½p) (background) or 'all-over' phosphor (others)*

993	477	6½p multicoloured	20	15	☐	☐
994	478	8½p multicoloured	20	20	☐	☐
995	479	11p multicoloured	30	35	☐	☐
996	480	13p multicoloured	40	40	☐	☐
		Set of 4	1·00	1·00	☐	☐
		First Day Cover		1·25		☐
		Presentation Pack	2·00		☐	
		Set of 4 Gutter Pairs	2·50		☐	
		Set of 4 Traffic Light Gutter Pairs	7·00		☐	

Collectors Pack 1975

1975 (26 NOV) *Comprises Nos 970/96*

		Collectors Pack	7·50		☐

481 Housewife

482 Policeman

483 District Nurse

484 Industrialist

Telephone Centenary

1976 (10 Mar.) 'All-over' phosphor

997	**481**	8½p multicoloured	20	20	☐	☐
998	**482**	10p multicoloured	25	25	☐	☐
999	**483**	11p multicoloured	30	30	☐	☐
1000	**484**	13p multicoloured	35	35	☐	☐
		Set of 4	1·00	1·00	☐	☐
		First Day Cover		1·25	☐	
		Presentation Pack	2·00		☐	
		Set of 4 Gutter Pairs	2·50		☐	
		Set of 4 Traffic Light Gutter Pairs	7·00		☐	

485 Hewing Coal (Thomas Hepburn)
486 Machinery (Robert Owen)

487 Chimney Cleaning (Lord Shaftesbury)
488 Hands clutching Prison Bars (Elizabeth Fry)

Social Reformers

1976 (28 Apr.) 'All-over' phosphor

1001	**485**	8½p multicoloured	20	20	☐	☐
1002	**486**	10p multicoloured	25	25	☐	☐
1003	**487**	11p black, slate-grey and drab	30	30	☐	☐
1004	**488**	13p slate-grey, black and green	35	35	☐	☐
		Set of 4	1·00	1·00	☐	☐
		First Day Cover		1·25	☐	
		Presentation Pack	2·25		☐	
		PHQ Card (No. 1001)	5·00	7·50	☐	☐
		Set of 4 Gutter Pairs	2·50		☐	
		Set of 4 Traffic Light Gutter Pairs	7·00		☐	

489 Benjamin Franklin (bust by Jean-Jacques Caffieri)

Bicentenary of American Independence

1976 (2 June) 'All-over' phosphor

1005	**489**	11p multicoloured	50	50	☐	☐
		First Day Cover		1·00		☐
		Presentation Pack	1·25		☐	
		PHQ Card	3·00	8·50	☐	☐
		Gutter Pair	1·00		☐	
		Traffic Light Gutter Pair	2·00		☐	

490 'Elizabeth of Glamis'
491 'Grandpa Dickson'

492 'Rosa Mundi'
493 'Sweet Briar'

Centenary of Royal National Rose Society

1976 (30 June) 'All-over' phosphor

1006	**490**	8½p multicoloured	20	20	☐	☐
1007	**491**	10p multicoloured	30	30	☐	☐
1008	**492**	11p multicoloured	55	50	☐	☐
1009	**493**	13p multicoloured	60	40	☐	☐
		Set of 4	1·50	1·25	☐	☐
		First Day Cover		1·75	☐	
		Presentation Pack	2·25		☐	
		PHQ Cards (set of 4)	28·00	11·00	☐	☐
		Set of 4 Gutter Pairs	3·00		☐	
		Set of 4 Traffic Light Gutter Pairs	9·00		☐	

494 Archdruid
495 Morris Dancing

496 Scots Piper

497 Welsh Harpist

British Cultural Traditions
1976 (4 Aug.) *'All-over' phosphor*

1010	494	8½p multicoloured	20	20	□	□
1011	495	10p multiccloured	25	25	□	□
1012	496	11p multicoloured	30	30	□	□
1013	497	13p multicoloured	35	35	□	□
		Set of 4	1·00	1·00	□	□
		First Day Cover		1·25		□
		Presentation Pack	2·00		□	
		PHQ Cards (set of 4)	14·00	10·00	□	□
		Set of 4 Gutter Pairs	2·50		□	
		Set of 4 Traffic Light Gutter Pairs	8·50		□	

498 *The Canterbury Tales*

499 *The Tretyse of Love*

500 *Game and Playe of Chesse*   501 Early Printing Press

500th Anniversary of British Printing
1976 (29 Sept.) *'All-over' phosphor*

1014	498	8½p blk, bl & gold	20	20	□	□
1015	499	10p blk, olive-grn & gold	25	25	□	□
1016	500	11p blk, grey & gold	30	30	□	□
1017	501	13p brn, ochre & gold	35	35	□	□
		Set of 4	1·00	1·00	□	□
		First Day Cover		1·50		□
		Presentation Pack	2·50		□	
		PHQ Cards (set of 4)	10·00	10·00	□	□
		Set of 4 Gutter Pairs	2·50		□	
		Set of 4 Traffic Light Gutter Pairs	7·00		□	

502 Virgin and Child

503 Angel with Crown

504 Angel appearing to Shepherds

505 The Three Kings

Christmas
1976 (24 Nov.) *Designs show English mediaeval embroidery. One phosphor band (6½p) or 'all-over' phosphor (others)*

1018	502	6½p multicoloured	15	15	□	□
1019	503	8½p multicoloured	20	20	□	□
1020	504	11p multicoloured	35	35	□	□
1021	505	13p multicoloured	40	40	□	□
		Set of 4	1·00	1·00	□	□
		First Day Cover		1·25		□
		Presentation Pack	2·25		□	
		PHQ Cards (set of 4)	3·00	8·00	□	□
		Set of 4 Gutter Pairs	2·50		□	
		Set of 4 Traffic Light Gutter Pairs	6·50		□	

Collectors Pack 1976
1976 (24 Nov.) *Comprises Nos. 997/1021*

	Collectors Pack	10·00	□

506 Lawn Tennis

507 Table Tennis

508 Squash

509 Badminton

Racket Sports

1977 (12 JAN) *Phosphorised paper*

1022	**506**	8½p multicoloured	20	20	☐	☐
1023	**507**	10p multicoloured	25	25	☐	☐
1024	**508**	11p multicoloured	30	30	☐	☐
1025	**509**	13p multicoloured	35	35	☐	☐
		Set of 4	1·00	1·00	☐	☐
		First Day Cover		1·50		☐
		Presentation Pack ..	2·00		☐	
		PHQ Cards (set of 4)	6·00	9·50	☐	☐
		Set of 4 Gutter Pairs	2·50		☐	
		Set of 4 Traffic Light Gutter Pairs	6·50		☐	

510

1977 (2 FEB)–**87** *Type* **510** *Ordinary paper*

1026	£1 green and olive	3·00	20	☐	☐
1026b	£1·30 drab & dp grnish bl ..	5·50	5·00	☐	☐
1026c	£1·33 pale mve & grey-blk ..	6·00	6·00	☐	☐
1026d	£1·41 drab & dp grnish bl ..	7·00	6·00	☐	☐
1026e	£1·50 pale mve & grey-blk ..	5·50	4·00	☐	☐
1026f	£1·60 drab and dp grnish bl	5·50	6·00	☐	☐
1027	£2 green and brown	5·50	75	☐	☐
1028	£5 pink and blue	13·00	2·00	☐	☐
	Presentation Pack (Nos. 1026, 1027/8)	22·00		☐	
	Presentation Pack (No. 1026f)	13·00		☐	
	Set of 8 Gutter Pairs	£100		☐	
	Set of 8 Traffic Light Gutter Pairs	£130		☐	

First Day Covers

2 Feb. 1977	Nos: 1026, 1027/8	7·00	☐
3 Aug. 1983	No. 1026b	5·50	☐
28 Aug. 1984	No. 1026c	6·00	☐
17 Sept. 1985	No. 1026d	6·00	☐
2 Sept. 1986	No. 1026e	4·00	☐
15 Sept. 1987	No. 1026f	6·00	☐

511 Steroids – Conformational Analysis

512 Vitamin C – Synthesis

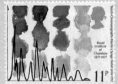

513 Starch – Chromatography

514 Salt – Crystallography

Centenary of Royal Institute of Chemistry

1977 (2 MAR) *'All-over' phosphor*

1029	**511**	8½p multicoloured	20	20	☐	☐
1030	**512**	10p multicoloured ..	30	30	☐	☐
1031	**513**	11p multicoloured	30	30	☐	☐
1032	**514**	13p multicoloured	30	30	☐	☐
		Set of 4	1·00	1·00	☐	☐
		First Day Cover		1·25		☐
		Presentation Pack	2·50		☐	
		PHQ Cards (set of 4)	7·00	10·00	☐	☐
		Set of 4 Gutter Pairs ..	2·50		☐	
		Set of 4 Traffic Light Gutter Pairs	6·00		☐	

515

Silver Jubilee

1977 (11 MAY–15 JUNE) *'All-over' phosphor*

1033	**515**	8½p multicoloured ..	20	20	☐	☐
1034		9p mult (15 June)	25	25	☐	☐
1035		10p multicoloured	25	25	☐	☐
1036		11p multicoloured	30	30	☐	☐
1037		13p multicoloured	40	40	☐	☐
		Set of 5	1·25	1·25	☐	☐
		First Day Covers (2)		1·50		☐
		Presentation Pack (ex 9p)	2·00		☐	
		Souvenir Book (ex 9p) ..	4·00		☐	
		PHQ Cards (set of 5)	9·50	9·00	☐	☐
		Set of 5 Gutter Pairs	2·75		☐	
		Set of 5 Traffic Light Gutter Pairs	4·50		☐	

519 'Gathering of Nations'

1977 (8 June) 'All-over' phosphor

1038	**519**	13p	black, deep green rose and silver	50	50	□	□
		First Day Cover			1·00		□
		Presentation Pack		1·00		□	
		PHQ Card		2·25	4·50	□	□
		Gutter Pair		1·00		□	
		Traffic Light Gutter Pair		1·25		□	

520 Hedgehog

521 Brown Hare

522 Red Squirrel

523 Otter

524 Badger

T **520/4** were printed together, *se-tenant*, throughout the sheet

British Wildlife

1977 (5 Oct.) 'All-over' phosphor

1039	**520**	9p multicoloured		25	20	□	□
		a. Strip of 5 Nos 1039/43		1·75	1·75	□	□
1040	**521**	9p multicoloured		25	20	□	□
1041	**522**	9p multicoloured		25	20	□	□
1042	**523**	9p multicoloured		25	20	□	□
1043	**524**	9p multicoloured		25	20	□	□
		Set of 5		1·75	90	□	□
		First Day Cover			2·50		□
		Presentation Pack		2·50		□	
		PHQ Cards (set of 5)		4·00	5·00	□	□
		Gutter Strip of 10		3·75		□	
		Traffic Light Gutter Strip of 10		4·00		□	

525 'Three French Hens. Two Turtle Doves and a Partridge in a Pear Tree'

526 'Six Geese a-laying. Five Gold Rings. Four Colly Birds'

527 'Eight Maids a-milking. Seven Swans a-swimming'

528 'Ten Pipers piping. Nine Drummers drumming'

529 'Twelve Lords a-leaping. Eleven Ladies dancing'

530 'A Partridge in a Pear Tree'

T **525/30** depict the carol 'The Twelve Days of Christmas'. T **525/29** were printed horizontally *se-tenant* throughout the sheet.

Christmas

1977 (23 Nov.) One centre phosphor band (7p) or 'all-over' phosphor (9p)

1044	**525**	7p multicoloured	15	15	□	□
		a Strip of 5 Nos 1044/8	90	1·25	□	□
1045	**526**	7p multicoloured	15	15	□	□
1046	**527**	7p multicoloured	15	15	□	□
1047	**528**	7p multicoloured	15	15	□	□
1048	**529**	7p multicoloured	15	15	□	□
1049	**530**	9p multicoloured	20	20	□	□
		Set of 6	1·00	85	□	□
		First Day Cover		1·40		□
		Presentation Pack	2·25		□	
		PHQ Cards (set of 6)	3·25	4·00	□	□
		Set of 6 Gutter Pairs	2·50		□	
		Set of 6 Traffic Light Gutter Pairs	4·50		□	

Collectors Pack 1977

1977 (23 Nov.) Comprises Nos. 1022/5. 1029/49

	Collectors Pack	6·50		□

531 Oil—North Sea Production Platform

532 Coal—Modern Pithead

533 Natural Gas—Flame Rising from Sea

534 Electricity—Nuclear Power Station and Uranium Atom

Energy Resources

1978 (25 Jan.) *'All-over' phosphor*

1050	**531**	9p multicoloured	..	25	20	☐ ☐
1051	**532**	10½p multicoloured	..	25	30	☐ ☐
1052	**533**	11p multicoloured	..	30	30	☐ ☐
1053	**534**	13p multicoloured	..	30	30	☐ ☐
	Set of 4	.. .. ..	..	1·00	1·00	☐ ☐
	First Day Cover ..		..		1·25	☐
	Presentation Pack	..	..	2·00		☐
	PHQ Cards (set of 4) ..		..	3·00	4·00	☐ ☐
	Set of 4 Gutter Pairs	..		2·50		☐
	Set of 4 Traffic Light					
	Gutter Pairs	..	..	4·00		☐

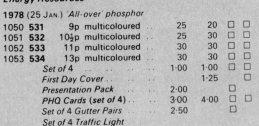

535 Tower of London

536 Holyroodhouse

537 Caernarvon Castle

538 Hampton Court Palace

British Architecture (Historic Buildings)

1978 (1 Mar.) *'All-over' phosphor*

1054	**535**	9p multicoloured	..	25	20	☐ ☐
1055	**536**	10½p multicoloured	..	25	30	☐ ☐
1056	**537**	11p multicoloured	..	30	30	☐ ☐
1057	**538**	13p multicoloured	..	30	30	☐ ☐
	Set of 4	.. .. ..		1·00	1·00	☐ ☐
	First Day Cover ..		..		1·25	☐
	Presentation Pack			2·00		☐
	PHQ Cards (set of 4) ..			2·50	4·00	☐ ☐
	Set of 4 Gutter Pairs			2·50		☐
	Set of 4 Traffic Light					
	Gutter Pairs	.. ..		4·00		☐
MS1058	121 × 90 mm. Nos. 1054/57			1·25	1·50	☐ ☐
	First Day Cover	.. ..			2·50	☐

No. **MS**1058 was sold at 53½p, the premium being used for the London 1980 Stamp Exhibition.

539 State Coach

540 St Edward's Crown

541 The Sovereign's Orb

542 Imperial State Crown

25th Anniversary of Coronation

1978 (31 May) *'All-over' phosphor*

1059	**539**	9p gold and blue	..	20	20	☐
1060	**540**	10½p gold and red	..	25	30	☐
1061	**541**	11p gold and green	..	30	30	☐
1062	**542**	13p gold and violet	..	35	30	☐
	Set of 4	.. .. ..		1·00	1·00	☐
	First Day Cover ..		..		1·25	
	Presentation Pack	..		2·25		☐
	Souvenir Book	..		4·00		
	PHQ Cards (set of 4) ..			2·50	4·00	☐
	Set of 4 Gutter Pairs			2·50		
	Set of 4 Traffic Light					
	Gutter Pairs	.. ..		4·00		

543 Shire Horse

544 Shetland Pony

545 Welsh Pony

546 Thoroughbred

Horses

1978 (5 July) *'All-over' phosphor*

1063	**543**	9p multicoloured	20	20	□	□
1064	**544**	10½p multicoloured	35	25	□	□
1065	**545**	11p multicoloured	40	30	□	□
1066	**546**	13p multicoloured	45	35	□	□
	Set of 4		1·25	1·00	□	□
	First Day Cover			1·25	□	
	Presentation Pack		2·25		□	
	PHQ Cards (set of 4)		2·50	5·00	□	□
	Set of 4 Gutter Pairs		2·50		□	
	Set of 4 Traffic Light					
	Gutter Pairs		4·00		□	

547 Penny-farthing and 1884 Safety Bicycle

548 1920 Touring Bicycles

549 Modern Small-wheel Bicycles

550 1978 Road-racers

Centenaries of Cyclists Touring Club and British Cycling Federation

1978 (2 Aug.) *'All-over' phosphor*

1067	**547**	9p multicoloured	20	20	□	□
1068	**548**	10½p multicoloured	25	25	□	□
1069	**549**	11p multicoloured	30	30	□	□
1070	**550**	13p multicoloured	35	35	□	□
	Set of 4		1·00	1·00	□	□
	First Day Cover			1·25	□	
	Presentation Pack		2·00		□	
	PHQ Cards (set of 4)		1·50	3·25	□	□
	Set of 4 Gutter Pairs		2·50		□	
	Set of 4 Traffic Light					
	Gutter Pairs		4·00		□	

551 Singing Carols round the Christmas Tree

552 The Waits

553 18th-Century Carol Singers

554 'The Boar's Head Carol'

Christmas

1978 (22 Nov.) *One centre phosphor band (7p) or 'all-over' phosphor (others)*

1071	**551**	7p multicoloured	20	20	□	□
1072	**552**	9p multicoloured	25	25	□	□
1073	**553**	11p multicoloured	30	30	□	□
1074	**554**	13p multicoloured	35	35	□	□
	Set of 4		1·00	1·00	□	□
	First Day Cover			1·25	□	
	Presentation Pack		1·75		□	
	PHQ Cards (set of 4)		1·50	4·00	□	□
	Set of 4 Gutter Pairs		2·50		□	
	Set of 4 Traffic Light					
	Gutter Pairs		3·00		□	

Collectors Pack 1978

1978 (22 Nov.) *Comprises Nos* 1050/7, 1059/74

	Collectors Pack		7·00	□

555 Old English Sheepdog

556 Welsh Springer Spaniel

557 West Highland Terrier

558 Irish Setter

Dogs

1979 (7 Feb.) *'All-over' phosphor*

1075	**555**	9p multicoloured	20	20	☐	☐
1076	**556**	10½p multicoloured	40	30	☐	☐
1077	**557**	11p multicoloured	40	30	☐	☐
1078	**558**	13p multicoloured	40	30	☐	☐
		Set of 4	1·25	1·00	☐	☐
		First Day Cover		1·25		☐
		Presentation Pack	2·25		☐	
		PHQ Cards (set of 4) ..	3·00	5·00	☐	☐
		Set of 4 Gutter Pairs .	2·50		☐	
		Set of 4 Traffic Light				
		Gutter Pairs	3·75		☐	

559 Primrose

561 Bluebell

560 Daffodil

562 Snowdrop

Spring Wild Flowers

1979 (21 Mar.) *'All-over' phosphor*

1079	**559**	9p multicoloured .	20	20	☐	☐
1080	**560**	10½p multicoloured .	40	30	☐	☐
1081	**561**	11p multicoloured	40	30	☐	☐
1082	**562**	13p multicoloured	40	30	☐	☐
		Set of 4 .	1·25	1·00	☐	☐
		First Day Cover ..		1·25		☐
		Presentation Pack	2·00		☐	
		PHQ Cards (set of 4)	2·00	4·00	☐	☐
		Set of 4 Gutter Pairs	2·50		☐	
		Set of 4 Traffic Light				
		Gutter Pairs	3·75		☐	

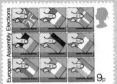

563

564

565

566

T **563/6** show hands placing the flags of the member nations into ballot boxes

First Direct Elections to European Assembly

1979 (9 May) *Phosphorised paper*

1083	**563**	9p multicoloured	20	20	☐	☐
1084	**564**	10½p multicoloured	30	30	☐	☐
1085	**565**	11p multicoloured	30	30	☐	☐
1086	**566**	13p multicoloured	30	30	☐	☐
		Set of 4	1·00	1·00	☐	☐
		First Day Cover		1·25		☐
		Presentation Pack	2·00		☐	
		PHQ Cards (set of 4)	1·50	3·50	☐	☐
		Set of 4 Gutter Pairs	2·50		☐	
		Set of 4 Traffic Light				
		Gutter Pairs	3·75		☐	

Saddling Mahmoud for The Derby 1936

567 'Saddling "Mahmoud" for
the Derby, 1936' (Sir
Alfred Munnings)

The Liverpool Great National Steeple Chase 1839

568 'The Liverpool Great
National Steeple Chase,
1839' (aquatint by F C
Turner)

The First Spring Meeting, Newmarket 1793

569 'The First Spring Meeting,
Newmarket, 1793' (J N
Sartorius)

Racing at Dorsett Ferry, Windsor 1684

570 'Racing at Dorsett Ferry,
Windsor, 1684' (Francis
Barlow)

Horseracing Paintings and Bicentenary of The Derby (9p)

1979 (6 June) 'All-over' phosphor

1087	**567**	9p multicoloured	25	25	☐	☐
1088	**568**	10½p multicoloured	30	30	☐	☐
1089	**569**	11p multicoloured	30	30	☐	☐
1090	**570**	13p multicoloured	30	30	☐	☐
		Set of 4	1·10	1·10	☐	☐
		First Day Cover		1·50		☐
		Presentation Pack	2·00		☐	
		PHQ Cards (set of 4)	1·50	3·00	☐	☐
		Set of 4 Gutter Pairs	2·50		☐	
		Set of 4 Traffic Light Gutter Pairs	3·75		☐	

571 *The Tale of Peter Rabbit* (Beatrix Potter)

572 *The Wind in the Willows* (Kenneth Grahame)

573 *Winnie-the-Pooh* (A. A. Milne)

574 *Alice's Adventures in Wonderland* (Lewis Carroll)

T **571/4** depict original illustrations from the four books

International Year of the Child

1979 (11 July) 'All-over' phosphor

1091	**571**	9p multicoloured	25	20	☐	☐
1092	**572**	10½p multicoloured	30	35	☐	☐
1093	**573**	11p multicoloured	35	40	☐	☐
1094	**574**	13p multicoloured	50	45	☐	☐
		Set of 4	1·25	1·25	☐	☐
		First Day Cover		2·00		☐
		Presentation Pack	2·25		☐	
		PHQ Cards (set of 4)	2·50	3·00	☐	☐
		Set of 4 Gutter Pairs	3·00		☐	
		Set of 4 Traffic Light Gutter Pairs	4·75		☐	

For full information on all future British issues, collectors should write to the British Post Office Philatelic Bureau, 20 Brandon Street, Edinburgh EH3 5TT

575 Sir Rowland Hill, 1795–1879

576 General Post. c 1839

577 London Post. c 1839

578 Uniform Postage. 1840

Death Centenary of Sir Rowland Hill (Postal Reformer)

1979 (22 Aug.–24 Oct.) 'All-over' phosphor

1095	**575**	10p multicoloured	25	25	☐	☐
1096	**576**	11½p multicoloured	30	35	☐	☐
1097	**577**	13p multicoloured	35	40	☐	☐
1098	**578**	15p multicoloured	50	40	☐	☐
		Set of 4	1·25	1·25	☐	☐
		First Day Cover		1·25		☐
		Presentation Pack	2·00		☐	
		PHQ Cards (set of 4)	1·50	3·00	☐	☐
		Set of 4 Gutter Pairs	2·50		☐	
		Set of 4 Traffic Light Gutter Pairs	3·75		☐	
MS1099	89×121 mm. Nos. 1095/8		1·25	1·25	☐	☐
	First Day Cover (24 Oct)			1·50		☐

No. **MS**1099 was sold at 59½p, the premium being used for the London 1980 Stamp Exhibition.

579 Policeman on the Beat

580 Policeman directing Traffic

581 Mounted Policewoman   **582** River Patrol Boat

150th Anniversary of Metropolitan Police

1979 (26 SEPT.) *Phosphorised paper*

1100	**579**	10p multicoloured	25	25	□	□
1101	**580**	11½p multicoloured	30	35	□	□
1102	**581**	13p multicoloured	35	40	□	□
1103	**582**	15p multicoloured	50	40	□	□
		Set of 4	1·25	1·25	□	□
		First Day Cover		1·25		□
		Presentation Pack	2·00		□	
		PHQ Cards (set of 4)	1·50	3·00	□	□
		Set of 4 Gutter Pairs	2·50		□	
		Set of 4 Traffic Light Gutter Pairs	3·75		□	

583 The Three Kings   **584** Angel appearing to the Shepherds

585 The Nativity   **586** Mary and Joseph travelling to Bethlehem

587 The Annunciation

Christmas

1979 (21 NOV.) *One centre phosphor band (8p) or phosphorised paper (others)*

1104	**583**	8p multicoloured	20	20	□	□
1105	**584**	10p multicoloured	25	25	□	□
1106	**585**	11½p multicoloured	30	35	□	□
1107	**586**	13p multicoloured	40	40	□	□
1108	**587**	15p multicoloured	50	45	□	□
		Set of 5	1·50	1·50	□	□
		First Day Cover		1·50		□
		Presentation Pack	2·25		□	
		PHQ Cards (set of 5)	1·50	3·50	□	□
		Set of 5 Gutter Pairs	3·00		□	
		Set of 5 Traffic Light Gutter Pairs	3·75		□	

Collectors Pack 1979

1979 (21 NOV.) *Comprises Nos. 1075/98, 1100/8*

Collectors Pack	8·50	□

588 Kingfisher   **589** Dipper

590 Moorhen   **591** Yellow Wagtails

Centenary of Wild Bird Protection Act

1980 (16 JAN.) *Phosphorised paper*

1109	**588**	10p multicoloured	25	25	□	□
1110	**589**	11½p multicoloured	40	35	□	□
1111	**590**	13p multicoloured	50	40	□	□
1112	**591**	15p multicoloured	55	45	□	□
		Set of 4	1·50	1·25	□	□
		First Day Cover		1·40		□
		Presentation Pack	2·00		□	
		PHQ Cards (set of 4)	1·50	3·00	□	□
		Set of 4 Gutter Pairs	3·00		□	

92 *Rocket* approaching Moorish Arch, Liverpool

593 First and Second Class Carriages passing through Olive Mount Cutting

94 Third Class Carriage and Cattle Truck crossing Chat Moss

595 Horsebox and Carriage Truck near Bridgewater Canal

596 Goods Truck and Mail-coach at Manchester

† 592/6 were printed together, *se-tenant* in horizontal strips of 5 throughout the sheet.

50th Anniversary of Liverpool and Manchester Railway

980 (12 MAR.) *Phosphorised paper*

113	**592**	12p multicoloured	25	25	□	□
		a. Strip of 5.				
		Nos. 1113/17	1·50	1·60	□	□
114	**593**	12p multicoloured	25	25	□	□
115	**594**	12p multicoloured	25	25	□	□
116	**595**	12p multicoloured	25	25	□	□
117	**596**	12p multicoloured	25	25	□	□
		Set of 5	1·50	1·10	□	□
		First Day Cover		1·25		□
		Presentation Pack	2·75		□	
		PHQ Cards (set of 5)	1·50	3·75	□	□
		Gutter block of 10	3·25		□	

597 Montage of London Buildings

"London 1980" International Stamp Exhibition

1980 (9 APR–7 MAY) *Phosphorised paper. Perf* $14\frac{1}{2} \times 14$

1118	**597**	50p agate		1·50	1·25	□	□
		First Day Cover			1·25		□
		Presentation Pack		2·00		□	
		PHQ Card		50	1·75	□	□
		Gutter Pair		3·00		□	
MS1119	90×123 mm. No. 1118		1·50	1·50	□	□
		First Day Cover (7 May)			1·50		□

No. **MS**1119 was sold at 75p, the premium being used for the exhibition.

598 Buckingham Palace

599 The Albert Memorial

600 Royal Opera House

601 Hampton Court

17½p Kensington Palace

602 Kensington Palace

607 Queen Elizabeth the
Queen Mother

London Landmarks

1980 (7 MAY) *Phosphorised paper*

1120	**598**	10½p multicoloured	25	25	☐	☐
1121	**599**	12p multicoloured	30	30	☐	☐
1122	**600**	13½p multicoloured	35	35	☐	☐
1123	**601**	15p multicoloured	40	40	☐	☐
1124	**602**	17½p multicoloured	40	40	☐	☐
		Set of 5	1·50	1·50	☐	☐
		First Day Cover		1·75		☐
		Presentation Pack	2·50		☐	
		PHQ Cards (set of 5)	1·50	3·00	☐	☐
		Set of 5 Gutter Pairs	3·00		☐	

80th Birthday of Queen Elizabeth the Queen Mother

1980 (4 AUG.) *Phosphorised paper*

1129	**607**	12p multicoloured	50	50	☐	☐
		First Day Cover		60		☐
		PHQ Card	50	1·25	☐	☐
		Gutter Pair	1·00		☐	

608 Sir Henry Wood

609 Sir Thomas Beecham

603 Charlotte Bronte
(*Jane Eyre*)

604 George Eliot (*The Mill
on the Floss*)

605 Emily Bronte
(*Wuthering Heights*)

606 Mrs Gaskell (*North and
South*)

T **603/6** show authoresses and scenes from their novels. T **603/4** also include the ''Europa'' C.E.P.T. emblem.

610 Sir Malcolm Sargent

611 Sir John Barbirolli

Famous Authoresses

1980 (9 JULY) *Phosphorised paper*

1125	**603**	12p multicoloured	30	30	☐	☐
1126	**604**	13½p multicoloured	35	35	☐	☐
1127	**605**	15p multicoloured	40	45	☐	☐
1128	**606**	17½p multicoloured	60	60	☐	☐
		Set of 4	1·50	1·50	☐	☐
		First Day Cover		1·50		☐
		Presentation Pack	2·50		☐	
		PHQ Cards (set of 4)	1·50	3·00	☐	☐
		Set of 4 Gutter Pairs	3·00		☐	

British Conductors

1980 (10 SEPT.) *Phosphorised paper*

1130	**608**	12p multicoloured	30	30	☐
1131	**609**	13½p multicoloured	35	40	☐
1132	**610**	15p multicoloured	45	45	☐
1133	**611**	17½p multicoloured	55	50	☐
		Set of 4	1·50	1·50	☐
		First Day Cover		1·50	
		Presentation Pack	2·00		☐
		PHQ Cards (set of 4)	1·50	2·50	☐
		Set of 4 Gutter Pairs	3·00		☐

612 Running

613 Rugby

614 Boxing

615 Cricket

618 Apples and Mistletoe

619 Crown, Chains and Bell

620 Holly

Sports Centenaries

1980 (10 Ост.) *Phosphorised paper. Perf 14 × 14½*

1134	**612**	12p multicoloured	30	30	☐	☐
1135	**613**	13½p multicoloured	35	40	☐	☐
1136	**614**	15p multicoloured	40	40	☐	☐
1137	**615**	17½p multicoloured	60	55	☐	☐
		Set of 4	1·50	1·50	☐	☐
		First Day Cover		1·50		☐
		Presentation Pack	2·00		☐	
		PHQ Cards (set of 4)	1·50	2·50	☐	☐
		Set of 4 Gutter Pairs	3·00		☐	

Centenaries:- 12p Amateur Athletics Association; 13½p Welsh Rugby Union; 15p Amateur Boxing Association; 17½p First England v Australia Test Match.

Christmas

1980 (19 Nov.) *One centre phosphor band (10p) or phosphorised paper (others)*

1138	**616**	10p multicoloured	25	25	☐	☐
1139	**617**	12p multicoloured	30	35	☐	☐
1140	**618**	13½p multicoloured	35	40	☐	☐
1141	**619**	15p multicoloured	40	40	☐	☐
1142	**620**	17½p multicoloured	40	40	☐	☐
		Set of 5	1·50	1·60	☐	☐
		First Day Cover		1·60		☐
		Presentation Pack	2·25		☐	
		PHQ Cards (set of 5)	1·50	2·50	☐	☐
		Set of 5 Gutter Pairs	3·00		☐	

Collectors Pack 1980

1980 (19 Nov.) *Comprises Nos.* 1109/18, 1120/42

	Collectors Pack	10·00	☐

616 Christmas Tree   **617** Candles

621 St. Valentine's Day

622 Morris Dancers

623 Lammastide

624 Medieval Mummers

629 *Aglais urticae*

630 *Maculinea arion*

T **621/22** also include the "Europa" C.E.P.T. emblem

Folklore

1981 (6 FEB.) *Phosphorised paper*

1143	**621**	14p multicoloured	35	35	□	□
1144	**622**	18p multicoloured	45	50	□	□
1145	**623**	22p multicoloured	60	60	□	□
1146	**624**	25p multicoloured	75	70	□	□
		Set of 4	2·00	2·00	□	□
		First Day Cover		2·00		□
		Presentation Pack	2·50		□	
		PHQ Cards (set of 4)	1·50	2·50	□	□
		Set of 4 Gutter Pairs	4·00		□	

631 *Inachis io*

632 *Carterocephalus palaemon*

625 Blind Man with Guide Dog

626 Hands spelling "Deaf" in Sign Language

Butterflies

1981 (13 MAY) *Phosphorised paper*

1151	**629**	14p multicoloured	35	35	□	□
1152	**630**	18p multicoloured	60	50	□	□
1153	**631**	22p multicoloured	70	65	□	□
1154	**632**	25p multicoloured	80	75	□	□
		Set of 4	2·25	2·00	□	□
		First Day Cover		2·00		□
		Presentation Pack	2·50		□	
		PHQ Cards (set of 4)	2·00	3·00	□	□
		Set of 4 Gutter Pairs	4·50		□	

627 Disabled Man in Wheelchair

628 Disabled Artist painting with Foot

633 Glenfinnan, Scotland

634 Derwentwater, England

International Year of the Disabled

1981 (25 MAR.) *Phosphorised paper*

1147	**625**	14p multicoloured	35	35	□	□
1148	**626**	18p multicoloured	45	50	□	□
1149	**627**	22p multicoloured	60	60	□	□
1150	**628**	25p multicoloured	75	70	□	□
		Set of 4	2·00	2·00	□	□
		First Day Cover		2·00		□
		Presentation Pack	2·50		□	
		PHQ Cards (set of 4)	1·50	2·75	□	□
		Set of 4 Gutter Pairs	4·00		□	

635 Stackpole Head, Wales

636 Giant's Causeway, N. Ireland

637 St Kilda, Scotland

641 "Service"

642 "Recreation"

50th Anniversary of National Trust for Scotland

1981 (24 JUNE) *Phosphorised paper*

1155	633	14p multicoloured ..	30	30	☐	☐
1156	634	18p multicoloured ..	40	40	☐	☐
1157	635	20p multicoloured ..	50	50	☐	☐
1158	636	22p multicoloured ..	60	60	☐	☐
1159	637	25p multicoloured ..	70	70	☐	☐
		Set of 5	2·25	2·25	☐	☐
		First Day Cover		2·25		☐
		Presentation Pack	2·75		☐	
		PHQ Cards (set of 5) ..	2·00	2·75	☐	☐
		Set of 5 Gutter Pairs ..	4·50		☐	

25th Anniversary of Duke of Edinburgh Award Scheme

1981 (12 AUG.) *Phosphorised paper. Perf* 14

1162	639	14p multicoloured ..	35	35	☐	☐
1163	640	18p multicoloured ..	50	50	☐	☐
1164	641	22p multicoloured ..	60	60	☐	☐
1165	642	25p multicoloured ..	70	70	☐	☐
		Set of 4	2·00	2·00	☐	☐
		First Day Cover		2·00		☐
		Presentation Pack	2·50		☐	
		PHQ Cards (set of 4) ..	1·60	2·25	☐	☐
		Set of 4 Gutter Pairs ..	4·00		☐	

638 Prince Charles and Lady Diana Spencer

643 Cockle-Dredging from *Linsey II*

644 Hauling Trawl Net

Royal Wedding

1981 (22 JULY) *Phosphorised paper*

1160	638	14p multicoloured ..	25	25	☐	☐
1161		25p multicoloured ..	75	75	☐	☐
		Set of 2	1·00	1·00	☐	☐
		First Day Cover		2·00		☐
		Presentation Pack	2·00		☐	
		Souvenir Book	4·00		☐	
		PHQ Cards (set of 2) ..	1·00	2·75	☐	☐
		Set of 2 Gutter Pairs ..	2·00		☐	

645 Lobster Potting

646 Hoisting Seine Net

Fishing Industry

1981 (23 SEPT.) *Phosphorised paper*

1166	643	14p multicoloured ..	35	35	☐	☐
1167	644	18p multicoloured ..	50	50	☐	☐
1168	645	22p multicoloured ..	60	60	☐	☐
1169	646	25p multicoloured ..	70	65	☐	☐
		Set of 4	2·00	2·00	☐	☐
		First Day Cover		2·00		☐
		Presentation Pack	2·50		☐	
		PHQ Cards (set of 4) ..	2·00	2·50	☐	☐
		Set of 4 Gutter Pairs ..	4·00		☐	

Nos. 1166/9 were issued on the occasion of the centenary of Royal National Mission to Deep Sea Fishermen.

639 "Expeditions"

640 "Skills"

647 Father Christmas

648 Jesus Christ

649 Flying Angel

650 Joseph and Mary
arriving at Bethlehem

651 Three Kings approaching
Bethlehem

Christmas. Children's Pictures

1981 (18 Nov.) *One phosphor band (11½p) or phosphorised paper (others)*

1170	**647**	11½p multicoloured	..	30	30	☐	☐
1171	**648**	14p multicoloured	..	40	40	☐	☐
1172	**649**	18p multicoloured	..	50	50	☐	☐
1173	**650**	22p multicoloured	..	60	60	☐	☐
1174	**651**	25p multicoloured	..	70	70	☐	☐
		Set of 5	.. .. ..	2·25	2·25	☐	☐
		First Day Cover			2·25	☐	
		Presentation Pack	..	3·00		☐	
		PHO Cards (set of 5)	..	2·00	3·50	☐	☐
		Set of 5 Gutter Pairs	.. ..	4·50		☐	

Collectors Pack 1981

1981 (18 Nov.) *Comprises Nos.* 1143/74

Collectors Pack	.. .. ..	16·00	☐

For full information on all future British issues, collectors should write to the British Post Office Philatelic Bureau, 20 Brandon Street, Edinburgh EH3 5TT.

652 Charles Darwin and Giant
Tortoises

653 Darwin and Marine
Iguanas

654 Darwin, Cactus Ground
Finch and Large Ground
Finch

655 Darwin and Prehistoric
Skulls

Death Centenary of Charles Darwin

1982 (10 Feb.) *Phosphorised paper*

1175	**652**	15½p multicoloured	..	35	35	☐	☐
1176	**653**	19½p multicoloured	..	60	60	☐	☐
1177	**654**	26p multicoloured	..	70	70	☐	☐
1178	**655**	29p multicoloured	..	75	75	☐	☐
		Set of 4	.. .. ..	2·25	2·25	☐	☐
		First Day Cover	.. ..		2·25		☐
		Presentation Pack	..	3·00		☐	
		PHQ Cards (set of 4)	..	2·50	6·50	☐	☐
		Set of 4 Gutter Pairs		4·50		☐	

656 Boys' Brigade

657 Girls' Brigade

658 Boy Scout
Movement

659 Girl Guide
Movement

Youth Organizations

1982 (24 MAR.) *Phosphorised paper*

1179	**656**	15½p multicoloured	..	35	35	☐ ☐
1180	**657**	19½p multicoloured	..	60	50	☐ ☐
1181	**658**	26p multicoloured	..	85	75	☐ ☐
1182	**659**	29p multicoloured	..	1·00	90	☐ ☐
		Set of 4	..	2·50	2·25	☐ ☐
		First Day Cover	..		2·25	☐
		Presentation Pack		3·50		☐
		PHQ Cards (set of 4)		2·50	6·50	☐ ☐
		Set of 4 Gutter Pairs	..	5·00		☐

Nos. 1179/82 were issued on the occasion of the 75th anniversary of the Boy Scout Movement, the 125th birth anniversary of Lord Baden-Powell and the centenary of the Boys' Brigade (1983).

660 Ballerina

661 Harlequin

662 Hamlet

663 Opera Singer

Europa. British Theatre

1982 (28 APR.) *Phosphorised paper*

1183	**660**	15½p multicoloured	..	35	35	☐ ☐
1184	**661**	19½p multicoloured	..	60	50	☐ ☐
1185	**662**	26p multicoloured	..	90	75	☐ ☐
1186	**663**	29p multicoloured	..	1·25	90	☐ ☐
		Set of 4	..	2·75	2·25	☐ ☐
		First Day Cover	..		2·25	☐
		Presentation Pack		3·25		☐
		PHQ Cards (set of 4)		2·50	6·50	☐ ☐
		Set of 4 Gutter Pairs	..	5·50		☐

664 Henry VIII and *Mary Rose*

665 Admiral Blake and *Triumph*

666 Lord Nelson and HMS *Victory*

667 Lord Fisher and HMS *Dreadnought*

668 Viscount Cunningham and HMS *Warspite*

Maritime Heritage

1982 (16 JUNE) *Phosphorised paper*

1187	**664**	15½p multicoloured	..	35	35	☐ ☐
1188	**665**	19½p multicoloured	..	60	60	☐ ☐
1189	**666**	24p multicoloured	..	70	70	☐ ☐
1190	**667**	26p multicoloured	..	80	80	☐ ☐
1191	**668**	29p multicoloured	..	90	90	☐ ☐
		Set of 5	..	3·00	3·00	☐ ☐
		First Day Cover	..		3·00	☐
		Presentation Pack		3·75		☐
		PHQ Cards (set of 5)		3·00	6·50	☐ ☐
		Set of 5 Gutter Pairs	..	6·00		☐

669 "Strawberry Thief" (William Morris)

670 Untitled (Steiner and Co)

671 "Cherry Orchard"
(Paul Nash)

672 "Chevron" (Andrew Foster)

British Textiles

1982 (23 July) *Phosphorised paper*

1192	**669**	15½p multicoloured ..	35	35	☐	☐
1193	**670**	19½p multicoloured ..	55	55	☐	☐
1194	**671**	26p multicoloured ..	70	70	☐	☐
1195	**672**	29p multicoloured ..	90	90	☐	☐
		Set of 4	2·25	2·25	☐	☐
		First Day Cover		2·50		☐
		Presentation Pack ..	3·25		☐	
		PHQ Cards (set of 4) ..	3·00	6·50	☐	☐
		Set of 4 Gutter Pairs ..	4·50		☐	

Nos 1192/5 were issued on the occasion of the 250th birth anniversary of Sir Richard Arkwright (inventor of spinning machine).

673 Development of Communications

674 Modern Technological Aids

Information Technology

1982 (8 Sept.) *Phosphorised paper. Perf 14 × 15*

1196	**673**	15½p multicoloured ..	45	50	☐	☐
1197	**674**	26p multicoloured ..	80	85	☐	☐
		Set of 2	1·25	1·25	☐	☐
		First Day Cover		1·50		☐
		Presentation Pack ..	2·00		☐	
		PHQ Cards (set of 2) ..	1·50	4·50	☐	☐
		Set of 2 Gutter Pairs ..	2·50		☐	

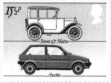

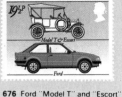

675 Austin "Seven" and "Metro" **676** Ford "Model T" and "Escort"

677 Jaguar "SS1" and "XJ6" **678** Rolls-Royce "Silver Ghost" and "Silver Spirit"

British Motor Industry

1982 (13 Oct.) *Phosphorised paper. Perf 14½ × 14*

1198	**675**	15½p multicoloured ..	50	50	☐	☐
1199	**676**	19½p multicoloured ..	70	70	☐	☐
1200	**677**	26p multicoloured ..	90	90	☐	☐
1201	**678**	29p multicoloured ..	1·25	1·25	☐	☐
		Set of 4	3·00	3·00	☐	☐
		First Day Cover		3·00		☐
		Presentation Pack	3·75		☐	
		PHQ Cards (set of 4)	3·00	7·00	☐	☐
		Set of 4 Gutter Pairs ..	6·00		☐	

679 "While Shepherds Watched" **680** "The Holly and the Ivy"

681 "I Saw Three Ships" **682** "We Three Kings"

683 ''Good King Wenceslas''

Christmas. Carols

1982 (17 Nov.) *One phosphor band* (12½p) *or phosphorised paper* (*others*)

1202	**679**	12½p multicoloured	30	30	☐	☐
1203	**680**	15½p multicoloured	40	40	☐	☐
1204	**681**	19½p multicoloured	60	60	☐	☐
1205	**682**	26p multicoloured	70	70	☐	☐
1206	**683**	29p multicoloured	80	80	☐	☐
		Set of 5	2·50	2·50	☐	☐
		First Day Cover		2·50		☐
		Presentation Pack	3·25		☐	
		PHQ Cards (set of 5)	3·00	7·00	☐	☐
		Set of 5 Gutter Pairs	5·00		☐	

Collectors Pack 1982

1982 (17 Nov.) *Comprises Nos.* 1175/1206

	Collectors Pack	21·00		☐

684 Salmon **685** Pike

686 Trout **687** Perch

British River Fishes

1983 (26 Jan.) *Phosphorised paper*

1207	**684**	15½p multicoloured	35	35	☐	☐
1208	**685**	19½p multicoloured	65	55	☐	☐
1209	**686**	26p multicoloured	80	70	☐	☐
1210	**687**	29p multicoloured	1·00	90	☐	☐
		Set of 4	2·50	2·25	☐	☐
		First Day Cover		2·50		☐
		Presentation Pack	3·00		☐	
		PHQ Cards (set of 4)	3·00	6·50	☐	☐
		Set of 4 Gutter Pairs	5·00		☐	

688 Tropical Island **689** Desert

690 Temperate Farmland **691** Mountain Range

Commonwealth Day. Geographical Regions

1983 (9 Mar.) *Phosphorised paper*

1211	**688**	15½p multicoloured	35	35	☐	☐
1212	**689**	19½p multicoloured	55	55	☐	☐
1213	**690**	26p multicoloured	70	70	☐	☐
1214	**691**	29p multicoloured	90	90	☐	☐
		Set of 4	2·25	2·25	☐	☐
		First Day Cover		2·50		☐
		Presentation Pack	3·25		☐	
		PHQ Cards (set of 4)	3·00	6·50	☐	☐
		Set of 4 Gutter Pairs	4·50		☐	

692 Humber Bridge **693** Thames Flood Barrier

694 *Iolair* (oilfield emergency support vessel)

Europa. Engineering Achievements

1983 (25 May) *Phosphorised paper*

1215	**692**	16p multicoloured	45	45	☐	☐
1216	**693**	20½p multicoloured	95	1·10	☐	☐
1217	**694**	28p multicoloured	1·10	1·25	☐	☐
		Set of 3	2·25	2·50	☐	☐
		First Day Cover		2·50		☐
		Presentation Pack	3·50		☐	
		PHQ Cards (set of 3)	2·50	6·00	☐	☐
		Set of 3 Gutter Pairs	4·50		☐	

British Army Uniforms

1983 (6 July) *Phosphorised paper*

1218	**695**	16p multicoloured	40	40	☐	☐
1219	**696**	20½p multicoloured	70	70	☐	☐
1220	**697**	26p multicoloured	85	85	☐	☐
1221	**698**	28p multicoloured	85	85	☐	☐
1222	**699**	31p multicoloured	1·10	1·10	☐	☐
		Set of 5	3·50	3·50	☐	☐
		First Day Cover		3·25		☐
		Presentation Pack	4·50		☐	
		PHQ Cards (set of 5)	3·00	6·00	☐	☐
		Set of 5 Gutter Pairs	7·00		☐	

Nos. 1218/22 were issued on the occasion of the 350th anniversary of The Royal Scots, the senior line regiment of the British Army.

695 Musketeer and Pikeman. The Royal Scots (1633)

696 Fusilier and Ensign. The Royal Welch Fusiliers (mid-18th century)

700 20th-Century Garden, Sissinghurst

701 19th-Century Garden, Biddulph Grange

697 Riflemen. 96th Rifles (The Royal Green Jackets) (1805)

698 Sergeant (khaki service uniform) and Guardsman (full dress). The Irish Guards (1900)

702 18th-Century Garden, Blenheim

703 17th-Century Garden, Pitmedden

British Gardens

1983 (24 Aug.) *Phosphorised paper. Perf* 14

1223	**700**	16p multicoloured	40	40	☐	☐
1224	**701**	20½p multicoloured	50	50	☐	☐
1225	**702**	28p multicoloured	70	90	☐	☐
1226	**703**	31p multicoloured	90	1·00	☐	☐
		Set of 4	2·25	2·50	☐	☐
		First Day Cover		2·75		☐
		Presentation Pack	3·50		☐	
		PHQ Cards (set of 4)	3·00	6·00	☐	☐
		Set of 4 Gutter Pairs	4·50		☐	

699 Paratroopers. The Parachute Regiment (1983)

704 Merry-go-round

705 Big Wheel, Helter-skelter and Performing Animals

706 Side-shows

707 Early Produce Fair

British Fairs

1983 (5 Oct) *Phosphorised paper.*

1227	**704**	16p multicoloured	..	40	40	☐	☐
1228	**705**	20½p multicoloured	..	65	65	☐	☐
1229	**706**	28p multicoloured	..	85	85	☐	☐
1230	**707**	31p multicoloured	..	90	90	☐	☐
	Set of 4		..	2·50	2·50	☐	☐
	First Day Cover		..		2·75		☐
	Presentation Pack		..	3·50		☐	
	PHQ Cards (set of 4)		..	3·00	6·00	☐	☐
	Set of 4 Gutter Pairs			5·00		☐	

Nos. 1227/30 were issued to mark the 850th Anniversary of St. Bartholomew's Fair, Smithfield, London.

708 "Christmas Post" (pillar-box)

709 "The Three Kings" (chimney-pots)

710 "World at Peace" (Dove and Blackbird)

711 "Light of Christmas" (street lamp)

712 "Christmas Dove" (hedge sculpture)

Christmas

1983 (16 Nov) One phosphor band (12½p) or phosphorised paper (*others*)

1231	**708**	12½p multicoloured	..	30	30	☐ ☐
1232	**709**	16p multicoloured	..	35	35	☐ ☐
1233	**710**	20½p multicoloured	..	60	60	☐ ☐
1234	**711**	28p multicoloured	..	70	80	☐ ☐
1235	**712**	31p multicoloured	..	85	1·00	☐ ☐
	Set of 5		..	2·50	2·75	☐ ☐
	First Day Cover				2·75	☐
	Presentation Pack		..	3·50		☐
	PHQ Cards (set of 5)		..	3·00	6·00	☐ ☐
	Set of 5 Gutter Pairs			5·00		☐

Collectors Pack 1983

1983 (16 Nov) *Comprises Nos.* 1207/35

	Collectors Pack	..	35·00	☐

713 Arms of the College of Arms

714 Arms of King Richard III (founder)

715 Arms of the Earl Marshal of England

716 Arms of the City of London

500th Anniversary of College of Arms

1984 (17 Jan) *Phosphorised paper. Perf* 14½

1236	**713**	16p multicoloured	40	40	☐	☐
1237	**714**	20½p multicoloured	60	60	☐	☐
1238	**715**	28p multicoloured	85	85	☐	☐
1239	**716**	31p multicoloured	95	95	☐	☐
		Set of 4	2·50	2·50	☐	☐
		First Day Cover		2·50		☐
		Presentation Pack	3·50		☐	
		PHQ Cards (set of 4)	3·00	6·00	☐	☐
		Set of 4 Gutter Pairs	5·00		☐	

717 Highland Cow   **718** Chillingham Wild Bull

719 Hereford Bull   **720** Welsh Black Bull

721 Irish Moiled Cow

British Cattle

1984 (6 Mar) *Phosphorised paper.*

1240	**717**	16p multicoloured	40	40	☐	☐
1241	**718**	20½p multicoloured	65	65	☐	☐
1242	**719**	26p multicoloured	70	70	☐	☐
1243	**720**	28p multicoloured	70	70	☐	☐
1244	**721**	31p multicoloured	90	90	☐	☐
		Set of 5	3·00	3·00	☐	☐
		First Day Cover		3·00		☐
		Presentation Pack	4·25		☐	
		PHQ Cards (set of 5)	3·00	6·00	☐	☐
		Set of 5 Gutter Pairs	6·00		☐	

Nos. 1240/4 marked the centenary of the Highland Cattle Society and the bicentenary of the Royal Highland and Agricultural Society of Scotland.

722 Festival Hall, Liverpool   **723** Milburngate Shopping Centre, Durham

724 Bush House, Bristol   **725** Commercial Street Housing Scheme, Perth

Urban Renewal

1984 (10 Apr) *Phosphorised paper.*

1245	**722**	16p multicoloured	40	40	☐	☐
1246	**723**	20½p multicoloured	60	60	☐	☐
1247	**724**	28p multicoloured	90	90	☐	☐
1248	**725**	31p multicoloured	90	90	☐	☐
		Set of 4	2·50	2·50	☐	☐
		First Day Cover		3·00		☐
		Presentation Pack	3·50		☐	
		PHQ Cards (set of 4)	3·00	6·00	☐	☐
		Set of 4 Gutter Pairs	5·00		☐	

Nos. 1245/8 mark the opening of the International Gardens Festival, Liverpool, and the 150th anniversaries of the Royal Institute of British Architects and the Chartered Institute of Building.

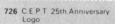 

726 C.E.P.T. 25th Anniversary Logo   **727** Abduction of Europa

Nos. 1249/50 and 1251/2 were each printed together, *se-tenant*, in horizontal pairs throughout the sheets.

Europa. 25th Anniversary of C.E.P.T. and 2nd European Parliamentary Elections

1984 (15 May) *Phosphorised paper.*

1249	**726**	16p	greenish slate, dp blue and gold	90	90	☐	☐
		a.	*Horiz pair. Nos 1249/50*	1·75	1·75	☐	☐
1250	**727**	16p	greenish slate, dp bl, blk and gold	90	90	☐	☐
1251	**726**	20½p	Venetian red, deep magenta and gold	1·50	1·50	☐	☐
		a.	*Horizontal pair. Nos. 1251/2*	3·00	3·00	☐	☐
1252	**727**	20½p	Venetian red, deep magenta, black and gold	1·50	1·50	☐	☐
			Set of 4	4·25	4·25	☐	☐
			First Day Cover		4·25		☐
			Presentation Pack	5·00		☐	
			PHQ Cards (set of 4)	3·00	6·00	☐	☐
			Set of 2 Gutter Blocks of 4	8·50		☐	

728 Lancaster House

London Economic Summit Conference

1984 (5 June) *Phosphorised paper.*

1253	**728**	31p	multicoloured	1·00	1·00	☐	☐
			First Day Cover		2·00		☐
			PHQ Card	1·00	2·75	☐	☐
			Gutter Pair	2·00			☐

729 View of Earth from "Apollo 11"

730 Navigational Chart of English Channel

731 Greenwich Observatory

732 Sir George Airey's Transit Telescope

Centenary of Greenwich Meridian

1984 (26 June) *Phosphorised paper. Perf 14 × 14½*

1254	**729**	16p	multicoloured	40	40	☐	☐
1255	**730**	20½p	multicoloured	65	65	☐	☐
1256	**731**	28p	multicoloured	85	90	☐	☐
1257	**732**	31p	multicoloured	90	1·10	☐	☐
			Set of 4	2·50	2·75	☐	☐
			First Day Cover		2·75		☐
			Presentation Pack	3·75		☐	
			PHQ Cards (set of 4)	3·00	6·00	☐	☐
			Set of 4 Gutter Pairs	5·00			

733 Bath Mail Coach, 1784

734 Attack on Exeter Mail, 1816

735 Norwich Mail in Thunderstorm, 1827

736 Holyhead and Liverpool Mails leaving London, 1828

737 Edinburgh Mail Snowbound, 1831

T **733/7** were printed together, *se-tenant* in horizontal strips of 5 throughout the sheet.

Bicentenary of First Mail Coach Run, Bath and Bristol to London

1984 (31 July) *Phosphorised paper*

1258	**733**	16p multicoloured	60	40	☐	☐
		a. Horiz strip of 5.				
		Nos. 1258/62	2·75	2·75	☐	☐
1259	**734**	16p multicoloured	60	40	☐	☐
1260	**735**	16p multicoloured	60	40	☐	☐
1261	**736**	16p multicoloured	60	40	☐	☐
1262	**737**	16p multicoloured	60	40	☐	☐
		Set of 5	2·75	1·75	☐	☐
		First Day Cover		2·75		☐
		Presentation Pack	3·75		☐	
		Souvenir Book	6·00		☐	
		PHQ Cards (set of 5)	3·00	6·50	☐	☐
		Gutter Block of 10	5·50		☐	

738 Nigerian Clinic

739 Violinist and Acropolis. Athens

740 Building Project. Sri Lanka

741 British Council Library

50th Anniversary of The British Council

1984 (25 Sept.) *Phosphorised paper*

1263	**738**	17p multicoloured	50	50	☐	☐
1264	**739**	22p multicoloured	65	65	☐	☐
1265	**740**	31p multicoloured	90	90	☐	☐
1266	**741**	34p multicoloured	1·00	1·00	☐	☐
		Set of 4	2·75	2·75	☐	☐
		First Day Cover		2·75		☐
		Presentation Pack	3·50		☐	
		PHQ Cards (set of 4)	3·00	6·00	☐	☐
		Set of 4 Gutter Pairs	5·50		☐	

For full information on all future British issues, collectors should write to the British Post Office Philatelic Bureau, 20 Brandon Street, Edinburgh EH3 5TT.

742 The Holy Family   **743** Arrival in Bethlehem

744 Shepherd and Lamb   **745** Virgin and Child

746 Offering of Frankincense

Christmas

1984 (20 Nov.) *One phosphor band (13p) or phosphorised paper (others)*

1267	**742**	13p multicoloured	30	30	☐	☐
1268	**743**	17p multicoloured	50	50	☐	☐
1269	**744**	22p multicoloured	60	60	☐	☐
1270	**745**	31p multicoloured	95	95	☐	☐
1271	**746**	34p multicoloured	1·00	1·00	☐	☐
		Set of 5	3·00	3·00	☐	☐
		First Day Cover		3·00		☐
		Presentation Pack	3·75		☐	
		PHQ Cards (set of 5)	3·00	6·00	☐	☐
		Set of 5 Gutter Pairs	6·00		☐	

Collectors Pack 1984

1984 (20 Nov.) *Comprises Nos. 1236/71*

	Collectors Pack	35·00	☐

Post Office Yearbook

1984 *Comprises Nos. 1236/71 in hardbound book with slip case.*

	Yearbook	75·00	☐

747 "The Flying Scotsman" 748 "The Golden Arrow"

749 "The Cheltenham Flyer" 750 "The Royal Scot"

751 "The Cornish Riviera"

Wart-Biter Bush-Cricket

Stag Beetle

754 *Decticus verrucivorus*
(bush-cricket)

755 *Lucanus cervus* (stag beetle)

Emperor Dragonfly

756 *Anax imperator* (dragonfly)

Famous Trains

1985 (22 Jan) *Phosphorised paper*

1272	**747**	17p multicoloured	..	50	50	☐	☐
1273	**748**	22p multicoloured	..	85	70	☐	☐
1274	**749**	29p multicoloured	..	1·00	90	☐	☐
1275	**750**	31p multicoloured	..	1·25	1·00	☐	☐
1276	**751**	34p multicoloured	..	1·40	1·10	☐	☐
		Set of 5	.. ..	4·50	4·00	☐	☐
		First Day Cover	.. ..		5·00	☐	
		Presentation Pack	.. ..	5·25		☐	
		PHQ Cards (set of 5)	.. ..	4·00	11·00	☐	☐
		Set of 5 Gutter Pairs	.. ..	9·00		☐	

Nos. 1272/6 were issued on the occasion of the 150th anniversary of the Great Western Railway Company.

Insects

1985 (12 March) *Phosphorised paper*

1277	**752**	17p multicoloured	..	40	40	☐	☐
1278	**753**	22p multicoloured	..	60	60	☐	☐
1279	**754**	29p multicoloured	..	80	80	☐	☐
1280	**755**	31p multicoloured	..	90	90	☐	☐
1281	**756**	34p multicoloured	..	90	90	☐	☐
		Set of 5	.. .. ..	3·25	3·25	☐	☐
		First Day Cover	.. ..		3·50	☐	
		Presentation Pack	.. ..	4·00		☐	
		PHQ Cards (set of 5)	..	3·00	6·50	☐	☐
		Set of 5 Gutter Pairs	.. ..	6·50		☐	

Nos. 1277/81 were issued on the occasion of the centenaries of the Royal Entomological Society of London's Royal Charter and of the Selborne Society.

Buff Tailed Bumble Bee

Seven Spotted Ladybird

752 *Bombus terrestris* (bee) 753 *Coccinella septempunctata* (ladybird)

SEVENTEEN · PENCE
WATER · MUSIC
George Frideric Handel

TWENTY · TWO · PENCE
THE · PLANETS · SUITE
Gustav Holst

757 "Water Music", by Handel 758 "The Planets", by Holst

THIRTY·ONE·PENCE

THE·FIRST·CUCKOO
Frederick Delius

THIRTY·FOUR·PENCE

SEA·PICTURES
Edward Elgar

759 "The First Cuckoo", by Delius

760 "Sea Pictures", by Elgar

Europa – European Music Year

1985 (14 MAY) *Phosphorised paper. Perf 14½*

1282	**757**	17p multicoloured	65	65	□	□
1283	**758**	22p multicoloured	90	90	□	□
1284	**759**	31p multicoloured	1·40	1·40	□	□
1285	**760**	34p multicoloured	1·50	1·50	□	□
		Set of 4	4·00	4·00	□	□
		First Day Cover		4·00	□	
		Presentation Pack	4·50		□	
		PHQ Cards (set of 4)	3·00	6·00	□	□
		Set of 4 Gutter Pairs	8·00		□	

Nos. 1282/5 were issued on the occasion of the 300th birth anniversary of Handel.

761 R.N.L.I. Lifeboat and Signal Flags

762 Beachy Head Lighthouse and Chart

763 "Marecs A" Communications Satellite and Dish Aerials

764 Buoys

Safety at Sea

1985 (18 JUNE) *Phosphorised paper. Perf 14*

1286	**761**	17p multicoloured	50	50	□	□
1287	**762**	22p multicoloured	65	65	□	□
1288	**763**	31p multicoloured	1·10	1·10	□	□
1289	**764**	34p multicoloured	1·10	1·10	□	□
		Set of 4	3·00	3·00	□	□
		First Day Cover		3·50	□	
		Presentation Pack	4·25		□	
		PHQ Cards (set of 4)	3·00	6·00	□	□
		Set of 4 Gutter Pairs	6·00		□	

Nos. 1286/9 were issued on the occasion of the bicentenary of the unimmersible lifeboat and the 50th anniversary of Radar.

765 Datapost Motorcyclist, City of London

766 Rural Postbus

767 Parcel Delivery in Winter

768 Town Letter Delivery

350 Years of Royal Mail Public Postal Service

1985 (30 JULY) *Phosphorised paper*

1290	**765**	17p multicoloured	50	50	□	□
1291	**766**	22p multicoloured	65	65	□	□
1292	**767**	31p multicoloured	1·10	1·10	□	□
1293	**768**	34p multicoloured	1·10	1·10	□	□
		Set of 4	3·00	3·00	□	□
		First Day Cover		3·25	□	
		Presentation Pack	4·25		□	
		PHQ Cards (set of 4)	3·00	6·00	□	□
		Set of 4 Gutter Pairs	6·00		□	

769 King Arthur and Merlin

770 The Lady of the Lake

QUALITY STAMPS
DIRECT TO YOUR DOOR

Irresistibly simple, exceptionally quick and reassuringly reliable
Stanley Gibbons Mail Order service enables you to economically build your
collection from the comfort of your own home.

WE PROVIDE:

- The world's largest stocks of guaranteed quality GB material.
- Regular well produced, illustrated brochures and lists.
- Fast 48 hour order despatch.
- Free telephone advice from our team of specialists.
- A detailed register of your collecting interests.
- Exclusive special offers mailed regularly.
- Specialist 'wants list' service available.
- Over 140 years philatelic experience.

ORDER STRAIGHT FROM THIS CATALOGUE

As the world's oldest established stamp dealer, we hold comprehensive stocks.
The majority of items in this catalogue are usually available, but if we are unable to
supply, we will record your requirements and notify you, without obligation, when
they do come into stock.

To order, complete your details and the SG numbers you require on the following
two pages, remove this section and return to:

Stanley Gibbons Limited, GB Department, 399 Strand, London WC2R 0LX England.

TERMS AND CONDITIONS:

1. **Minimum order £20** (excluding P&P)
2. **Please order complete sets only,** we are unable to supply individual items from sets.
3. **Please submit alternatives should your preferred requests be unavailable.** Alternatively you will be sent a credit note for use against your next order, if paying by cheque.
4. **All orders will be despatched within 48 hours of receipt of payment.** We cannot accept responsibility for delays caused in the mail.
5. **Quality of our stamps is guaranteed,** if you are dissatisfied in any way please return your stamps within 14 days for a full refund.

SPECIAL COMMEMORATIVE
YEAR SET OFFERS
Over the Page

COMPLETE COMMEMORATIVE YEAR SET OFFERS

Year	Unmounted Mint	Used	Presentation Pack	First Day Cover
1963	☐ £12.50	☐ £11.50	–	☐ £122.00
1964	☐ £11.00	☐ £11.00	☐ £375.00	☐ £50.00
1965	☐ £15.00	☐ £17.00	☐ £85.00	☐ £99.00
1966	☐ £7.50	☐ £9.00	☐ £90.00	☐ £48.00
1967	☐ £3.50	☐ £3.50	☐ £15.00	☐ £17.50
1968	☐ £1.75	☐ £1.75	☐ £10.00	☐ £11.00
1969	☐ £6.25	☐ £7.00	☐ £18.75	☐ £20.00
1970	☐ £4.40	☐ £5.00	☐ £16.50	☐ £11.50
1971	☐ £4.80	☐ £4.80	☐ £22.50	☐ £14.00
1972	☐ £6.50	☐ £6.80	☐ £21.00	☐ £17.00
1973	☐ £11.50	☐ £12.00	☐ £23.50	☐ £19.50
1974	☐ £5.00	☐ £5.00	☐ £13.00	☐ £10.00
1975	☐ £6.50	☐ £6.00	☐ £13.50	☐ £9.00
1976	☐ £6.00	☐ £6.00	☐ £13.00	☐ £8.00
1977	☐ £5.50	☐ £6.00	☐ £11.00	☐ £8.00
1978	☐ £6.50	☐ £6.70	☐ £11.00	☐ £9.00
1979	☐ £9.50	☐ £9.50	☐ £15.00	☐ £11.40
1980	☐ £12.50	☐ £12.40	☐ £16.00	☐ £12.00
1981	☐ £14.00	☐ £13.50	☐ £18.00	☐ £14.50
1982	☐ £17.50	☐ £16.50	☐ £23.00	☐ £17.00
1983	☐ £15.50	☐ £16.00	☐ £22.00	☐ £17.00
1984	☐ £21.50	☐ £22.00	☐ £27.50	☐ £23.00
1985	☐ £25.00	☐ £25.00	☐ £33.00	☐ £28.00
1986	☐ £27.50	☐ £26.75	☐ £36.50	☐ £34.00
1987	☐ £22.50	☐ £22.50	☐ £32.50	☐ £27.50
1988	☐ £29.50	☐ £28.75	☐ £31.00	☐ £33.00
1989	☐ £50.50	☐ £45.40	☐ £33.25	☐ £51.00
1990	☐ £52.50	☐ £48.50	☐ £36.00	☐ £61.00
1991	☐ £45.00	☐ £44.00	☐ £31.50	☐ £50.00
1992	☐ £28.50	☐ £29.00	☐ £35.00	☐ £38.00
1993	☐ £34.50	☐ £33.00	☐ £38.50	☐ £40.50
1994	☐ £32.00	☐ £32.00	☐ £37.50	☐ £41.00
1995	☐ £28.00	☐ £28.00	☐ £29.00	☐ £31.00

Please tick the sets you require in the boxes provided.

CUSTOMER DETAILS

☐ **Please send me the items I have listed below**

Account No. (if valid) ☐☐☐☐☐☐☐☐☐

(Mr/Mrs/Miss/Ms) _____ Initial _____

Surname _____

Address _____

_____

_____ Postcode _____

Telephone _____

☐ I enclose cheque/postal order made payable to **Stanley Gibbons Ltd** for: £ _____

☐ I authorise you to charge my

Mastercard ☐ [MasterCard] Amex ☐ [AMERICAN EXPRESS]

Diners ☐ [◯◯] Visa ☐ [VISA]

Card No ☐☐☐☐☐☐☐☐☐☐☐☐☐☐☐☐

Expiry date ☐☐☐☐

Signature _____

PRESTIGE PAYMENT PLAN 0% INTEREST FREE CREDIT ON PURCHASES OVER £1000. All items are subject to status. A written quotation is available on request. TELEPHONE TODAY FOR AN APPLICATION FORM

ORDER FORM

Please list the items you would like supplied in the spaces below:

S.G. Cat No.	Description	Mint or Used	S.G. Cat Price	Office use only
	Please continue on a separate page			
	Plus Commemorative Year Sets from previous page			
	Allow £2.00 for recorded postage and packing		£2.00	
	Total payable		£	

☐ Please also send me the brochures and/or lists I have indicated on the next page

CBS1/97

FREE ILLUSTRATED
GB MAIL ORDER LISTING!

- Produced twice yearly and used by thousands of collectors worldwide.
- Packed full of popular material from one of the world's largest stocks.
- Includes a number of rare and specialised items.
- Contains illustrations (many in colour), accurate descriptions and SG catalogue numbers throughout.
- Also features a number of special offers, a useful checklist and a pull out mail order form in the centre pages.

☐ Please send me your latest GB mail order listing.

☐ Please also send me mail order lists available for:
   ☐ Australia   ☐ Canada   ☐ Channel Islands & Isle of Man
   ☐ Falkland Islands ☐ New Zealand

LUXURY COLOUR BROCHURE

- A twice yearly publication containing superb rare and specialised items, each expertly described with many illustrations in colour.
- Sections devoted to Great Britain, Commonwealth and Foreign Countries.
- An outstanding reference for all serious collectors.
- Only a limited number are produced. A yearly subscription of £10 ensures you receive both editions POST FREE by priority despatch.
- FREE INSIDE each brochure you will receive £20 of vouchers to spend on any of the items featured.

☐ Please send me the next two issues of your Luxury Brochure. I enclose a cheque/postal order for £10 made payable to Stanley Gibbons Limited.

Return to:
Stanley Gibbons Limited, GB Department,
399 Strand, London WC2R 0LX, England
Tel: 0171 836 8444 Fax: 0171 836 7342

e.mail sales@stangib.demon.co.uk

BY APPOINTMENT TO
HER MAJESTY THE QUEEN
STANLEY GIBBONS LTD
LONDON PHILATELISTS

STANLEY GIBBONS

• **OUR NAME IS YOUR GUARANTEE OF QUALITY** •

771 Queen Guinevere and Sir Lancelot

772 Sir Galahad

777 Alfred Hitchcock (from photo by Howard Coster)

Arthurian Legends

1985 (3 SEPT.) *Phosphorised paper*

1294	**769**	17p multicoloured	50	50	□	□
1295	**770**	22p multicoloured	65	75	□	□
1296	**771**	31p multicoloured	1·10	1·10	□	□
1297	**772**	34p multicoloured	1·10	1·25	□	□
		Set of 4	3·00	3·25	□	□
		First Day Cover		3·50		□
		Presentation Pack	5·00		□	
		PHQ Cards (set of 4)	3·00	6·00	□	□
		Set of 4 Gutter Pairs	6·00		□	

Nos. 1294/7 were issued on the occasion of the 500th anniversary of the printing of Sir Thomas Malory's *Morte d'Arthur*.

British Film Year

1985 (8 OCT.) *Phosphorised paper. Perf 14½*

1298	**773**	17p multicoloured	50	50	□	□
1299	**774**	22p multicoloured	75	75	□	□
1300	**775**	29p multicoloured	1·10	1·10	□	□
1301	**776**	31p multicoloured	1·25	1·25	□	□
1302	**777**	34p multicoloured	1·40	1·40	□	□
		Set of 5	4·50	4·50	□	□
		First Day Cover		4·75		□
		Presentation Pack	6·50		□	
		Souvenir Book	7·50		□	
		PHQ Cards (set of 5)	3·00	6·00	□	□
		Set of 5 Gutter Pairs	9·00		□	

778 Principal Boy

779 Genie

773 Peter Sellers (from photo by Bill Brandt)

774 David Niven (from photo by Cornell Lucas)

780 Dame

781 Good Fairy

775 Charlie Chaplin (from photo by Lord Snowdon)

776 Vivien Leigh (from photo by Angus McBean)

782 Pantomime Cat

Christmas. Pantomime Characters

1985 (19 Nov.) One phosphor band (12p) or phosphorised paper (others)

1303	778	12p multicoloured	35	30	☐	☐
1304	779	17p multicoloured	45	40	☐	☐
1305	780	22p multicoloured	70	80	☐	☐
1306	781	31p multicoloured	95	1·00	☐	☐
1307	782	34p multicoloured	1·00	1·10	☐	☐
		Set of 5	3·00	3·25	☐	☐
		First Day Cover		3·75	☐	
		Presentation Pack	4·50		☐	
		PHQ Cards (Set of 5)	3·00	6·00	☐	☐
		Set of 5 Gutter Pairs	6·00		☐	

Collectors Pack 1985

1985 (19 Nov.) Comprises Nos. 1272/1307

	Collectors Pack	35·00	☐

Post Office Yearbook

1985 Comprises Nos. 1272/1307 in hardbound book with slip case.

	Yearbook	75·00	☐

783 Light Bulb and North Sea Oil Drilling Rig (Energy)

784 Thermometer and Pharmaceutical Laboratory (Health)

785 Garden Hoe and Steel Works (Steel)

786 Loaf of Bread and Cornfield (Agriculture)

Industry Year

1986 (14 Jan.) Phosphorised paper. Perf 14½ × 14

1308	783	17p multicoloured	45	45	☐	☐
1309	784	22p multicoloured	60	60	☐	☐
1310	785	31p multicoloured	90	90	☐	☐
1311	786	34p multicoloured	1·10	1·10	☐	☐
		Set of 4	2·75	2·75	☐	☐
		First Day Cover		3·25	☐	
		Presentation Pack	4·00		☐	
		PHQ Cards (set of 4)	3·00	6·00	☐	☐
		Set of 4 Gutter Pairs	5·50		☐	

787 Dr. Edmond Halley as Comet

788 Giotto Spacecraft approaching Comet

789 "Twice in a Lifetime"

790 Comet orbiting Sun and Planets

Appearance of Halley's Comet

1986 (18 Feb.) Phosphorised paper.

1312	787	17p multicoloured	45	45	☐	☐
1313	788	22p multicoloured	70	70	☐	☐
1314	789	31p multicoloured	1·10	1·10	☐	☐
1315	790	34p multicoloured	1·10	1·10	☐	☐
		Set of 4	3·00	3·00	☐	☐
		First Day Cover		4·00	☐	
		Presentation Pack	4·75		☐	
		PHQ Cards (set of 4)	4·00	6·00	☐	☐
		Set of 4 Gutter Pairs	6·00		☐	

791 Queen Elizabeth II in 1928, 1942 and 1952

792 Queen Elizabeth II in 1958, 1973 and 1982

Nos. 1316/17 and 1318/19 were each printed together, *se-tenant*, in horizontal pairs throughout the sheets.

60th Birthday of Queen Elizabeth II

1986 (21 Apr.) Phosphorised paper.

1316	791	17p multicoloured	70	40	☐	☐
		a. Horiz pair.				
		Nos.1316/17	1·40	1·40	☐	
1317	792	17p multicoloured	70	40	☐	☐
1318	791	34p multicoloured	1·25	1·00	☐	☐
		a. Horiz pair.				
		Nos.1318/19	2·50	2·50		☐
1319	792	34p multicoloured	1·25	1·00	☐	☐
		Set of 4	3·50	2·50	☐	
		First Day Cover		4·00	☐	
		Presentation Pack	5·00		☐	
		Souvenir Book	7·00		☐	
		PHQ Cards (set of 4)	3·00	6·00	☐	☐
		Set of 2 Gutter Blocks of 4	7·00		☐	

793 Barn Owl

794 Pine Marten

795 Wild Cat

796 Natterjack Toad

Europa. Nature Conservation. Endangered Species

1986 (20 May) *Phosphorised paper. Perf* $14\frac{1}{2} \times 14$

1320	**793**	17p multicoloured	50	50	□	□
1321	**794**	22p multicoloured	90	75	□	□
1322	**795**	31p multicoloured	1·25	1·10	□	□
1323	**796**	34p multicoloured	1·50	1·25	□	□
	Set of 4		3·75	3·25	□	□
	First Day Cover			4·00		□
	Presentation Pack		4·50		□	
	PHQ Cards (set of 4)		3·00	6·00	□	□
	Set of 4 Gutter Pairs		7·50		□	

797 Peasants working in Fields

798 Freemen working at Town Trades

799 Knight and Retainers

800 Lord at Banquet

900th Anniversary of Domesday Book

1986 (17 June) *Phosphorised paper*

1324	**797**	17p multicoloured	50	50	□	□
1325	**798**	22p multicoloured	75	75	□	□
1326	**799**	31p multicoloured	1·10	1·10	□	□
1327	**800**	34p multicoloured	1·25	1·25	□	□
	Set of 4		3·25	3·25	□	□
	First Day Cover			4·00		□
	Presentation Pack		4·50		□	
	PHQ Cards (set of 4)		3·00	6·00	□	□
	Set of 4 Gutter Pairs		6·50		□	

801 Athletics

802 Rowing

803 Weightlifting

804 Rifle-Shooting

805 Hockey

Thirteenth Commonwealth Games, Edinburgh (Nos. 1328 31) and World Men's Hockey Cup, London (No. 1332)

1986 (15 July) *Phosphorised paper.*

1328	**801**	17p multicoloured	50	50	□	□
1329	**802**	22p multicoloured	70	70	□	□
1330	**803**	29p multicoloured	90	90	□	□
1331	**804**	31p multicoloured	1·10	1·10	□	□
1332	**805**	34p multicoloured	1·25	1·25	□	□
	Set of 5		4·00	4·00	□	□
	First Day Cover			4·25		□
	Presentation Pack		5·25		□	
	PHQ Cards (Set of 5)		4·00	6·00	□	□
	Set of 5 Gutter Pairs		8·00		□	

No. 1332 also marked the centenary of the Hockey Association.

806 Prince Andrew and Miss Sarah Ferguson 807

Royal Wedding

1986 (22 July) *One side band (12p) or phosphorised paper (17p)*

1333	**806**	12p multicoloured	..	60	60	☐	☐
1334	**807**	17p multicoloured	..	90	90	☐	☐
		Set of 2	.. .. ..	1·25	1·25	☐	☐
		First Day Cover	.. ..		2·50		☐
		Presentation Pack	.. ..	2·00		☐	
		PHQ Cards (set of 2)	..	1·50	5·00	☐	☐
		Set of 2 Gutter Pairs	..	2·50		☐	

808 Stylised Cross on Ballot Paper

32nd Commonwealth Parliamentary Conference, London

1986 (19 Aug.) *Phosphorised paper. Perf 14 × 14½*

1335	**808**	34p multicoloured	..	1·25	1·25	☐	☐
		First Day Cover	.. .. ..		2·00		☐
		PHQ Card	.. .. ..	1·00	2·50	☐	☐
		Gutter Pair	.. .. ..	2·50		☐	

809 Lord Dowding and Hawker Hurricane Mk I   810 Lord Tedder and Hawker Typhoon 1B

811 Lord Trenchard and De Havilland D.H.9A   812 Sir Arthur Harris and Avro Type 683 Lancaster

813 Lord Portal and De Havilland D.H.98 Mosquito

History of the Royal Air Force

1986 (16th Sept.) *Phosphorised paper. Perf 14½ × 14.*

1336	**809**	17p multicoloured	..	50	40	☐	☐
1337	**810**	22p multicoloured	..	75	85	☐	☐
1338	**811**	29p multicoloured	..	1·00	1·00	☐	☐
1339	**812**	31p multicoloured	..	1·25	1·10	☐	☐
1340	**813**	34p multicoloured	..	1·50	1·25	☐	☐
		Set of 5	.. .. ..	4·50	4·25	☐	☐
		First Day Cover	.. ..		5·00		☐
		Presentation Pack	.. ..	6·00		☐	
		PHQ Cards (set of 5)	..	4·00	6·50	☐	☐
		Set of 5 Gutter Pairs	..	9·00		☐	

Nos. 1336/40 were issued to celebrate the 50th anniversary of the first R.A.F. Commands.

814 The Glastonbury Thorn   815 The Tanad Valley Plygain

816 The Hebrides Tribute   817 The Dewsbury Church Knell

818 The Hereford Boy Bishop

Christmas. Folk Customs

1986 *One phosphor band (12p, 13p) or phosphorised paper (others)*

1341	**814**	12p mult. (2 Dec.)	..	50	50	☐	☐
1342		13p mult. (18 Nov.)	..	30	30	☐	☐
1343	**815**	18p mult. (18 Nov.)	..	45	45	☐	☐
1344	**816**	22p mult. (18 Nov.)	..	65	65	☐	☐
1345	**817**	31p mult. (18 Nov.)	..	80	80	☐	☐
1346	**818**	34p mult. (18 Nov.)	..	90	90	☐	☐
		Set of 6	..	3·25	3·25	☐	☐
		First Day Covers (2)	..		5·25		☐
		Presentation Pack (Nos. 1342/6)		5·00		☐	
		PHQ Cards (set of 5) (Nos. 1342/6)	..	3·00	6·00	☐	☐
		Set of 6 Gutter Pairs	..	6·50		☐	

Collectors Pack 1986

1986 (18 Nov.) *Comprises Nos. 1308/40, 1342/6*

	Collectors Pack	..	35·00	☐

Post Office Yearbook

1986 *Comprises Nos. 1308/40, 1342/6 in hardbound book with slip case.*

	Yearbook	..	65·00	☐

819 North American Blanket Flower

820 Globe Thistle

821 Echeveria

822 Autumn Crocus

Flower Photographs by Alfred Lammer

1987 (20 Jan) *Phosphorised paper. Perf 14½ × 14*

1347	**819**	18p multicoloured		50	50	☐	☐
1348	**820**	22p multicoloured		80	70	☐	☐
1349	**821**	31p multicoloured		1·25	1·10	☐	☐
1350	**822**	34p multicoloured		1·40	1·25	☐	☐
		Set of 4		3·50	3·25	☐	☐
		First Day Cover			4·25		☐
		Presentation Pack	..	4·75		☐	
		PHQ Cards (set of 4)		3·00	6·00	☐	☐
		Set of 4 Gutter Pairs	..	7·00		☐	

823 The Principia Mathematica

824 Motion of Bodies in Ellipses

825 Optick Treatise

826 The System of the World

300th Anniversary of The Principia Mathematica by Sir Isaac Newton

1987 (24 Mar) *Phosphorised paper.*

1351	**823**	18p multicoloured	..	50	50	☐	☐
1352	**824**	22p multicoloured		70	70	☐	☐
1353	**825**	31p multicoloured		1·10	1·10	☐	☐
1354	**826**	34p multicoloured		1·25	1·25	☐	☐
		Set of 4		3·25	3·25	☐	☐
		First Day Cover	..		3·50		☐
		Presentation Pack		4·50		☐	
		PHQ Cards (set of 4)		3·00	6·00	☐	☐
		Set of 4 Gutter Pairs		6·50		☐	

For full information on all future British issues, collectors should write to the British Post Office Philatelic Bureau, 20 Brandon Street, Edinburgh EH3 5TT

827 Willis Faber and Dumas Building. Ipswich

828 Pompidou Centre. Paris

829 Staatsgalerie, Stuttgart

830 European Investment Bank. Luxembourg

Europa. British Architects in Europe

1987 (12 MAY) *Phosphorised paper.*

1355	**827**	18p multicoloured		50	50	☐	☐
1356	**828**	22p multicoloured		70	70	☐	☐
1357	**829**	31p multicoloured		1·10	1·10	☐	☐
1358	**830**	34p multicoloured		1·25	1·25	☐	☐
		Set of 4		3·25	3·25	☐	☐
		First Day Cover			3·50	☐	
		Presentation Pack		4·50		☐	
		PHQ Cards (set of 4)		3·00	6·00	☐	☐
		Set of 4 Gutter Pairs		6·50		☐	

831 Brigade Members with Ashford Litter, 1887

832 Bandaging Blitz Victim, 1940

833 Volunteer with fainting Girl, 1965

834 Transport of Transplant Organ by Air Wing, 1987

Centenary of St. John Ambulance Brigade

1987 (16 JUNE) *Phosphorised paper. Perf 14 × 14½*

1359	**831**	18p multicoloured		50	50	☐	☐
1360	**832**	22p multicoloured		65	65	☐	☐
1361	**833**	31p multicoloured		1·10	1·10	☐	☐
1362	**834**	34p multicoloured		1·10	1·10	☐	☐
		Set of 4		3·00	3·00	☐	☐
		First Day Cover			3·50	☐	
		Presentation Pack		4·50		☐	
		PHQ Cards (set of 4)		3·00	6·00	☐	☐
		Set of 4 Gutter Pairs		6·00		☐	

835 Arms of the Lord Lyon King of Arms

836 Scottish Heraldic Banner of Prince Charles

837 Arms of Royal Scottish Academy of Painting, Sculpture and Architecture

838 Arms of Royal Society of Edinburgh

300th Anniversary of Revival of Order of the Thistle

1987 (21 JULY) *Phosphorised paper. Perf 14½*

1363	**835**	18p multicoloured		50	50	☐	☐
1364	**836**	22p multicoloured		65	65	☐	☐
1365	**837**	31p multicoloured		1·10	1·10	☐	☐
1366	**838**	34p multicoloured		1·10	1·10	☐	☐
		Set of 4		3·00	3·00	☐	☐
		First Day Cover			4·25	☐	
		Presentation Pack		4·50		☐	
		PHQ Cards (set of 4)		3·00	6·00	☐	☐
		Set of 4 Gutter Pairs		6 00		☐	

839 Crystal Palace, 'Monarch of the Glen' (Landseer) and Grace Darling

840 Great Eastern, Beeton's Book of Household Management and Prince Albert

841 Albert Memorial, Ballot Box and Disraeli

842 Diamond Jubilee Emblem, Morse Key and Newspaper Placard for Relief of Mafeking

150th Anniversary of Queen Victoria's Accession

1987 (8 Sept) *Phosphorised paper.*

1367	**839**	18p multicoloured		50	50	□	□
1368	**840**	22p multicoloured		65	65	□	□
1369	**841**	31p multicoloured		1·10	1·10	□	□
1370	**842**	34p multicoloured		1·10	1·10	□	□
		Set of 4		3·00	3·00	□	□
		First Day Cover			4·25		□
		Presentation Pack		4·75		□	
		PHQ Cards (set of 4)		3·00	6·00	□	□
		Set of 4 Gutter Pairs		6·00		□	

843 Pot by Bernard Leach

844 Pot by Elizabeth Fritsch

845 Pot by Lucie Rie

846 Pot by Hans Coper

Studio Pottery

1987 (13 Oct) *Phosphorised paper. Perf 14½ × 14*

1371	**843**	18p multicoloured		50	50	□	□
1372	**844**	26p multicoloured		70	70	□	□
1373	**845**	31p multicoloured		1·10	1·10	□	□
1374	**846**	34p multicoloured		1·25	1·25	□	□
		Set of 4		3·25	3·25	□	□
		First Day Cover			3·50		□
		Presentation Pack		4·50		□	
		PHQ Cards (set of 4)		3·00	6·00	□	□
		Set of 4 Gutter Pairs		6·50		□	

Nos. 1371/4 also mark the birth centenary of Bernard Leach, the potter.

847 Decorating the Christmas tree

848 Waiting for Father Christmas

849 Sleeping Child and Father Christmas in Sleigh

850 Child reading

851 Child playing Flute and Snowman

Christmas

1987 (17 Nov) *One phosphor band (13p) or phosphorised paper (others)*

1375	**847**	13p multicoloured		30	30	□	□
1376	**848**	18p multicoloured		50	50	□	□
1377	**849**	26p multicoloured		75	75	□	□
1378	**850**	31p multicoloured		95	1·10	□	□
1379	**851**	34p multicoloured		1·10	1·25	□	□
		Set of 5		3·25	3·50	□	□
		First Day Cover			4·25		□
		Presentation Pack		4·50		□	
		PHQ Cards (set of 5)		3·00	6·00	□	□
		Set of 5 Gutter Pairs		6·50		□	

Collectors Pack 1987

1987 (17 Nov.) Comprises Nos. 1347/79
    Collectors Pack   32·00   ☐

Post Office Yearbook

1987 Comprises Nos. 1347/79 in hardbound book with slip case
    Yearbook   40·00   ☐

852 Bull-rout (Jonathan Couch)

853 Yellow Waterlily (Major Joshua Swatkin)

854 Whistling ("Bewick's") Swan (Edward Lear)

855 *Morchella esculenta* (James Sowerby)

Bicentenary of Linnean Society. Archive Illustrations

1988 (19 Jan.) *Phosphorised paper*

1380	**852**	18p multicoloured		60	45	☐ ☐
1381	**853**	26p multicoloured		80	70	☐ ☐
1382	**854**	31p multicoloured		1·25	1·10	☐ ☐
1383	**855**	34p multicoloured		1·25	1·10	☐ ☐
		Set of 4		3·50	3·00	☐ ☐
		First Day Cover			3·50	☐
		Presentation Pack		4·50		☐
		PHQ Cards (set of 4)		3·00	6·00	☐ ☐
		Set of 4 Gutter Pairs		7·00		☐

856 Revd William Morgan (Bible translator, 1588)

857 William Salesbury (New Testament translator, 1567)

858 Bishop Richard Davies (New Testament translator, 1567)

859 Bishop Richard Parry (editor of Revised Welsh Bible, 1620)

400th Anniversary of Welsh Bible

1988 (1 Mar.) *Phosphorised paper. Perf* $14\frac{1}{2} \times 14$

1384	**856**	18p multicoloured		45	45	☐ ☐
1385	**857**	26p multicoloured		70	70	☐ ☐
1386	**858**	31p multicoloured		1·10	1·10	☐ ☐
1387	**859**	34p multicoloured		1·10	1·10	☐ ☐
		Set of 4		3·00	3·00	☐ ☐
		First Day Cover			4·00	☐
		Presentation Pack		4·50		☐
		PHQ Cards (set of 4)		3·00	6·00	☐ ☐
		Set of 4 Gutter Pairs		6·00		☐

860 Gymnastics (Centenary of British Amateur Gymnastics Association)

861 Downhill Skiing (Ski Club of Great Britain)

862 Tennis (Centenary of Lawn Tennis Association)

863 Football (Centenary of Football League)

Sports Organizations

1988 (22 Mar.) *Phosphorised paper. Perf* 14½

1388	**860**	18p multicoloured	45	45	☐	☐
1389	**861**	26p multicoloured	70	70	☐	☐
1390	**862**	31p multicoloured	1·10	1·10	☐	☐
1391	**863**	34p multicoloured	1·10	1·10	☐	☐
		Set of 4	3·00	3·00	☐	☐
		First Day Cover		4·00		☐
		Presentation Pack	4·50		☐	
		PHQ Cards (set of 4)	2·25	5·00	☐	☐
		Set of 4 Gutter Pairs	6·00		☐	

864 *Mallard* and Mailbags on Pick-up Arms

865 Loading Transatlantic Mail on Liner *Queen Elizabeth*

866 Glasgow Tram No 1173 and Pillar Box

867 Imperial Airways Handley Page H.P.45 *Horatius* and Airmail Van

Europa. Transport and Mail Services in 1930's

1988 (10 May) *Phosphorised paper*

1392	**864**	18p multicoloured	50	50	☐	☐
1393	**865**	26p multicoloured	80	80	☐	☐
1394	**866**	31p multicoloured	1·10	1·10	☐	☐
1395	**867**	34p multicoloured	1·25	1·25	☐	☐
		Set of 4	3·25	3·25	☐	☐
		First Day Cover		3·50		☐
		Presentation Pack	4·50		☐	
		PHQ Cards (set of 4)	2·00	5·00	☐	☐
		Set of 4 Gutter Pairs	6·50		☐	

868 Early Settler and Sailing Clipper

869 Queen Elizabeth II with British and Australian Parliament Buildings

870 W. G. Grace (cricketer) and Tennis Racquet

871 Shakespeare, John Lennon (entertainer) and Sydney Landmarks

Nos. 1396/7 and 1398/9 were each printed together, *se-tenant*, in horizontal pairs throughout the sheets, each pair showing a background design of the Australian flag.

Bicentenary of Australian Settlement

1988 (21 June) *Phosphorised paper. Perf* 14½

1396	**868**	18p multicoloured	60	60	☐	☐
		a. Horiz pair.				
		Nos. 1396/7	1·25	1·25	☐	☐
1397	**869**	18p multicoloured	60	60	☐	☐
1398	**870**	34p multicoloured	1·10	1·10	☐	☐
		a. Horiz pair.				
		Nos. 1398/9	2·40	2·40	☐	☐
1399	**871**	34p multicoloured	1·10	1·10	☐	☐
		Set of 4	3·25	3·25	☐	☐
		First Day Cover		3·50		☐
		Presentation Pack	4·50		☐	
		Souvenir Book	6·00		☐	
		PHQ Cards (set of 4)	2·00	5·00	☐	☐
		Set of 2 Gutter Blocks of 4	6·50		☐	

Stamps in similar designs were also issued by Australia. These are included in the Souvenir Book.

872 Spanish Galeasse off The Lizard

873 English Fleet leaving Plymouth

874 Engagement off Isle of Wight

875 Attack of English Fire-ships, Calais

876 Armada in Storm, North Sea

Nos. 1400/4 were printed together, *se-tenant*, in horizontal strips of 5 throughout the sheet, forming a composite design.

400th Anniversary of Spanish Armada

1988 (19 JULY) *Phosphorised paper*

1400	**872**	18p multicoloured	65	65	□	□
		a. Horiz strip of 5.				
		Nos. 1400/4	2·75	2·75	□	□
1401	**873**	18p multicoloured	65	65	□	□
1402	**874**	18p multicoloured	65	65	□	□
1403	**875**	18p multicoloured	65	65	□	□
1404	**876**	18p multicoloured	65	65	□	□
		Set of 5	2·75	2·75	□	□
		First Day Cover		3·25		□
		Presentation Pack	4·00		□	
		PHQ Cards (set of 5)	2·50	5·50	□	□
		Gutter Block of 10	5·50		□	

877 "The Owl and the Pussy-cat"

878 "Edward Lear as a Bird" (self-portrait)

879 "Cat" (from alphabet book)

880 "There was a Young Lady whose Bonnet . . ." (limerick)

Death Centenary of Edward Lear (artist and author)

1988 (6–27 SEPT.) *Phosphorised paper*

1405	**877**	19p black, pale cream and carmine	50	50	□	□
1406	**878**	27p black, pale cream and yellow	65	80	□	□
1407	**879**	32p black, pale cream and emerald	1·10	1·10	□	□
1408	**880**	35p black, pale cream and blue	1·10	1·25	□	□
		Set of 4	3·00	3·25	□	□
		First Day Cover		4·00		□
		Presentation Pack	4·50		□	
		PHQ Cards (set of 4)	2·00	5·00	□	□
		Set of 4 Gutter Pairs	6·00		□	
MS1409		122 × 90 mm. Nos. 1405/8	8·00	7·00	□	□
		First Day Cover (27 Sept.)		7·00		□

No. **MS**1409 was sold at £1·35, the premium being used for the "Stamp World London 90" International Stamp Exhibition.

881 Carrickfergus Castle

882 Caernarvon Castle

883 Edinburgh Castle

884 Windsor Castle

1988 (18 OCT.) *Ordinary paper*

1410	**881**	£1 deep green	2·75	50	□	□
1411	**882**	£1·50 maroon	4·00	1·25	□	□
1412	**883**	£2 indigo	6·00	1·75	□	□
1413	**884**	£5 deep brown	14·00	3·50	□	□
		Set of 4	24·00	6·25	□	□
		First Day Cover		45·00		□
		Presentation Pack	26·00		□	
		Set of 4 Gutter Pairs	48·00		□	

For similar designs, but with silhouette Queen's head see Nos. 1611/14.

885 Journey to Bethlehem

886 Shepherds and Star

887 Three Wise Men

888 Nativity

889 The Annunciation

890 Atlantic Puffin

891 Avocet

892 Oystercatcher

893 Northern Gannet

Christmas

1988 (15 Nov.) *One phosphor band (14p) or phosphorised paper (others)*

1414	**885**	14p multicoloured	..	35	35	☐ ☐
1415	**886**	19p multicoloured	..	40	45	☐ ☐
1416	**887**	27p multicoloured	..	70	70	☐ ☐
1417	**888**	32p multicoloured	..	90	1·00	☐ ☐
1418	**889**	35p multicoloured	..	1·00	1·10	☐ ☐
		Set of 5		3·00	3·25	☐ ☐
		First Day Cover			4·25	☐
		Presentation Pack ..		4·25		☐
		PHQ Cards (set of 5) ..		2·50	5·25	☐ ☐
		Set of 5 Gutter Pairs		6·00		☐

Collectors Pack 1988

1988 (15 Nov.) *Comprises Nos.* 1380/1408, 1414/18
   Collectors Pack .. .. .. 32·00 ☐

Post Office Yearbook

1988 *Comprises Nos.* 1380/1404. **MS**1409, 1414/18 *in hardbound book with slip case*
   Yearbook .. .. 40·00 ☐

Centenary of Royal Society for the Protection of Birds

1989 (17 Jan.) *Phosphorised paper*

1419	**890**	19p multicoloured	..	45	45	☐ ☐
1420	**891**	27p multicoloured	..	1·25	1·10	☐ ☐
1421	**892**	32p multicoloured	..	1·25	1·10	☐ ☐
1422	**893**	35p multicoloured	..	1·50	1·25	☐ ☐
		Set of 4		4·00	3·50	☐ ☐
		First Day Cover			4·50	☐
		Presentation Pack ..		4·50		☐
		PHQ Cards (set of 4) ..		2·50	5·00	☐ ☐
		Set of 4 Gutter Pairs ..		8·00		☐

894 Rose

895 Cupid

896 Yachts

897 Fruit

898 Teddy Bear

Nos. 1423/7 were printed together, *se-tenant*, in horizontal strips of five, two such strips forming the booklet pane with twelve half stamp-size labels.

Greetings Booklet Stamps

1989 (31 Jan.) *Phosphorised paper*

1423	**894**	19p multicoloured	..	4·50	3·00	☐	☐
		a. *Booklet pane*.					
		Nos. 1423/7 × 2		38·00		☐	
1424	**895**	19p multicoloured	..	4·50	3·00	☐	☐
1425	**896**	19p multicoloured	..	4·50	3·00	☐	☐
1426	**897**	19p multicoloured	..	4·50	3·00	☐	☐
1427	**898**	19p multicoloured	..	4·50	3·00	☐	☐
		Set of 5		20·00	13·50	☐	☐
		First Day Cover			16·00		☐

899 Fruit and Vegetables

900 Meat Products

901 Dairy Produce

902 Cereal Products

Food and Farming Year

1989 (7 Mar.) *Phosphorised paper. Perf* $14 \times 14\frac{1}{2}$

1428	**899**	19p multicoloured	..	50	50	☐	☐
1429	**900**	27p multicoloured	..	80	80	☐	☐
1430	**901**	32p multicoloured	..	1·10	1·10	☐	☐
1431	**902**	35p multicoloured	..	1·25	1·25	☐	☐
		Set of 4		3·25	3·25	☐	☐
		First Day Cover			4·25		☐
		Presentation Pack		4·50		☐	
		PHQ Cards (set of 4) ..		2·00	5·00	☐	☐
		Set of 4 Gutter Pairs ..		6·50		☐	

903 Mortar Board (150th Anniv of Public Education in England)

904 Cross on Ballot Paper (3rd Direct Elections to European Parliament)

905 Posthorn (26th Postal, Telegraph and Telephone International Congress Brighton)

906 Globe (Inter-Parliamentary Union Centenary Conference, London)

Nos. 1432/3 and 1434/5 were each printed together, *se-tenant*, in horizontal pairs throughout the sheets.

Anniversaries

1989 (11 Apr.) *Phosphorised paper. Perf* $14 \times 14\frac{1}{2}$

1432	**903**	19p multicoloured	..	1·25	1·25	☐	☐
		a. *Horiz pair*.					
		Nos. 1432/3	..	2·50	2·50	☐	☐
1433	**904**	19p multicoloured	..	1·25	1·25	☐	☐
1434	**905**	35p multicoloured	..	1·75	1·75	☐	☐
		a. *Horiz pair*.					
		Nos. 1434/5	..	3·50	3·50	☐	☐
1435	**906**	35p multicoloured	..	1·75	1·75	☐	☐
		Set of 4		5·50	5·50	☐	☐
		First Day Cover			6·00		☐
		Presentation Pack		6·50		☐	
		PHQ Cards (set of 4) ..		2·00	7·00	☐	☐
		Set of 2 Gutter Strips of 4 ..		11·00		☐	

907 Toy Train and Airplane

908 Building Bricks

909 Dice and Board Games

910 Toy Robot, Boat and Doll's House

Europa. Games and Toys

1989 (16 MAY) *Phosphorised paper*

1436	**907**	19p multicoloured	..	50	50	☐	☐
1437	**908**	27p multicoloured	..	90	90	☐	☐
1438	**909**	32p multicoloured	..	1·25	1·25	☐	☐
1439	**910**	35p multicoloured	..	1·40	1·40	☐	☐
		Set of 4	..	3·50	3·50	☐	☐
		First Day Cover	..		4·25		☐
		Presentation Pack	..	4·50		☐	
		PHQ Cards (set of 4)	..	2·00	5·00	☐	☐
		Set of 4 Gutter Pairs	..	7·00		☐	

911 Ironbridge, Shropshire

912 Tin Mine, St. Agnes Head, Cornwall

913 Cotton Mills, New Lanark, Strathclyde

914 Pontcysyllte Aqueduct, Clwyd

915

Industrial Archaeology

1989 (4–25 JULY) *Phosphorised paper*

1440	**911**	19p multicoloured	..	50	50	☐	☐
1441	**912**	27p multicoloured	..	80	80	☐	☐
1442	**913**	32p multicoloured	..	1·00	1·00	☐	☐
1443	**914**	35p multicoloured	..	1·10	1·10	☐	☐
		Set of 4	..	3·00	3·00	☐	☐
		First Day Cover	..		4·25		☐
		Presentation Pack	..	4·50		☐	
		PHQ Cards (set of 4)	..	2·00	5·00	☐	☐
		Set of 4 Gutter Pairs	..	6·50		☐	
MS1444		122 × 90 mm. **915** As Nos.					
		1440/3 but designs horizontal		6·50	5·50	☐	☐
		First Day Cover (25 July)	..		5·50		☐

No. **MS**1444 was sold at £1.40, the premium being used for the "Stamp World London 90" International Stamp Exhibition.

916

917

Booklet Stamps

1989 (22 AUG.)–**92**

(a) Printed in photogravure by Harrison and Sons. Perf 15 × 14

1445	**916**	(2nd) bright blue (1 centre band)	.. ..	60	35	☐	☐
1446		(2nd bright blue (1 side band) (20.3.90)		2·25	2·25	☐	☐
1447	**917**	(1st) black (phosphorised paper	.. ..	1·25	50	☐	☐
1448		(1st brownish black (2 bands) (20.3.90)	.. ..	2·25	2·25	☐	☐

(b) Printed in lithography by Walsall. Perf 14

1449	**916**	(2nd) bright blue (1 centre band)	.. .. ..	75	75	☐	☐
1450	**917**	(1st) black (2 bands)	..	1·75	1·50	☐	☐

(c) Printed in lithography by Questa. Perf 15 × 14

1451	**916**	(2nd) bright blue (1 centre band) (19.9.89)	70	70	☐	☐
1451*a*		(2nd) bright blue (1 side band) (25.2.92) ..	1·00	1·00	☐	☐
1452	**917**	(1st) black (phosphorised paper) (19.9.89)	1·10	1·10	☐	☐
		First Day Cover (Nos. 1445, 1447)		3·50	☐	

For similar stamps showing changed colours see Nos. 1511/16 and for those with elliptical perforations Nos. 1663*a*/6.

No. 1451*a* exists with the phosphor band at the left or right of the stamp.

918 Snowflake (× 10)

919 *Calliphora erythrocephala* (fly) (× 5)

920 Blood Cells (× 500)

921 Microchip (× 600)

150th Anniversary of Royal Microscopical Society

1989 (5 Sept.) *Phosphorised paper. Perf* 14½ × 14

1453	**918**	19p multicoloured ..	50	50	☐	☐
1454	**919**	27p multicoloured ..	85	85	☐	☐
1455	**920**	32p multicoloured ..	1·25	1·25	☐	☐
1456	**921**	35p multicoloured ..	1·40	1·40	☐	☐
		Set of 4	3·50	3·50	☐	☐
		First Day Cover		4·25		☐
		Presentation Pack ..	4·00		☐	
		PHQ Cards (set of 4) ..	2·00	5·00	☐	☐
		Set of 4 Gutter Pairs ..	7·00		☐	

922 Royal Mail Coach

923 Escort of Blues and Royals

924 Lord Mayor's Coach

925 Coach Team passing St Paul's

926 Blues and Royals Drum Horse

Nos. 1457/61 were printed together, *se-tenant*, in horizontal strips of 5 throughout the sheet, forming a composite design.

Lord Mayor's Show, London

1989 (17 Oct.) *Phosphorised paper*

1457	**922**	20p multicoloured ..	60	70	☐	☐
		a. Horiz strip of 5 Nos. 1457/61 ..	3·25	3·25	☐	☐
1458	**923**	20p multicoloured ..	60	70	☐	☐
1459	**924**	20p multicoloured ..	60	70	☐	☐
1460	**925**	20p multicoloured ..	60	70	☐	☐
1461	**926**	20p multicoloured ..	60	70	☐	☐
		Set of 5	3·25	3·25	☐	☐
		First Day Cover		3·75		☐
		Presentation Pack	4·50		☐	
		PHQ Cards (set of 5) ..	2·50	5·00	☐	☐
		Gutter Strip of 10 ..	6·50		☐	

Nos. 1457/61 commemorate the 800th anniversary of the installation of the first Lord Mayor of London.

927 14th-century Peasants from Stained-glass Window

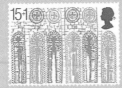

928 Arches and Roundels, West Front

929 Octagon Tower

930 Arcade from West Transept

931 Triple Arch from West Front

Christmas. 800th Anniversary of Ely Cathedral

1989 (14 Nov.) *One phosphor band (Nos. 1462/3) or phosphorised paper (others)*

1462	**927**	15p gold, silver and blue	35	35	☐	☐
1463	**928**	15p + 1p gold, silver and blue	50	40	☐	☐
1464	**929**	20p + 1p gold, silver and rosine	60	50	☐	☐
1465	**930**	34p + 1p gold, silver and emerald	1·25	1·40	☐	☐
1466	**931**	37p + 1p gold, silver and yellow-olive	1·25	1·40	☐	☐
		Set of 5	3·50	3·50	☐	☐
		First Day Cover		4·00		☐
		Presentation Pack	4·50		☐	
		PHQ Cards (set of 5)	2·50	5·00	☐	☐
		Set of 5 Gutter Pairs	7·00		☐	

Collectors Pack 1989

1989 (14 Nov.) *Comprises Nos.* 1419/22, 1428/43 *and* 1453/66

	Collectors Pack	.. ..	35·00	☐

Post Office Yearbook

1989 (14 Nov) *Comprises Nos.* 1419/22, 1428/44 *and* 1453/66 *in hardback book with slip case.*

	Yearbook	.. ..	40·00	☐

932 Queen Victoria and Queen Elizabeth II

150th Anniversary of the Penny Black

1990 (10 Jan.–17 Apr.)

(a) Printed in photogravure by Harrison and Sons. Perf 15 × 14

1467	**932**	15p bright blue (1 centre band)	50	50	☐	☐
1468		15p bright blue (1 side band) (30 Jan)	1·50	1·75	☐	☐
1469		20p brownish black and cream (phosphorised paper)	75	75	☐	☐
1470		20p brnish blk & cream (2 bands) (30 Jan)	1·50	1·50	☐	☐
1471		29p deep mauve (phosphorised paper)	1·00	1·25	☐	☐
1472		29p deep mauve (2 bands) (20 Mar)	8·00	7·00	☐	☐
1473		34p deep bluish grey (phosphorised paper)	1·25	1·25	☐	☐
1474		37p rosine (phosphorised paper)	1·25	1·50	☐	☐
		Set of 5 (Nos. 1467, 1469, 1471, 1473/4)	4·50	4·75	☐	☐
		First Day Cover (Nos. 1467, 1469, 1471, 1473/4)		5·00		☐
		Presentation Pack (Nos. 1467, 1469, 1471, 1473/4)	5·75		☐	

(b) Litho Walsall. Perf 14 (30 Jan)

1475	**932**	15p bright blue (1 centre band)	90	60	☐	☐
1476		20p brnish blk & cream (phosphorised paper)	1·25	80	☐	☐

(c) Litho Questa. Perf 15 × 14 (17 Apr)

1477	**932**	15p bright blue (1 centre band)	1·25	1·25	☐	☐
1478		20p brnish black (phosphorised paper)	1·25	1·25	☐	☐

No. 1468 exists with the phosphor band at the left or right of the stamp.

933 Kitten

934 Rabbit

87

935 Duckling

936 Puppy

150th Anniversary of Royal Society for Prevention of Cruelty to Animals

1990 (23 Jan.) *Phosphorised paper. Perf* $14 \times 14\frac{1}{2}$.

1479	**933**	20p multicoloured	..	65	50	☐ ☐
1480	**934**	29p multicoloured	..	1·00	80	☐ ☐
1481	**935**	34p multicoloured	..	1·40	1·10	☐ ☐
1482	**936**	37p multicoloured	..	1·40	1·10	☐ ☐
		Set of 4	.. .. ..	4·00	3·25	☐ ☐
		First Day Cover	.. ..		4·25	☐
		Presentation Pack	.. ..	5·00		☐
		PHQ Cards (set of 4)	..	2·50	5·50	☐ ☐
		Set of 4 Gutter Pairs	.. ..	8·00		☐

937 Teddy Bear

938 Dennis the Menace

939 Punch

940 Cheshire Cat

941 The Man in the Moon

942 The Laughing Policeman

943 Clown

944 Mona Lisa

945 Queen of Hearts

946 Stan Laurel (comedian)

T **937**/**46** were printed together, *se-tenant*, in booklet panes of 10.

Greetings Booklet Stamps. ''Smiles''

1990 (6 Feb.) *Two phosphor bands*

1483	**937**	20p multicoloured	..	2·40	2·00	☐ ☐
		a. Booklet pane.				
		Nos. 1483/92	..	22·00		☐
1484	**938**	20p multicoloured	..	2·40	2·00	☐ ☐
1485	**939**	20p multicoloured	..	2·40	2·00	☐ ☐
1486	**940**	20p multicoloured	..	2·40	2·00	☐ ☐
1487	**941**	20p multicoloured	..	2·40	2·00	☐ ☐
1488	**942**	20p multicoloured	..	2·40	2·00	☐ ☐
1489	**943**	20p multicoloured	..	2·40	2·00	☐ ☐
1490	**944**	20p multicoloured	..	2·40	2·00	☐ ☐
1491	**945**	20p multicoloured	..	2·40	2·00	☐ ☐
1492	**946**	20p gold and grey-black	..	2·40	2·00	☐ ☐
		Set of 10	.. ..	22·00	18·00	☐ ☐
		First Day Cover	.. ..		22·00	☐

For those designs with the face value expressed as ''1st'' see Nos. 1550/9.

947 Alexandra Palace (''Stamp World London 90'' Exhibition)

948 Glasgow School of Art

88

949 British Philatelic Bureau, Edinburgh

950 Templeton Carpet Factory, Glasgow

Europa (Nos. 1493 and 1495) and "Glasgow 1990 European City of Culture" (Nos. 1494 and 1496)

1990 (6 Mar.) *Phosphorised paper*

1493	**947**	20p multicoloured	..	50	50	☐ ☐
1494	**948**	20p multicoloured	..	50	50	☐ ☐
1495	**949**	29p multicoloured	..	1·10	1·10	☐ ☐
1496	**950**	37p multicoloured	..	1·25	1·25	☐ ☐
		Set of 4	.. ..	3·00	3·00	☐ ☐
		First Day Cover	.. ..		4·25	☐
		Presentation Pack	..	4·00		☐
		PHQ Cards (set of 4)	..	2·50	5·25	☐ ☐
		Set of 4 Gutter Pairs	..	6·00		☐

951 Export Achievement Award

952 Technological Achievement Award

Nos. 1497/8 and 1499/500 were each printed together, *se-tenant*, in horizontal pairs throughout the sheets.

25th Anniversary of Queen's Awards for Export and Technology

1990 (10 Apr.) *Phosphorised paper. Perf* $14 \times 14\frac{1}{2}$.

1497	**951**	20p multicoloured	..	70	70	☐ ☐
		a. Horiz. pair. Nos. 1497/8	..	1·40	1·40	☐ ☐
1498	**952**	20p multicoloured	..	70	70	☐ ☐
1499	**951**	37p multicoloured	..	1·25	1·25	☐ ☐
		a. Horiz. pair. Nos. 1499/500	..	2·50	2·50	☐ ☐
1500	**952**	37p multicoloured	..	1·25	1·25	☐ ☐
		Set of 4	.. ..	3·50	3·50	☐ ☐
		First Day Cover	.. ..		4·50	☐
		Presentation Pack	..	4·00		☐
		PHQ Cards (set of 4)	..	2·50	5·25	☐ ☐
		Set of 2 Gutter Strips of 4	..	7·00		☐

953

"Stamp World 90" International Stamp Exhibition, London

1990 (3 May) *Sheet* 122 × 90 *mm. Phosphorised paper*

MS1501	**953**	20p. brownish black and cream		4·25	4·25	☐ ☐
		First Day Cover	.. ..		4·75	☐
		Souvenir Book (Nos. 1467, 1469, 1471, 1473/4 and **MS**1501)	..	17·00		☐

No. **MS**1501 was sold at £1, the premium being used for the exhibition.

954 Cycad and Sir Joseph Banks Building

955 Stone Pine and Princess of Wales Conservatory

956 Willow Tree and Palm House

957 Cedar Tree and Pagoda

150th Anniversary of Kew Gardens

1990 (5 June) *Phosphorised paper*

1502	**954**	20p multicoloured	..	50	50	☐ ☐
1503	**955**	29p multicoloured	..	80	80	☐ ☐

1504	956	34p multicoloured	..	1·10	1·25	☐	☐
1505	957	37p multicoloured	..	1·25	1·40	☐	☐
		Set of 4	..	3·25	3·50	☐	☐
		First Day Cover	..		4·50		☐
		Presentation Pack	..	4·00		☐	
		PHQ Cards (set of 4)	..	2·50	5·00	☐	☐
		Set of 4 Gutter Pairs	..	6·50		☐	

958 Thomas Hardy and Clyffe Clump, Dorset

150th Birth Anniversary of Thomas Hardy (author)

1990 (10 JULY) *Phosphorised paper*

1506	958	20p multicoloured	..	60	70	☐	☐
		First Day Cover	..		2·00		☐
		Presentation Pack	..	1·75		☐	
		PHQ Card	..	75	2·00	☐	☐
		Gutter Pair	..	1·25		☐	

959 Queen Elizabeth the Queen Mother

960 Queen Elizabeth

961 Elizabeth, Duchess of York

962 Lady Elizabeth Bowes-Lyon

90th Birthday of Queen Elizabeth the Queen Mother

1990 (2 AUG.) *Phosphorised paper*

| 1507 | 959 | 20p multicoloured | .. | 50 | 50 | ☐ | ☐ |
| 1508 | 960 | 29p silver, indigo and grey-blue | .. | 80 | 80 | ☐ | ☐ |

1509	961	34p multicoloured	..	1·10	1·25	☐	☐
1510	962	37p silver, sepia and stone	..	1·25	1·40	☐	☐
		Set of 4	..	3·25	3·50	☐	☐
		First Day Cover	..		4·50		☐
		Presentation Pack	..	4·50		☐	
		PHQ Cards (set of 4)	..	2·50	5·50	☐	☐
		Set of 4 Gutter Pairs ..	..	6·50		☐	

Booklet Stamps

1990 (7 AUG.)-**92** *As Types* **916/17**, *but colours changed*

(a) Photo Harrison, Perf 15 × 14

| 1511 | 916 | (2nd) dp blue (1 centre band) | .. | 80 | 80 | ☐ | ☐ |
| 1512 | 917 | (1st) brt orge-red (phosphorised paper) | .. | 70 | 70 | ☐ | ☐ |

(b) Litho Questa. Perf 15 × 14

1513	916	(2nd) dp blue (1 centre band)	..	1·40	1·40	☐	☐
1514	917	(1st) brt orge-red (phosphorised paper)	..	75	75	☐	☐
1514*a*		(1st) brt orange-red (2 bands) (25.2.92)	..	1·00	1·10	☐	☐

(c) Litho Walsall. Perf 14

1515	916	(2nd) dp blue (1 centre band)	..	60	60	☐	☐
1516	917	(1st) brt orge-red (phosphorised paper)	..	60	60	☐	☐
		c. Perf 13	..	1·75	1·75	☐	☐
		First Day Cover (Nos. 1515/16)	..		3·50		☐

For similar stamps with elliptical perforations see Nos. 1663*a*/6.

963 Victoria Cross

964 George Cross

965 Distinguished Service Cross and Distinguished Service Medal

966 Military Cross and Military Medal

967 Distinguished Flying Cross and Distinguished Flying Medal

Gallantry Awards

1990 (11 Sept.) *Phosphorised paper*

1517	**963**	20p multicoloured	..	80	65	☐ ☐
1518	**964**	20p multicoloured	..	80	65	☐ ☐
1519	**965**	20p multicoloured	..	80	65	☐ ☐
1520	**966**	20p multicoloured	..	80	65	☐ ☐
1521	**967**	20p multicoloured	..	80	65	☐ ☐
		Set of 5	..	3·50	3·00	☐ ☐
		First Day Cover			3·75	☐
		Presentation Pack	..	4·00		☐
		PHQ Cards (set of 5)	..	3·00	5·50	☐ ☐
		Set of 5 Gutter Pairs		7·00		☐

968 Armagh Observatory, Jodrell Bank Radio Telescope and La Palma Telescope

969 Newton's Moon and Tides Diagram with Early Telescopes

970 Greenwich Old Observatory and Early Astronomical Equipment

971 Stonehenge, Gyroscope and Navigating by Stars

Astronomy

1990 (16 Oct.) *Phosphorised paper. Perf* 14 × 14½

1522	**968**	22p multicoloured	..	50	40	☐ ☐
1523	**969**	26p multicoloured	..	80	90	☐ ☐
1524	**970**	31p multicoloured	..	1·00	1·00	☐ ☐
1525	**971**	37p multicoloured	..	1·10	1·10	☐ ☐
		Set of 4	..	3·00	3·00	☐ ☐
		First Day Cover	..		4·25	☐
		Presentation Pack	..	4·00		☐
		PHQ Cards (set of 4)	..	2·50	5·50	☐ ☐
		Set of 4 Gutter Pairs	..	6·00		☐

Nos. 1522/5 commemorate the centenary of the British Astronomical Association and the bicentenary of the Armagh Observatory.

972 Building a Snowman

973 Fetching the Christmas Tree

974 Carol Singing

975 Tobogganing

976 Ice-skating

Christmas

1990 (13 Nov.) *One phosphor band* (17p) *or phosphorised paper (others)*

1526	**972**	17p multicoloured	..	45	35	☐ ☐
1527	**973**	22p multicoloured	..	55	65	☐ ☐
1528	**974**	26p multicoloured	..	80	80	☐ ☐
1529	**975**	31p multicoloured	..	1·00	1·00	☐ ☐
1530	**976**	37p multicoloured	..	1·10	1·10	☐ ☐
		Set of 5	..	3·50	3·50	☐ ☐
		First Day Cover	..		4·50	☐
		Presentation Pack	..	4·25		☐
		PHQ Cards (set of 5)	..	3·25	6·00	☐ ☐
		Set of 5 Gutter Pairs	..	7·00		☐

Collectors Pack 1990

1990 (13 Nov.) *Comprises Nos.* 1479/82, 1493/1510 *and* 1517/30

	Collectors Pack	..	32·00	☐

Post Office Yearbook

1990 *Comprises Nos.* 1479/82, 1493/500, 1502/10 *and* 1517/30 *in hardback book with slip case.*

	Yearbook	.. .. ..	40·00	☐

KING CHARLES SPANIEL
GEORGE STUBBS

977 "King Charles Spaniel"

A POINTER
GEORGE STUBBS

978 "A Pointer"

TWO HOUNDS IN A LANDSCAPE
GEORGE STUBBS

979 "Two Hounds in a Landscape"

A ROUGH DOG
GEORGE STUBBS

980 "A Rough Dog"

FINO AND TINY
GEORGE STUBBS

981 "Fino and Tiny"

Dogs. Paintings by George Stubbs

1991 (8 JAN.) *Phosphorised paper. Perf* 14 × 14½

1531	**977**	22p multicoloured	..	75	75	☐	☐
1532	**978**	26p multicoloured	..	90	80	☐	☐
1533	**979**	31p multicoloured	..	1·00	85	☐	☐
1534	**980**	33p multicoloured	..	1·10	95	☐	☐
1535	**981**	37p multicoloured	..	1·25	1·10	☐	☐
		Set of 5	.. ..	4·50	4·00	☐	☐
		First Day Cover	..		4·25		☐
		Presentation Pack		5·00		☐	
		PHQ Cards (set of 5)		3·25	6·00	☐	☐
		Set of 5 Gutter Pairs	..	9·00		☐	

982 Thrush's Nest

983 Shooting Star and Rainbow

984 Magpies and Charm Bracelet

985 Black Cat

986 Common Kingfisher with Key

987 Mallard and Frog

988 Four-leaf Clover in Boot and Match Box

989 Pot of Gold at End of Rainbow

990 Heart-shaped Butterflies

991 Wishing Well and Sixpence

T 982/91 were printed together, *se-tenant*, in booklet panes of 10 stamps and 12 half stamp-size labels, the backgrounds of the stamps forming a composite design.

Greetings Booklet Stamps. "Good Luck"

1991 (5 FEB.) *Two phosphor bands.*

1536	**982**	(1st) multicoloured	..	1·40	1·40	☐	☐
		a. Booklet pane. Nos.					
		1536/45	.. ..	12·50		☐	
1537	**983**	(1st) multicoloured	..	1·40	1·40	☐	☐
1538	**984**	(1st) multicoloured	..	1·40	1·40	☐	☐
1539	**985**	(1st) multicoloured	..	1·40	1·40	☐	☐
1540	**986**	(1st) multicoloured	..	1·40	1·40	☐	☐
1541	**987**	(1st) multicoloured	..	1·40	1·40	☐	☐
1542	**988**	(1st) multicoloured	..	1·40	1·40	☐	☐
1543	**989**	(1st) multicoloured	..	1·40	1·40	☐	☐
1544	**990**	(1st) multicoloured	..	1·40	1·40	☐	☐
1545	**991**	(1st) multicoloured	..	1·40	1·40	☐	☐
		Set of 10	.. .. ..	12·50	12·50	☐	☐
		First Day Cover	.. .. ..		13·00		☐

992 Michael Faraday (inventor of electric motor) (Birth Bicentenary)

993 Charles Babbage (computer science pioneer) (Birth Bicentenary)

994 Radar Sweep of East Anglia (50th Anniv of Discovery by Sir Robert Watson-Watt)

995 Gloster Whittle E28/39 Aircraft over East Anglia (50th Anniv of First Flight of Sir Frank Whittle's Jet Engine)

Scientific Achievements

1991 (5 Mar.) *Phosphorised paper*

1546	**992**	22p multicoloured	..	65	65	☐	☐
1547	**993**	22p multicoloured	..	65	65	☐	☐
1548	**994**	31p multicoloured	..	95	95	☐	☐
1549	**995**	37p multicoloured	..	1·10	1·10	☐	☐
		Set of 4	.. .. ..	3·00	3·00	☐	☐
		First Day Cover	.. ..		4·00		☐
		Presentation Pack	.. ..	3·75		☐	
		PHQ Cards (set of 4)	.. ..	3·00	5·50	☐	☐
		Set of 4 Gutter Pairs	.. ..	6·00		☐	

996 Teddy Bear

Nos. 1550/9 were printed together, *se-tenant*, in booklet panes of 10 stamps and 12 half stamp-size labels.

Greetings Booklet Stamps. "Smiles"

1991 (26 Mar.) *As Nos. 1483/92, but inscribed "1st" as T 996. Two phosphor bands.*

1550	**996**	(1st) multicoloured	..	90	90	☐	☐
		a. Booklet pane. Nos. 1550/9	.. ..	8·00		☐	
1551	**938**	(1st) multicoloured		90	90	☐	☐
1552	**939**	(1st) multicoloured		90	90	☐	☐
1553	**940**	(1st) multicoloured		90	90	☐	☐
1554	**941**	(1st) multicoloured		90	90	☐	☐
1555	**942**	(1st) multicoloured		90	90	☐	☐
1556	**943**	(1st) multicoloured		90	90	☐	☐
1557	**944**	(1st) multicoloured		90	90	☐	☐
1558	**945**	(1st) multicoloured		90	90	☐	☐
1559	**946**	(1st) multicoloured		90	90	☐	☐
		Set of 10	.. .. ..	8·00	8·00	☐	☐
		First Day Cover ..	.. ..		9·00		☐

997 Man looking at Space

998

999 Space looking at Man

1000

Nos. 1560/1 and 1562/3 were each printed together, *se-tenant*, in horizontal pairs throughout the sheets, each pair forming a composite design.

Europa. Europe in Space

1991 (23 Apr.) *Phosphorised paper.*

1560	**997**	22p multicoloured	..	55	55	☐	☐
		a. Horiz pair. Nos. 1560/1		1·10	1·10	☐	☐
1561	**998**	22p multicoloured	..	55	55	☐	☐
1562	**999**	37p multicoloured	..	1·10	1·10	☐	☐
		a. Horiz pair. Nos. 1562/3		2·25	2·25	☐	☐
1563	**1000**	37p multicoloured	..	1·10	1·10	☐	☐
		Set of 4	.. .. ..	3·00	3·00	☐	☐
		First Day Cover	.. ..		4·00		☐
		Presentation Pack	.. ..	4·00		☐	
		PHQ Cards (set of 4)	.. ..	3·00	5·50	☐	☐
		Set of 2 Gutter Strips of 4	..	6·00		☐	

1001 Fencing

1002 Hurdling

1003 Diving

1004 Rugby

World Student Games, Sheffield (Nos. 1564/6) and World Cup Rugby Championship, London (No. 1567)

1991 (11 June) *Phosphorised paper. Perf* 14½ × 14

1564	**1001**	22p multicoloured	..	50	50	☐ ☐
1565	**1002**	26p multicoloured	..	80	80	☐ ☐
1566	**1003**	31p multicoloured	..	95	95	☐ ☐
1567	**1004**	37p multicoloured	..	1·10	1·10	☐ ☐
		Set of 4	.. ..	3·00	3·00	☐ ☐
		First Day Cover	.. ..		4·00	☐
		Presentation Pack	..	4·00		☐
		PHQ Cards (set of 4)	..	3·00	5·50	☐ ☐
		Set of 4 Gutter Pairs	.. ..	6·00		☐

1005 "Silver Jubilee"

1006 "Mme Alfred Carrière"

1007 Rosa moyesii

1008 "Harvest Fayre"

1009 "Mutabilis"

9th World Congress of Roses, Belfast

1991 (16 July) *Phosphorised paper. Perf* 14½ × 14

1568	**1005**	22p multicoloured	..	75	50	☐ ☐
1569	**1006**	26p multicoloured	..	90	80	☐ ☐
1570	**1007**	31p multicoloured	..	1·00	85	☐ ☐
1571	**1008**	33p multicoloured	..	1·10	95	☐ ☐
1572	**1009**	37p multicoloured	..	1·25	1·25	☐ ☐
		Set of 5	.. ..	4·50	4·00	☐ ☐
		First Day Cover	.. ..		4·50	☐
		Presentation Pack	..	4·50		☐
		PHQ Cards (set of 5)	.. ..	3·25	7·00	☐ ☐
		Set of 5 Gutter Pairs	.. ..	9·00		☐

1010 Iguanodon

1011 Stegosaurus

1012 Tyrannosaurus

1013 Protoceratops

1014 Triceratops

150th Anniversary of Dinosaurs' Identification by Owen

1991 (20 Aug.) *Phosphorised paper. Perf* 14½ × 14

1573	**1010**	22p multicoloured	..	75	50	☐	☐
1574	**1011**	26p multicoloured	..	90	1·00	☐	☐
1575	**1012**	31p multicoloured	..	1·10	1·10	☐	☐
1576	**1013**	33p multicoloured	..	1·40	1·10	☐	☐
1577	**1014**	37p multicoloured	..	1·50	1·25	☐	☐
		Set of 5	.. ..	5·00	4·50	☐	☐
		First Day Cover	..		5·00		☐
		Presentation Pack	..	5·50		☐	
		PHQ Cards (set of 5)	..	3·25	6·00	☐	☐
		Set of 5 Gutter Pairs	..	10·00		☐	

1015 Map of 1816

1016 Map of 1906

1017 Map of 1959

1018 Map of 1991

Bicentenary of Ordnance Survey: Maps of Hamstreet, Kent

1991 (17 Sept.) *Phosphorised paper. Perf* 14½ × 14

1578	**1015**	24p multicoloured	..	50	50	☐	☐
1579	**1016**	28p multicoloured	..	80	85	☐	☐
1580	**1017**	33p multicoloured	..	95	1·00	☐	☐
1581	**1018**	39p multicoloured	..	1·10	1·25	☐	☐
		Set of 4	.. ..	3·00	3·25	☐	☐
		First Day Cover	..		4·25		☐
		Presentation Pack	..	4·00		☐	
		PHQ Cards (set of 4)	..	3·00	6·00	☐	☐
		Set of 4 Gutter Pairs	..	6·00		☐	

1019 Adoration of the Magi

1020 Mary and Baby Jesus in the Stable

1021 The Holy Family and Angel

1022 The Annunciation

1023 The Flight into Egypt

Christmas. Illuminated Manuscripts from the Bodleian Library, Oxford

1991 (12 Nov.) *One phosphor band (18p) or phosphorised paper (others)*

1582	**1019**	18p multicoloured	..	70	40	☐	☐
1583	**1020**	24p multicoloured	..	80	50	☐	☐
1584	**1021**	28p multicoloured	..	85	1·00	☐	☐
1585	**1022**	33p multicoloured	..	95	1·10	☐	☐
1586	**1023**	39p multicoloured	..	1·10	1·40	☐	☐
		Set of 5	.. ..	4·00	4·00	☐	☐
		First Day Cover	..		4·50		☐
		Presentation Pack	..	4·25		☐	
		PHQ Cards (set of 5)	..	3·00	6·00	☐	☐
		Set of 5 Gutter Pairs	..	8·00		☐	

Collectors Pack 1991

1991 (12 Nov.) *Comprises Nos.* 1531/5, 1546/9 *and* 1560/86.

Collectors Pack		32·00	☐

Post Office Yearbook

1991 *Comprises Nos.* 1531/5, 1546/9 *and* 1560/86. *in hardback book with slip case.*

Yearbook		40·00	☐

1024 Fallow Deer in Scottish Forest

1025 Hare on North Yorkshire Moors

1026 Fox in the Fens

1027 Redwing and Home Counties Village

1028 Welsh Mountain Sheep in Snowdonia

The Four Seasons. Wintertime

1992 (14 Jan.) One phosphor band (18p) or phosphorised paper (others)

1587	**1024**	18p multicoloured	..	45	50	☐ ☐
1588	**1025**	24p multicoloured	..	60	65	☐ ☐
1589	**1026**	28p multicoloured	..	80	75	☐ ☐
1590	**1027**	33p multicoloured	..	95	90	☐ ☐
1591	**1028**	39p multicoloured	..	1·10	1·10	☐ ☐
		Set of 5	.. ..	3·50	3·50	☐ ☐
		First Day Cover ..	..		3·75	☐
		Presentation Pack	..	4·25		☐
		PHQ Cards (set of 5) ..		3·00	7·00	☐ ☐
		Set of 5 Gutter Pairs ..	..	7·00		☐

1029 Flower Spray

1030 Double Locket

1031 Key

1032 Model Car and Cigarette Cards

1033 Compass and Map

1034 Pocket Watch

1035 1854 1d. Red Stamp and Pen

1036 Pearl Necklace

1037 Marbles

1038 Bucket, Spade and Starfish

T **1029/38** were printed together, se-tenant, in booklet panes of 10 stamps and 12 half stamp-size labels, the backgrounds of the stamps forming a composite design.

Greetings Stamps. "Memories".

1992 (28 Jan.) Two phosphor bands

1592	**1029**	(1st) multicoloured	..	40	45	☐ ☐
		a. Booklet pane. Nos.				
		1592/1601 ..	..	4·00		☐
1593	**1030**	(1st) multicoloured	..	40	45	☐ ☐
1594	**1031**	(1st) multicoloured	..	40	45	☐ ☐
1595	**1032**	(1st) multicoloured	..	40	45	☐ ☐
1596	**1033**	(1st) multicoloured	..	40	45	☐ ☐
1597	**1034**	(1st) multicoloured	..	40	45	☐ ☐
1598	**1035**	(1st) multicoloured	..	40	45	☐ ☐
1599	**1036**	(1st) multicoloured	..	40	45	☐ ☐
1600	**1037**	(1st) multicoloured	..	40	45	☐ ☐
1601	**1038**	(1st) multicoloured	..	40	45	☐ ☐
		Set of 10	..	4·00	4·50	☐ ☐
		Presentation Pack	..	6·00		☐
		First Day Cover	..		8·50	☐

1039 Queen Elizabeth in Coronation Robes and Parliamentary Emblem

1040 Queen Elizabeth in Garter Robes and Archiepiscopal Arms

1041 Queen Elizabeth with Baby Prince Andrew and Royal Arms

1042 Queen Elizabeth at Trooping the Colour and Service Emblems

1043 Queen Elizabeth and Commonwealth Emblem

Nos. 1602/6 were printed together, *se-tenant*, in horizontal strips of 5 throughout the sheet, forming a composite design

40th Anniversary of Accession

1992 (6 FEB) *Two phosphor bands. Perf* $14\frac{1}{2} \times 14$.

1602	**1039**	24p multicoloured		90	90	☐ ☐
		a. Horiz strip of 5. Nos. 1602/6		4·00	4·00	☐ ☐
1603	**1040**	24p multicoloured		90	90	☐ ☐
1604	**1041**	24p multicoloured		90	90	☐ ☐
1605	**1042**	24p multicoloured		90	90	☐ ☐
1606	**1043**	24p multicoloured		90	90	☐ ☐
		Set of 5		4·00	4·00	☐ ☐
		First Day Cover			4·25	☐
		Presentation Pack		4·25		☐
		PHQ Cards (set of 5)		3·00	5·00	☐ ☐
		Gutter Block of 10		8·00		☐

1044 Tennyson in 1888 and "The Beguiling of Merlin" (Sir Edward Burne-Jones)

1045 Tennyson in 1864 and "I am Sick of the Shadows" (John Waterhouse)

1046 Tennyson in 1856 and "April Love" (Arthur Hughes)

1047 Tennyson as a Young Man and "Mariana" (Dante Gabriel Rossetti)

Death Centenary of Alfred, Lord Tennyson (poet)

1992 (10 MAR) *Phosphorised paper. Perf* $14\frac{1}{2} \times 14$

1607	**1044**	24p multicoloured		50	50	☐ ☐
1608	**1045**	28p multicoloured		65	65	☐ ☐
1609	**1046**	33p multicoloured		1·10	1·10	☐ ☐
1610	**1047**	39p multicoloured		1·10	1·10	☐ ☐
		Set of 4		3·00	3·00	☐ ☐
		First Day Cover			3·50	☐
		Presentation Pack		3·75		☐
		PHQ Cards (set of 4)		2·50	5·00	☐ ☐
		Set of 4 Gutter Pairs		6·00		☐

£1

CARRICKFERGUS CASTLE

1048 Carrickfergus Castle

1992 (24 MAR.)–**95**. *Designs as Nos. 1410/13, but showing Queen's head in silhouette as T* **1048**. *Perf* 15 × 14 (*with one elliptical hole on each vertical side*)

1611	**1048**	£1 bottle green and gold†		2·50	1·50	☐ ☐
1612	**882**	£1·50 maroon and gold†		2·25	2·25	☐ ☐
1613	**883**	£2 indigo and gold†		3·00	3·00	☐ ☐
1613a	**1048**	£3 reddish violet and gold†		4·50	4·50	☐ ☐
1614	**884**	£5 deep brown and gold†		7·50	7·50	☐ ☐
		Set of 5		18·00	18·00	☐ ☐
		First Day Cover (Nos 1611, 1612, 1613, 1614)			30·00	☐
		First Day Cover (22 Aug 1995). (No. 1613a)			7·00	☐
		Presentation Pack (Nos. 1611/13, 1614)		14·50		☐
		Presentation Pack (No. 1613a)		5·00		☐
		PHQ Cards (Nos. 1611/14)		1·40		☐
		PHQ Card (No. 1613a)		40	7·50	☐ ☐
		Set of 5 Gutter Pairs		39·00		☐

†The Queen's head on these stamps is printed in optically variable ink which changes colour from gold to green when viewed from different angles.

PHQ cards for Nos. 1611/13 and 1614 were not issued until 2 March 1993.

1049 British Olympic Association Logo (Olympic Games, Barcelona)

1050 British Paralympic Association Symbol (Paralympics '92, Barcelona)

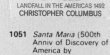

1051 *Santa Maria* (500th Anniv of Discovery of America by Columbus)

1052 *Kaisei* (Japanese cadet brigantine) (Grand Regatta Columbus, 1992)

1053 British Pavilion, "EXPO '92", Seville

Nos. 1615/16 were printed together, *se-tenant*, in horizontal pairs throughout the sheet.

Europa. International Events

1992 (7 APR.) *Phosphorised paper. Perf* 14 × 14½

1615	**1049**	24p multicoloured	..	65	65	☐ ☐
		a. Horiz. pair.				
		Nos. 1615/16	..	1·25	1·25	☐ ☐
1616	**1050**	24p multicoloured	..	65	65	☐ ☐
1617	**1051**	24p multicoloured	..	65	65	☐ ☐
1618	**1052**	39p multicoloured	..	1·10	1·10	☐ ☐
1619	**1053**	39p multicoloured	..	1·10	1·10	☐ ☐
		Set of 5	..	3·75	3·75	☐ ☐
		First Day Cover	..		4·50	☐
		Presentation Pack		4·25		☐
		PHQ Cards (set of 5)	..	3·00	6·00	☐ ☐
		Set of 3 Gutter Pairs and a				
		Gutter Strip of 4	.. ..	7·50		☐

1054 Pikeman

1055 Drummer

1056 Musketeer

1057 Standard Bearer

350th Anniversary of the Civil War

1992 (16 JUNE) *Phosphorised paper. Perf* 14½ × 14

1620	**1054**	24p multicoloured	..	55	55	☐ ☐
1621	**1055**	28p multicoloured		70	70	☐ ☐
1622	**1056**	33p multicoloured		1·00	1·00	☐ ☐
1623	**1057**	39p multicoloured		1·10	1·10	☐ ☐
		Set of 4	.. ..	3·00	3·00	☐ ☐
		First Day Cover	.. ..		4·00	☐
		Presentation Pack	..	3·75		☐
		PHQ Cards (set of 4)	..	2·00	5·00	☐ ☐
		Set of 4 Gutter Pairs	..	6·00		☐

1058 The Yeomen of the Guard

1059 The Gondoliers

1060 The Mikado

1061 The Pirates of Penzance

1062 *Iolanthe*

1067 European Star

150th Birth Anniversary of Sir Arthur Sullivan (composer). Gilbert and Sullivan Operas

1992 (21. JULY) *One phosphor band (18p) or phosphorised paper (others) Perf 14½ × 14*

1624	**1058**	18p multicoloured	..	40	45	□ □
1625	**1059**	24p multicoloured		55	55	□ □
1626	**1060**	28p multicoloured		70	70	□ □
1627	**1061**	33p multicoloured		1·10	1·10	□ □
1628	**1062**	39p multicoloured		1·25	1·25	□ □
		Set of 5	.. .. ..	3·50	3·50	□ □
		First Day Cover	.. ..		4·75	□
		Presentation Pack	..	4·00		□
		PHQ Cards (set of 5)	..	2·25	6·00	□ □
		Set of 5 Gutter Pairs		7·00		□

1063 "Acid Rain Kills"

1064 "Ozone Layer"

1065 "Greenhouse Effect"

1066 "Bird of Hope"

Protection of the Environment. Children's Paintings

1992 (15 SEPT.) *Phosphorised paper. Perf 14 × 14½*

1629	**1063**	24p multicoloured	..	60	45	□ □
1630	**1064**	28p multicoloured		85	90	□ □
1631	**1065**	33p multicoloured	..	90	1·00	□ □
1632	**1066**	39p multicoloured		1·00	1·00	□ □
		Set of 4	.. .. ..	3·00	3·00	□ □
		First Day Cover	.. ..		3·75	□
		Presentation Pack	..	3·50		□
		PHQ Cards (set of 4)	..	2·00	5·50	□ □
		Set of 4 Gutter Pairs		6·00		□

Single European Market

1992 (13 OCT.) *Phosphorised paper*

1633	**1067**	24p multicoloured	..	60	60	□ □
		First Day Cover ..			1·50	□
		Presentation Pack		1·40		□
		PHQ Card ..		60	1·60	□ □
		Gutter Pair..		1·25		□

1068 "Angel Gabriel", St. James's, Pangbourne

1069 "Madonna and Child", St. Mary's, Bilbury

1070 "King with Gold", Our Lady and St. Peter, Leatherhead

1071 "Shepherds", All Saints, Porthcawl

1072 "Kings with Frankincense and Myrrh", Our Lady and St. Peter, Leatherhead

Christmas. Stained Glass Windows

1992 (10 Nov.) *One phosphor band (18p) or phosphorised paper (others).*

1634	**1068**	18p multicoloured	..	40	40	□ □
1635	**1069**	24p multicoloured		65	65	□ □
1636	**1070**	28p multicoloured	..	80	80	□ □
1637	**1071**	33p multicoloured	..	95	95	□ □
1638	**1072**	39p multicoloured		1·10	1·10	□ □
		Set of 5	.. ..	3·50	3·50	□ □
		First Day Cover	.. ..		4·25	□
		Presentation Pack	..	4·00		□
		PHQ Cards (set of 5)	..	2·25	5·50	□ □
		Set of 5 Gutter Pairs	..	7·00		□

Collectors Pack 1992

1992 (10 Nov.) *Comprises Nos.* 1587/91, 1602/10 *and* 1615/38

    Collectors Pack .. .. .. 24·00 ☐

Post Office Yearbook

1992 (11 Nov.) *Comprises Nos.* 1587/91, 1602/10 *and* 1615/38 *in hardback book with slip case.*

    Yearbook .. .. 40·00 ☐

600th Anniversary of Abbotsbury Swannery

1993 (19 JAN.) *One phosphor band* (18p) *or phosphorised paper* (others)

1639	**1073**	18p multicoloured	..	50	40	☐	☐
1640	**1074**	24p multicoloured	..	75	65	☐	☐
1641	**1075**	28p multicoloured	..	1·10	90	☐	☐
1642	**1076**	33p multicoloured	..	1·25	1·00	☐	☐
1643	**1077**	39p multicoloured	..	1·40	1·25	☐	☐
		Set of 5		4·50	3·75	☐	☐
		First Day Cover			4·50		☐
		Presentation Pack		5·00		☐	
		PHQ Cards (set of 5)		2·25	5·00	☐	☐
		Set of 5 Gutter Pairs		9·00		☐	

1073 Mute Swan Cob and St. Catherine's, Abbotsbury

1074 Cygnet and Decoy

1078 Long John Silver and Parrot (*Treasure Island*)

1079 Tweedledum and Tweedledee (*Alice Through the Looking-Glass*)

1075 Swans and Cygnet

1076 Eggs in Nest and Tithe Barn, Abbotsbury

1080 William (*William* books)

1081 Mole and Toad (*The Wind in the Willows*)

1082 Teacher and Wilfrid ("The Bash Street Kids")

1083 Peter Rabbit and Mrs Rabbit (*The Tale of Peter Rabbit*)

1077 Young Swan and the Fleet

1084 Snowman (*The Snowman*) and Father Christmas (*Father Christmas*)

1085 The Big Friendly Giant and Sophie (*The BFG*)

1086 Bill Badger and Rupert
Bear

1087 Aladdin and the Genie

T **1078/87** were printed together, *se-tenant*, in booklet panes of 10
stamps and 20 half stamp-size labels.

Greetings Stamps. "Gift Giving"

1993 (2 FEB.) *Two phosphor bands. Perf* 15 × 14 (*with one
elliptical hole on each vertical side*)

1644	**1078**	(1st) multicoloured	..	75	75	☐ ☐
		a. Booklet pane. Nos.				
		1644/53	.. .. ..	6·50		☐
1645	**1079**	(1st) gold, cream and				
		black	.. .. ..	75	75	☐ ☐
1646	**1080**	(1st) multicoloured	..	75	75	☐ ☐
1647	**1081**	(1st) multicoloured	..	75	75	☐ ☐
1648	**1082**	(1st) multicoloured	..	75	75	☐ ☐
1649	**1083**	(1st) multicoloured	..	75	75	☐ ☐
1650	**1084**	(1st) multicoloured	..	75	75	☐ ☐
1651	**1085**	(1st) multicoloured	..	75	75	☐ ☐
1652	**1086**	(1st) multicoloured	..	75	75	☐ ☐
1653	**1087**	(1st) multicoloured	..	75	75	☐ ☐
		Set of 10	.. .. ..	6·50	6·50	☐ ☐
		First Day Cover ..	.. ..		7·50	☐
		Presentation Pack	.. ..	7·00		☐
		PHQ Cards (set of 10)	.. ..	3·00	7·75	☐ ☐

1088 Decorated Enamel
Dial

1089 Escapement,
Remontoire and
Fusee

1090 Balance, Spring and
Temperature
Compensator

1091 Back of Movement

300th Birth Anniversary of John Harrison (inventor of the marine chronometer). Details of "H4" Clock

1993 (16 FEB.) *Phosphorised paper. Perf* 14½ × 14

1654	**1088**	24p multicoloured	..	50	50	☐ ☐
1655	**1089**	28p multicoloured	..	80	80	☐ ☐
1656	**1090**	33p multicoloured	..	95	95	☐ ☐
1657	**1091**	39p multicoloured	..	1·10	1·10	☐ ☐
		Set of 4		3·00	3·00	☐ ☐
		First Day Cover			4·00	☐
		Presentation Pack		4·00		☐
		PHQ Cards (set of 4)		2·00	4·50	☐ ☐
		Set of 4 Gutter Pairs		6·00		

1092 Britannia

1993 (2 MAR.) *Granite paper. Perf* 14 × 14½ (*with two
elliptical holes on each horizontal side*)

1658	**1092**	£10 multicoloured	..	15·00	8·00	☐ ☐
		First Day Cover			22·00	☐
		Presentation Pack		15·00		☐
		PHQ Card		35	22·00	☐ ☐

1093 Dendrobium
hellwigianum

1094 Paphiopedilum Maudiae
"Magnificum"

1095 Cymbidium lowianum

1096 Vanda Rothschildiana

1097 *Dendrobium vexillarius var albiviride*

14th World Orchid Conference, Glasgow

1993 (16 Mar.) *One phosphor band* (18p) *or phosphorised paper* (others).

1659	**1093**	18p multicoloured	..	40	40	☐ ☐
1660	**1094**	24p multicoloured	..	65	65	☐ ☐
1661	**1095**	28p multicoloured	..	90	90	☐ ☐
1662	**1096**	33p multicoloured	..	1·10	1·00	☐ ☐
1663	**1097**	39p multicoloured	..	1·40	1·25	☐ ☐
	Set of 5	.. .. ..	..	4·00	3·50	☐ ☐
	First Day Cover	.. ..			4·50	☐
	Presentation Pack	..		4·50		☐
	PHQ Cards (set of 5)	..	..	2·25	5·00	☐ ☐
	Set of 5 Gutter Pairs	..	..	8·00		☐

Booklet Stamps

1993 (6 Apr.)–95 *As T* **916/17,** *but perf* 15 × 14 (*with one elliptical hole on each vertical side*)

(a) Photo Harrison

1663a	**916**	(2nd)	bright blue (centre band)	30	35	☐ ☐
1664	**917**	(1st)	bright orange-red (phosphorised paper)	60	55	☐ ☐
1664a		(1st)	bright orange-red (2 phosphor bands)	40	45	☐ ☐

(b) Litho Questa or Walsall

1665	**916**	(2nd)	bright blue (1 centre band)	30	35	☐ ☐
1666	**917**	(1st)	bright orange-red (2 phosphor bands)	40	45	☐ ☐

Nos. 1665/6 also come from sheets.

1993–96 *As Nos.* X841, *etc, but perf* 15 × 14 (*with one elliptical hole on each vertical side*)

(a) Photo Enschedé. Two phosphor bands

Y1667	**369**	1p crimson	10	10	☐ ☐
Y1668		2p deep green	10	10	☐ ☐
Y1669		4p new blue	10	10	☐ ☐
Y1670		5p dull red-brown ..	10	10	☐ ☐
Y1671		6p yellow-olive	10	15	☐ ☐
Y1672		10p dull orange	15	20	☐ ☐
Y1673		20p turquoise-green ..	30	35	☐ ☐
Y1674		29p grey	45	50	☐ ☐
Y1675		30p deep olive-grey ..	45	50	☐ ☐
Y1676		31p deep mauve	50	55	☐ ☐
Y1677		35p yellow	55	60	☐ ☐
Y1678		36p bright ultramarine	55	60	☐ ☐
Y1679		37p bright mauve ..	60	65	☐ ☐
Y1680		38p rosine	60	65	☐ ☐
Y1681		39p bright magenta ..	60	65	☐ ☐
Y1682		41p grey-brown	65	70	☐ ☐
Y1683		43p deep olive-brown	65	70	☐ ☐
Y1684		50p ochre	75	80	☐ ☐
Y1685		63p light emerald ..	95	1·00	☐ ☐
Y1686		£1 bluish violet	1·50	1·60	☐ ☐

(b) Photo Harrison or Enschedé (*some printings of No. Y1703 in 1995*)

Y1700	**369**	19p bistre (1 centre band)	30	35	☐ ☐
Y1701		20p bright green (1 centre band) ..	30	35	☐ ☐
Y1702		25p rose-red (phosphorised paper) ..	60	60	☐ ☐
Y1703		25p rose-red (2 bands)	40	45	☐ ☐
Y1704		26p red-brown (2 bands)	40	45	☐ ☐
Y1705		35p yellow (phosphorised paper)	55	60	☐ ☐
Y1706		41p drab (phosphorised paper)	65	70	☐ ☐
Y1707		43p sepia (2 bands) ..	65	70	☐ ☐

(c) Litho Walsall (37, 60, 63p), *Questa or Walsall* (25, 35, 41p) *or Questa* (others). *One side band* (19p), *one centre band* (20p) *or two phosphor bands* (others)

Y1743	**369**	1p lake	10	10	☐ ☐
Y1748		6p yellow-olive	2·50	2·50	☐ ☐
Y1749		10p dull orange	2·00	2·00	☐ ☐
Y1750		19p bistre	1·00	1·00	☐ ☐
Y1751		20p bright yellow-green	30	35	☐ ☐
Y1752		25p red	40	45	☐ ☐
Y1753		26p chestnut	40	45	☐ ☐
Y1754		30p olive-grey	2·00	2·00	☐ ☐
Y1755		35p yellow	55	60	☐ ☐
Y1756		37p bright mauve	60	65	☐ ☐
Y1757		41p drab	65	70	☐ ☐
Y1758		60p dull blue-grey ..	90	95	☐ ☐
Y1759		63p light emerald	95	1·00	☐ ☐
	First Day Cover (Nos. Y1674, Y1678, Y1680, Y1682, Y1700, Y1702) (26.10.93)		4·50		☐
	First Day Cover (No. Y1758) (9.8.94)		2·00		☐

First Day Cover (No. Y1686) (22.8.95)	2·75	☐	
First Day Cover (Nos. Y1676, Y1679, Y1681, Y1683, Y1685, Y1701, Y1704) (25.6.96)	5·50	☐	
Presentation Pack (Nos. Y1674, Y1678, Y1680, Y1682, Y1700, Y1702) ..	3·25	☐	
Presentation Pack (Nos. Y1667/75, Y1677/8, Y1680, Y1682, Y1684, Y1686, Y1700, Y1703, Y1758)	8·25	☐	
Presentation Pack (Nos. Y1676, Y1679, Y1681, Y1683, Y1685, Y1701, Y1704)	4·50	☐	
PHQ Card (No. Y1686) 40	2·75	☐	☐

No. Y1686 is printed in Iriodin ink which gives a shiny effect to the solid part of the background behind the Queen's head.

Nos. Y1705/7 were only issued in coils and Nos. Y1743/59 only in booklets.

No. Y1750 exists with the phosphor band at the left or right of the stamp.

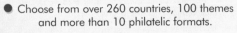

1098 "Family Group" (bronze sculpture) (Henry Moore)

1099 "Kew Gardens" (lithograph) (Edward Bawden)

1100 "St. Francis and the Birds" (Stanley Spencer)

1101 "Still Life. Odyssey I" (Ben Nicholson)

Europa. Contemporary Art

1993 (11 May) *Phosphorised paper. Perf 14 × 14½*

1767	1098	24p multicoloured	..	50	50	☐	☐
1768	1099	28p multicoloured		80	80	☐	☐
1769	1100	33p multicoloured		95	95	☐	☐
1770	1101	39p multicoloured		1·10	1·10	☐	☐
		Set of 4 ..	..	3·00	3·00	☐	☐
		First Day Cover ..	..		4·00		☐
		Presentation Pack	..	3·50		☐	
		PHQ Cards (set of 4)	..	2·00	4·50	☐	☐
		Set of 4 Gutter Pairs	..	6·00		☐	

1102 Emperor Claudius (from gold coin)

1103 Emperor Hadrian (bronze head)

1104 Goddess Roma (from gemstone)

1105 Christ (Hinton St. Mary mosaic)

Roman Britain

1993 (15 June) *Phosphorised paper with two phosphor bands. Perf 14 × 14½*

1771	1102	24p multicoloured	..	..	50	50	☐	☐
1772	1103	28p multicoloured			80	80	☐	☐
1773	1104	33p multicoloured			95	95	☐	☐
1774	1105	39p multicoloured			1·10	1·10	☐	☐
		Set of 4 ..	..	..	3·00	3·00	☐	☐
		First Day Cover ..				4·00		☐
		Presentation Pack			3·50		☐	
		PHQ Cards (set of 4)			1·40	4·00	☐	☐
		Set of 4 Gutter Pairs		..	6·00		☐	

1106 *Midland Maid* and other Narrow Boats, Grand Junction Canal

1107 *Yorkshire Maid* and other Humber Keels, Stainforth and Keadby Canal

1108 *Valley Princess* and other Horse-drawn Barges, Brecknock and Abergavenny Canal

1109 Steam Barges, including *Pride of Scotland*, and Fishing Boats, Crinan Canal

Inland Waterways

1993 (20 July) *Two phosphor bands. Perf 14½ × 14*

1775	1106	24p multicoloured	..	50	50	☐	☐
1776	1107	28p multicoloured		80	80	☐	☐
1777	1108	33p multicoloured		95	95	☐	☐
1778	1109	39p multicoloured		1·10	1·10	☐	☐
		Set of 4 ..	..	3·00	3·00	☐	☐
		First Day Cover ..	..		4·00		☐
		Presentation Pack	..	3·50		☐	
		PHQ Cards (set of 4)	..	1·40	4·50	☐	☐
		Set of 4 Gutter Pairs	..	6·00		☐	

Nos. 1775/8 commemorate the bicentenaries of the Acts of Parliament authorising the canals depicted.

1110 Horse Chestnut

1111 Blackberry

1112 Hazel

1113 Rowan

1114 Pear

The Four Seasons. Autumn. Fruits and Leaves

1993 (14 SEPT.) *One phosphor band* (18p) *or phosphorised paper* (*others*)

1779	**1110**	18p multicoloured	..	40	40	☐	☐
1780	**1111**	24p multicoloured	..	65	65	☐	☐
1781	**1112**	28p multicoloured	..	90	80	☐	☐
1782	**1113**	33p multicoloured	..	1·10	95	☐	☐
1783	**1114**	39p multicoloured	..	1·40	1·10	☐	☐
		Set of 5		4·00	3·50	☐	☐
		First Day Cover			4·50		☐
		Presentation Pack		4·25		☐	
		PHQ Cards (*set of* 5) ..		1·50	5·00	☐	☐
		Set of 5 *Gutter Pairs* ..		8·00		☐	

1115 The Reigate Squire

1116 The Hound of the Baskervilles

1117 The Six Napoleons

1118 The Greek Interpreter

1119 The Final Problem

T **1115/19** were printed together, *se-tenant*, in horizontal strips of 5 throughout the sheet.

Sherlock Holmes. Centenary of the Publication of The Final Problem

1993 (12 OCT.) *Phosphorised paper. Perf* 14 × 14½

1784	**1115**	24p multicoloured	..	90	90	☐	☐
		a. Horiz strip of 5.					
		Nos. 1784/8	..	4·00	4·00	☐	☐
1785	**1116**	24p multicoloured	..	90	90	☐	☐
1786	**1117**	24p multicoloured	..	90	90	☐	☐
1787	**1118**	24p multicoloured	..	90	90	☐	☐
1788	**1119**	24p multicoloured	..	90	90	☐	☐
		Set of 5		4·00	4·00	☐	☐
		First Day Cover			4·50		☐
		Presentation Pack ..		4·50		☐	
		PHQ Cards (*set of* 5) ..		1·50	5·50	☐	☐
		Gutter strip of 10 ..		8·00		☐	

1120

Self-adhesive Booklet Stamp

1993 (19 OCT.) *Two phosphor bands. Die-cut perf* 14 × 15 (*with one elliptical hole on each vertical side*)

1789	**1120**	(1st) orange-red..	..	75	75	☐	
		First Day Cover			3·25		☐
		Presentation Pack (*booklet pane of* 20)		10·00		☐	
		PHQ Card		30	3·25	☐	☐

1121 Bob Cratchit and Tiny Tim

1122 Mr. and Mrs. Fezziwig

1123 Scrooge

1124 The Prize Turkey

1125 Mr. Scrooge's Nephew

Christmas. 150th Anniversary of Publication of A Christmas Carol

1993 (9 Nov.) *One phosphor band. (19p) or phosphorised paper (others)*

1790	**1121**	19p multicoloured	..	40	40	☐ ☐
1791	**1122**	25p multicoloured	..	65	65	☐ ☐
1792	**1123**	30p multicoloured	..	80	80	☐ ☐
1793	**1124**	35p multicoloured	..	95	95	☐ ☐
1794	**1125**	41p multicoloured	..	1·10	1·10	☐ ☐
		Set of 5		3·50	3·50	☐
		First Day Cover			4·50	☐
		Presentation Pack		4·00		☐
		PHQ Cards (set of 5)		1·90	5·25	☐ ☐
		Set of 5 Gutter Pairs ..		7·25		☐

Collectors Pack 1993

1993 (9 Nov.) *Comprises Nos. 1639/43, 1654/7, 1659/63, 1767/88 and 1790/4*

	Collectors Pack	24·00			☐

Post Office Yearbook

1993 (9 Nov.) *Comprises Nos. 1639/43, 1654/7, 1659/63, 1767/88 and 1790/4 in hardback book with slip case*

Yearbook	45·00			☐

126 Class "5" No. 44957 and Class "B1" No. 61342 on West Highland Line

1127 Class "A1" No. 60149 *Amadis* at Kings Cross

1128 Class "4" No. 43000 on Turntable at Blyth North

1129 Class "4" No. 42455 near Wigan Central

1130 Class "Castle" No. 7002 *Devizes Castle* on Bridge crossing Worcester and Birmingham Canal

The Age of Steam. Railway Photographs by Colin Gifford

1994 (18 Jan.) *One phosphor band. (19p) or phosphorised paper with two bands (others). Perf 14½*

1795	**1126**	19p deep blue-green, grey-black and black	45	40	☐ ☐
1796	**1127**	25p slate-lilac, grey-black and black ..	75	65	☐ ☐
1797	**1128**	30p lake-brown, grey-black and black ..	90	80	☐ ☐
1798	**1129**	35p deep claret, grey-black and black	1·10	95	☐ ☐
1799	**1130**	41p indigo, grey-black and black	1·25	1·10	☐ ☐
		Set of 5	4·00	3·50	☐
		First Day Cover		4·50	☐
		Presentation Pack	4·25		☐
		PHQ Cards (set of 5)	1·90	5·25	☐ ☐
		Set of 5 Gutter Pairs	8·00		☐

1131 Dan Dare and the Mekon

1132 The Three Bears

1133 Rupert Bear

1134 Alice (*Alice in Wonderland*)

1135 Noggin and the Ice Dragon

1136 Peter Rabbit posting Letter

1137 Red Riding Hood and Wolf

1138 Orlando the Marmalade Cat

1139 Biggles

1140 Paddington Bear on Station

1141 Castell Y Waun (Chirk Castle), Clwyd, Wales

1142 Ben Arkle, Sutherland, Scotland

1143 Mourne Mountains, County Down, Northern Ireland

1144 Dersingham, Norfolk, England

1145 Dolwyddelan, Gwynedd, Wales

1806	**1137**	(1st) multicoloured	..	40	45	☐	☐
1807	**1138**	(1st) multicoloured	..	40	45	☐	☐
1808	**1139**	(1st) multicoloured	..	40	45	☐	☐
1809	**1140**	(1st) multicoloured	..	40	45	☐	☐
		Set of 10	..	4·00	4·50	☐	
		First Day Cover			7·50	☐	
		Presentation Pack		6·00		☐	
		PHQ Cards (set of 10)		4·25	10·00	☐	☐

T **1131/40** were printed together, *se-tenant*, in booklet panes of 10 stamps and 20 half stamp-size labels.

Greetings Stamps. "Messages"

1994 (1 FEB.) *Two phosphor bands. Perf* 15 × 14 (*with one elliptical hole on each vertical side*)

1800	**1131**	(1st) multicoloured	..	40	45	☐	☐
		a. Booklet pane.					
		Nos. 1800/9 ..	..	4·00		☐	
1801	**1132**	(1st) multicoloured	..	40	45	☐	☐
1802	**1133**	(1st) multicoloured	..	40	45	☐	☐
1803	**1134**	(1st) gold, bistre-yellow					
		and black	..	40	45	☐	☐
1804	**1135**	(1st) multicoloured	..	40	45	☐	☐
1805	**1136**	(1st) multicoloured	..	40	45	☐	☐

25th Anniversary of Investiture of the Prince Wales. Paintings by Prince Charles

1994 (1 MAR.) *One phosphor band* (19p) *or phosphorise paper* (*others*)

1810	**1141**	19p multicoloured ..	..	40	40	☐
1811	**1142**	25p multicoloured ..	..	65	65	☐
1812	**1143**	30p multicoloured ..	..	80	80	☐
1813	**1144**	35p multicoloured ..	..	95	95	☐
1814	**1145**	41p multicoloured ..	..	1·10	1·10	☐
		Set of 5		3·50	3·50	☐
		First Day Cover			4·00	☐
		Presentation Pack		4·00		☐
		PHQ Cards (set of 5)		1·90	5·25	☐
		Set of 5 *Gutter Pairs*		7·25		☐

146 Bather at Blackpool

1147 "Where's my Little Lad?"

148 "Wish You were Here!"

1149 Punch and Judy Show

1150 "The Tower Crane" Machine

entenary of Picture Postcards

994 (12 APR.) *One side band (19p) or two phosphor bands thers). Perf 14 × 14½*

15	**1146**	19p multicoloured	.. ..	40	40	☐ ☐
16	**1147**	25p multicoloured	.. ..	65	65	☐ ☐
17	**1148**	30p multicoloured	.. ..	80	80	☐ ☐
18	**1149**	35p multicoloured	.. ..	95	95	☐ ☐
19	**1150**	41p multicoloured	.. ..	1·10	1·10	☐ ☐
		Set of 5	.. ..	3·50	3·50	☐ ☐
		First Day Cover ..	.. ..		4·00	☐
		Presentation Pack	.. ..	4·00		☐
		PHQ Cards (set of 5)	.. ..	1·90	5·25	☐ ☐
		Set of 5 Gutter Pairs	.. ..	7·25		☐

1151 British Lion and French Cockerel over Tunnel

1152 Symbolic Hands over Train

Nos. 1820/1 and 1822/3 were printed together, *se-tenant*, in horizontal pairs throughout the sheets.

Opening of Channel Tunnel

1994 (3 MAY) *Phosphorised paper. Perf 14 × 14½*

1820	**1151**	25p multicoloured	..	55	55	☐ ☐
		a. Horiz pair. Nos.				
		1820/1		1·10	1·10	☐ ☐
1821	**1152**	25p multicoloured	..	55	55	☐ ☐
1822	**1151**	41p multicoloured	..	1·25	1·25	☐ ☐
		a. Horiz pair. Nos.				
		1822/3		2·50	2·50	☐ ☐
1823	**1152**	41p multicoloured		1·25	1·25	☐ ☐
		Set of 4		3·25	3·25	☐ ☐
		First Day Cover			5·00	☐
		Presentation Pack		4·00		☐
		PHQ Cards (set of 4)		1·75	4·50	☐ ☐

Stamps in similar designs were also issued by France.

1153 Groundcrew replacing Smoke Canisters on Douglas Boston of 88 Sqn

1154 H.M.S. *Warspite* (battleship) shelling Enemy Positions

1155 Commandos landing on Gold Beach

1156 Infantry regrouping on Sword Beach

1157 Tank and Infantry advancing. Ouistreham

Nos. 1824/8 were printed together, *se-tenant*, in horizontal strips of 5 throughout the sheet.

50th Anniversary of D-Day

1994 (6 June) *Two phosphor bands. Perf* $14\frac{1}{2} \times 14$

1824	**1153**	25p multicoloured	.. ..	65	65	□ □
	a.	Horiz strip of 5.				
		Nos. 1824/8	.. ..	3·00	3·00	□ □
1825	**1154**	25p multicoloured	.. ..	65	65	□ □
1826	**1155**	25p multicoloured	.. ..	65	65	□ □
1827	**1156**	25p multicoloured	.. ..	65	65	□ □
1828	**1157**	25p multicoloured	.. ..	65	65	□ □
		Set of 5	.. .. ..	3·00	3·00	□ □
		First Day Cover	.. .. ..		4·00	□
		Presentation Pack	.. ..	3·50		□
		PHQ Cards (set of 5)	.. ..	1·90	4·75	□ □
		Gutter Block of 10	.. .. ..	6·00		□

1158 The Old Course, St. Andrews

1159 The 18th Hole, Muirfield

1160 The 15th Hole ("Luckyslap"), Carnoustie

1161 The 8th Hole ("The Postage Stamp"), Royal Troon

1162 The 9th Hole, Turnberry

Scottish Golf Courses

1994 (5 July) *One phosphor band* (19p) *or phosphorised paper* (others). *Perf* $14\frac{1}{2} \times 14$

1829	**1158**	19p multicoloured	.. ..	50	50	□ □
1830	**1159**	25p multicoloured	.. ..	70	70	□ □
1831	**1160**	30p multicoloured	.. ..	90	90	□ □
1832	**1161**	35p multicoloured	.. ..	1·10	1·10	□ □
1833	**1162**	41p multicoloured	.. ..	1·25	1·25	□ □
		Set of 5	.. .. ..	4·00	4·00	□ □
		First Day Cover	.. .. ..		4·25	□
		Presentation Pack	.. ..	4·25		□
		PHQ Cards (set of 5)	.. ..	1·90	5·25	□ □
		Set of 5 Gutter Pairs	.. ..	8·00		□

Nos. 1829/33 commemorate the 250th anniversary of golf's first set of rules produced by the Honourable Company of Edinburgh Golfers.

1163 Royal Welsh Show. Llanelwedd

1164 All England Tennis Championships, Wimbledon

1165 Cowes Week

1166 Test Match, Lord's

SUMMERTIME *Braemar*

1167 Braemar Gathering

1172 Virgin Mary and Joseph

1173 Three Wise Men

The Four Seasons. Summertime. Events

1994 (2 Aug.) *One phosphor band* (19p) *or phosphorised paper* (*others*)

1834	**1163** 19p multicoloured	50	50	☐	☐
1835	**1164** 25p multicoloured	70	70	☐	☐
1836	**1165** 30p multicoloured	90	80	☐	☐
1837	**1166** 35p multicoloured	1·00	90	☐	☐
1838	**1167** 41p multicoloured	1·10	1·00	☐	☐
	Set of 5	3·75	3·50	☐	☐
	First Day Cover		4·25	☐
	Presentation Pack	4·00		☐
	PHQ Cards (*set of 5*)	1·90	5·25	☐	☐
	Set of 5 Gutter Pairs	7·50		☐

1174 Virgin and Child

1175 Shepherds

1168 Ultrasonic Imaging

1169 Scanning Electron Microscopy

1176 Angels

Christmas, Children's Nativity Plays

1994 (1 Nov.) *One phosphor band* (19p) *or phosphorised paper* (*others*)

1843	**1172** 19p multicoloured	50	50	☐	☐
1844	**1173** 25p multicoloured	70	70	☐	☐
1845	**1174** 30p multicoloured	80	80	☐	☐
1846	**1175** 35p multicoloured	90	90	☐	☐
1847	**1176** 41p multicoloured	1·00	1·00	☐	☐
	Set of 5	3·50	3·50	☐	☐
	First Day Cover		4·25	☐
	Presentation Pack	4·00		☐
	PHQ Cards (*set of 5*)	1·90	5·25	☐	☐
	Set of 5 Gutter Pairs	7·00		☐

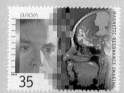

1170 Magnetic Resonance Imaging

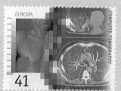

1171 Computed Tomography

Europa. Medical Discoveries

1994 (27 Sept.) *Phosphorised paper. Perf* $14 \times 14\frac{1}{2}$

1839	**1168** 25p multicoloured	65	65	☐	☐
1840	**1169** 30p multicoloured	85	85	☐	☐
1841	**1170** 35p multicoloured	90	90	☐	☐
1842	**1171** 41p multicoloured	1·00	1·00	☐	☐
	Set of 4	3·00	3·00	☐	☐
	First Day Cover		4·00	☐
	Presentation Pack	4·00		☐
	PHQ Cards (*set of 4*)	1·50	3·50	☐	☐
	Set of 4 Gutter Pairs	6·00		☐

Collectors Pack 1994

1994 (14 Nov.) *Comprises Nos.* 1795/1847.
       Collectors Pack .. .. 28·00   ☐

Post Office Yearbook

1994 (14 Nov.) *Comprises Nos.* 1795/9 *and* 1810/47 *in hardback book with slip case.*
       Yearbook .. .. 45·00   ☐

1177 Sophie (black cat)

1178 Puskas (Siamese) and Tigger (tabby)

1179 Chloe (ginger cat)

1180 Kikko (tortoiseshell) and Rosie (Abyssinian)

1181 Fred (black and white cat)

Cats

1995 (17 Jan.) *One phosphor band* (19p) *or two phosphor bands* (*others*). *Perf* 14½ × 14

1848	**1177**	19p multicoloured	..	..	45	45
1849	**1178**	25p multicoloured	..	..	55	55
1850	**1179**	30p multicoloured	..	..	65	65
1851	**1180**	35p multicoloured	..	..	75	75
1852	**1181**	41p multicoloured	..	..	85	85
		Set of 5	..	..	3·00	3·00
		First Day Cover ..	..	..		3·75
		Presentation Pack	..	..	3·25	
		PHQ Cards (*set of* 5)	..	..	2·25	5·50
		Set of 5 *Gutter Pairs*	..	..	6·00	

1182 Dandelions

1183 Sweet Chestnut Leaves

1184 Garlic Leaves

1185 Hazel Leaves

1186 Spring Grass

The Four Seasons. Springtime. Plant Sculptures by Andy Goldsworthy

1995 (14 Mar.) *One phosphor band* (19p) *or two phosphor bands* (*others*).

1853	**1182**	19p multicoloured	..	..	45	45
1854	**1183**	25p multicoloured	..	..	55	55
1855	**1184**	30p multicoloured	..	..	65	65
1856	**1185**	35p multicoloured	..	..	75	75
1857	**1186**	41p multicoloured	..	..	85	85
		Set of 5	..	..	3·00	3·00
		First Day Cover ..	..	..		3·75
		Presentation Pack		..	3·25	
		PHQ Cards (*set of* 5)	..	..	2·25	5·25
		Set of 5 *Gutter Pairs*	..	..	6·00	

1187 ''La Danse a la Campagne'' (Renoir)

1188 ''Troilus and Criseyde'' (Peter Brookes)

1189 ''The Kiss'' (Rodin)

1190 ''Girls on the Town'' (Beryl Cook)

1191 "Jazz" (Andrew Mockett)

1192 "Girls performing a Kathal Dance" (Aurangzeb period)

1197 Fireplace Decoration, Attingham Park, Shropshire

1198 Oak Seedling

1193 "Alice Keppel with her Daughter" (Alice Hughes)

1194 "Children Playing" (L. S. Lowry)

1199 Carved Table Leg, Attingham Park

1200 St. David's Head, Dyfed, Wales

1195 "Circus Clowns" (Emily Firmin and Justin Mitchell)

1196 Decoration from "All the Love Poems of Shakespeare" (Eric Gill)

T **1187/96** were printed together, *se-tenant*, in booklet panes of 10 stamps and 20 half stamp-size labels.

Greetings Stamp. "Greetings in Art"

1995 (21 Mar.) *Two phosphor bands. Perf 14½ × 14 (with one elliptical hole on each vertical side)*

1858	**1187** (1st) multicoloured ..	40	45 □ □
	a. *Booklet pane. Nos.*		
	1858/67	4·00	□
1859	**1188** (1st) multicoloured ..	40	45 □ □
1860	**1189** (1st) multicoloured ..	40	45 □ □
1861	**1190** (1st) multicoloured ..	40	45 □ □
1862	**1191** (1st) multicoloured ..	40	45 □ □
1863	**1192** (1st) multicoloured ..	40	45 □ □
1864	**1193** (1st) purple-brown and silver	40	45 □ □
1865	**1194** (1st) multicoloured ..	40	45 □ □
1866	**1195** (1st) multicoloured ..	40	45 □ □
1867	**1196** (1st) black, greenish yellow & silver ..	40	45 □ □
	Set of 10	4·00	4·10 □ □
	First Day Cover		5·00 □
	Presentation Pack	4·25	□
	PHQ Cards (set of 10) ..	3·75	8·75 □ □

The National Trust
Repairing Buildings 41

1201 Elizabethan Window, Little Moreton Hall, Cheshire

Centenary of The National Trust

1995 (11 Apr.) *One phosphor band (19p), two phosphor bands (25p, 35p) or phosphorised paper (30p, 41p).*

1868	**1197** 19p multicoloured	45	45 □ □
1869	**1198** 25p multicoloured	55	55 □ □
1870	**1199** 30p multicoloured	65	65 □ □
1871	**1200** 35p multicoloured	75	75 □ □
1872	**1201** 41p multicoloured	85	85 □ □
	Set of 5	3·00	3·00 □ □
	First Day Cover		3·25 □
	Presentation Pack	2·75	□
	PHQ Cards (set of 5) ..	1·90	5·25 □ □
	Set of 5 Gutter Pairs ..	6·25	□

1202 British Troops and French Civilians celebrating

1203 Symbolic Hands and Red Cross

1204 St. Paul's Cathedral and Searchlights

1205 Symbolic Hand releasing Peace Dove

1206 Symbolic Hands

Europa. Peace and Freedom

1995 (2 MAY) *One phosphor band* (*Nos.* 1873/4) *or two phosphor bands* (*others*). *Perf* 14½ × 14

1873	**1202**	19p silver, bistre-brown and grey-black	..	50	50	☐	☐
1874	**1203**	19p multicoloured ..	..	50	50	☐	☐
1875	**1204**	25p silver, blue and grey-black	..	65	65	☐	☐
1876	**1205**	25p multicoloured ..	..	65	65	☐	☐
1877	**1206**	30p multicoloured ..	..	75	75	☐	☐
		Set of 5	..	2·75	2·75	☐	☐
		First Day Cover ..	..		3·00		☐
		Presentation Pack	..	3·00		☐	
		PHQ Cards (set of 5)	..	1·90	4·50	☐	☐
		Set of 5 Gutter Pairs	..	5·50		☐	

Nos. 1873 and 1875 commemorate the 50th anniversary of the end of the Second World War, No. 1874 the 125th anniversary of the British Red Cross Society and Nos. 1876/7 the 50th anniversary of the United Nations.

Nos. 1876/7 include the "EUROPA" emblem.

1207 *The Time Machine*

1208 *The First Men in the Moon*

1209 *The War of the Worlds*

1210 *The Shape of Things to Come*

Science Fiction. Novels by H. G. Wells

1995 (6 JUNE) *Two phosphor bands. Perf* 14½ × 14

1878	**1207**	25p multicoloured ..	..	65	65	☐	☐
1879	**1208**	30p multicoloured ..	..	85	85	☐	☐
1880	**1209**	35p multicoloured ..	..	90	90	☐	☐
1881	**1210**	41p multicoloured ..	..	1·00	1·00	☐	☐
		Set of 4	..	3·00	3·00	☐	☐
		First Day Cover ..	..		3·50		☐
		Presentation Pack	..	3·50		☐	
		PHQ Cards (set of 4)	..	1·50	4·50	☐	☐
		Set of 4 Gutter Pairs	..	6·50		☐	

Nos. 1878/81 commemorate the centenary of publication of Wells's *The Time Machine.*

1211 The Swan, 1595

1212 The Rose, 1592

1213 The Globe, 1599

1214 The Hope, 1613

1215 The Globe, 1614

T **1211/15** were printed together, *se-tenant*, in horizontal strips of 5 throughout the sheet, the backgrounds forming a composite design.

Reconstruction of Shakespeare's Globe Theatre

1995 (8 Aug.) *Two phosphor bands. Perf 14½*

1882	**1211**	25p multicoloured	55	55	□	□
		a. Horiz strip of 5.				
		Nos. 1882/6	2·50	2·50	□	□
1883	**1212**	25p multicoloured	55	55	□	□
1884	**1213**	25p multicoloured	55	55	□	□
1885	**1214**	25p multicoloured	55	55	□	□
1886	**1215**	25p multicoloured	55	55	□	□
		Set of 5	2·50	2·50	□	□
		First Day Cover		3·00		□
		Presentation·Pack	2·75		□	
		PHQ Cards (set of 5)	1·90	4·75	□	□
		Gutter Strip of 10	5·00		□	

1218 Guglielmo Marconi and Early Wireless

1219 Marconi and Sinking of *Titanic* (liner)

Pioneers of Communications

1995 (5 Sept.) *One phosphor band* (19p.) *or phosphorised paper* (others). *Perf 14½ × 14*

1887	**1216**	19p silver, red and black	50	50	□	□
1888	**1217**	25p silver, brown and black	70	70	□	□
1889	**1218**	41p silver, grey-green and black	1·00	1·00	□	□
1890	**1219**	60p silver, deep ultra-marine and black ..	1·40	1·40	□	□
		Set of 4	3·25	3·25	□	□
		First Day Cover ..		3·50		□
		Presentation Pack ..	3·50		□	
		PHQ Cards (set of 4)	1·50	4·75	□	□
		Set of 4 Gutter Pairs	6·50		□	

Nos. 1887/8 mark the birth bicentenary of Sir Rowland Hill and Nos. 1889/90 the centenary of the first radio transmissions.

1220 Harold Wagstaff

1221 Gus Risman

1216 Sir Rowland Hill and Uniform Penny Postage Petition

1217 Hill and Penny Black

1222 Jim Sullivan

1223 Billy Batten

1224 Brian Bevan

Centenary of Rugby League

1995 (3 Oct.) One phosphor band (19p) or two phosphor bands (others). Perf 14 × 14½

1891	**1220**	19p multicoloured	.. ..	45	45	☐	☐
1892	**1221**	25p multicoloured	.. ..	60	60	☐	☐
1893	**1222**	30p multicoloured	.. ..	70	70	☐	☐
1894	**1223**	35p multicoloured	.. ..	95	95	☐	☐
1895	**1224**	41p multicoloured	.. ..	1·25	1·25	☐	☐
		Set of 5	.. ..	3·50	3·50	☐	☐
		First Day Cover ..	.. .. ..		3·75		☐
		Presentation Pack	.. ..	3·75		☐	
		PHQ Cards (set of 5)	..	1·90	5·25	☐	☐
		Set of 5 Gutter Pairs	.. ..	7·00		☐	

1225 European Robin in Mouth of Pillar Box

1226 European Robin on Railings and Holly

1227 European Robin on Snow-covered Milk Bottles

1228 European Robin on Road Sign

1229 European Robin on Door Knob and Christmas Wreath

Christmas. Christmas Robins

1995 (30 Oct.) One phosphor band (19p) or two phosphor bands (others)

1896	**1225**	19p multicoloured	.. ..	45	45	☐	☐
1897	**1226**	25p multicoloured	.. ..	60	60	☐	☐
1898	**1227**	30p multicoloured	.. ..	70	70	☐	☐
1899	**1228**	41p multicoloured	.. ..	95	95	☐	☐
1900	**1229**	60p multicoloured	.. ..	1·25	1·25	☐	☐
		Set of 5	.. ..	3·50	3·50	☐	☐
		First Day Cover ..	.. .. ..		3·75		☐
		Presentation Pack	.. ..	3·75		☐	
		PHQ Cards (set of 5)	..	1·90	5·75	☐	☐
		Set of 5 Gutter Pairs	.. ..	7·00		☐	

Collectors Pack 1995

1995 (30 Oct.) Comprises Nos. 1848/1900.

	Collectors Pack ..	.. .. ..	24·00	☐

Post Office Yearbook

1995 (30 Oct.) Comprises Nos. 1848/57 and 1868/1900 in hardback book with slip case.

	Yearbook	.. ..	35·00	☐

1230 Opening Lines of "To a Mouse" and Fieldmouse

1231 "O my Luve's like a red, red rose" and Wild Rose

1232 "Scots, wha hae wi Wallace bled" and Sir William Wallace

1233 "Auld Lang Syne" and Highland Dancers

Death Bicentenary of Robert Burns (Scottish poet)

1996 (25 Jan.) *One phosphor band (19p) or two phosphor bands (others). Perf 14½*

1901	**1230**	19p cream, bistre-brown and black	.. ..	30	35	☐ ☐
1902	**1231**	25p multicoloured		60	65	☐ ☐
1903	**1232**	41p multicoloured		65	70	☐ ☐
1904	**1233**	60p multicoloured		90	95	☐ ☐
		Set of 4		2·50	2·75	☐ ☐
		First Day Cover			3·25	☐
		Presentation Pack ..		2·50		☐
		PHQ Cards (set of 4)		1·50	4·75	☐ ☐
		Set of 4 Gutter Pairs		4·25		☐

1234 "MORE! LOVE" (Mel Calman)

1235 "Sincerely" (Charles Barsotti)

1236 "Do you have something for the HUMAN CONDITION?" (Mel Calman)

1237 "MENTAL FLOSS" (Leo Cullum)

1238 "4.55 P.M." (Charles Barsotti)

1239 "Dear lottery prize winner" (Larry)

1240 "I'm writing to you because...." (Mel Calman)

1241 "FETCH THIS, FETCH THAT" (Charles Barsotti)

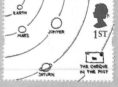

1242 "My day starts before I'm ready for it" (Mel Calman)

1243 "THE CHEQUE IN THE POST" (Jack Ziegler)

T **1234/43** were printed together, *se-tenant*, in booklet panes of 10 stamps and 20 half stamp-size labels.

Greetings Stamps. Cartoons

1996 (26 Feb.) *'All-over' phosphor. Perf 14½ × 14 (with one elliptical hole on each vertical side)*

1905	**1234**	(1st) black and bright mauve	40	45	☐ ☐
		a. Booklet pane. Nos. 1905/14	4·00		☐
1906	**1235**	(1st) black and blue-green	40	45	☐ ☐
1907	**1236**	(1st) black and new blue	40	45	☐ ☐
1908	**1237**	(1st) black and bright violet	40	45	☐ ☐
1909	**1238**	(1st) black and vermilion	40	45	☐ ☐
1910	**1239**	(1st) black and new blue	40	45	☐ ☐
1911	**1240**	(1st) black and vermilion	40	45	☐ ☐
1912	**1241**	(1st) black and bright violet	40	45	☐ ☐
1913	**1242**	(1st) black and blue-green	40	45	☐ ☐
1914	**1243**	(1st) black and bright mauve	40	45	☐ ☐
		Set of 10	4·00	4·50	☐ ☐
		First Day Cover		5·00	☐
		Presentation Pack	4·25		☐
		PHQ Cards (set of 10)	3·75	8·75	☐ ☐

1244 "Muscovy Duck"

1245 "Lapwing"

1246 "White-fronted Goose"

1247 "Bittern"

1248 "Whooper Swan"

50th Anniversary of the Wildfowl and Wetlands Trust. Bird Paintings by C. F. Tunnicliffe

1996 (12 MAR.) *One phosphor band (19p) or phosphorised paper (others). Perf* $14 \times 14\frac{1}{2}$

1915	**1244**	19p multicoloured	..	30	35	☐	☐
1916	**1245**	25p multicoloured	..	40	45	☐	☐
1917	**1246**	30p multicoloured	..	45	50	☐	☐
1918	**1247**	35p multicoloured	..	55	60	☐	☐
1919	**1248**	41p multicoloured	..	65	70	☐	☐
		Set of 5	.. ..	2·40	2·50	☐	☐
		First Day Cover ..	.. .. ..		3·25		☐
		Presentation Pack	.. ..	2·75		☐	
		PHQ Cards (set of 5)	.. ..	1·90	5·25	☐	☐
		Set of 5 Gutter Pairs	.. ..	5·00		☐	

1249 The Odeon, Harrogate

1250 Laurence Olivier and Vivien Leigh in *Lady Hamilton* (film)

1251 Old Cinema Ticket

1252 Pathé News Still

1253 Cinema Sign, The Odeon, Manchester

Centenary of Cinema

1996 (16 APR.) *One phosphor band (19p) or two phosphor bands (others). Perf* $14 \times 14\frac{1}{2}$

1920	**1249**	19p multicoloured	..	30	35	☐	☐
1921	**1250**	25p multicoloured	..	40	45	☐	☐
1922	**1251**	30p multicoloured	..	45	50	☐	☐
1923	**1252**	35p black, red and silver		55	60	☐	☐
1924	**1253**	41p multicoloured	..	65	70	☐	☐
		Set of 5	.. ..	2·40	2·50	☐	☐
		First Day Cover ..	.. .. ..		3·25		☐
		Presentation Pack	.. .. ..	2·75		☐	
		PHQ Cards (set of 5)	.. ..	1·90	5·25	☐	☐
		Set of 5 Gutter Pairs	.. ..	5·00		☐	

1254 Dixie Dean

1255 Bobby Moore

1256 Duncan Edwards

1257 Billy Wright

1258 Danny Blanchflower

European Football Championship

1996 (14 May). One phosphor band (19p) or two phosphor bands (others). Perf 14½ × 14

1925	**1254**	19p multicoloured	..	30	35	□ □
1926	**1255**	25p multicoloured	..	40	45	□ □
1927	**1256**	35p multicoloured	..	55	60	□ □
1928	**1257**	41p multicoloured	..	65	70	□ □
1929	**1258**	60p multicoloured	..	90	95	□ □
	Set of 5		..	2·75	3·00	□ □
	First Day Cover		..		3·75	□
	Presentation Pack ..		..	3·25		□
	PHQ Cards (set of 5) ..		..	1·90	5·75	□ □
	Set of 5 Gutter Pairs ..		..	6·25		□

1259 Athlete on Starting Blocks

1260 Throwing the Javelin

1261 Basketball

1262 Swimming

1263 Athlete celebrating and Olympic Rings

Nos. 1930/4 were printed together, *se-tenant*, in horizontal strips of 5 throughout the sheet.

Olympic and Paralympic Games, Atlanta

1996 (9 July) Two phosphor bands. Perf 14½ × 14

1930	**1259**	26p multicoloured	..	40	45	□ □
		a. Horiz strip of 5.				
		Nos. 1930/4	..	2·00		□
1931	**1260**	26p multicoloured	..	40	45	□ □
1932	**1261**	26p multicoloured	..	40	45	□ □
1933	**1262**	26p multicoloured	..	40	45	□ □
1934	**1263**	26p multicoloured	..	40	45	□ □
	Set of 5		..	2·00	2·25	□ □
	First Day Cover				2·75	□
	Presentation Pack ..		..	2·40		□
	PHQ Cards (set of 5) ..		..	1·90	4·75	□ □
	Gutter Strip of 10		..	4·25		□

1264 Prof. Dorothy Hodgkin (scientist)

1265 Dame Margot Fonteyn (ballerina)

1266 Dame Elisabeth Frink (sculptress)

1267 Dame Daphne du Maurier (novelist)

1268 Dame Marea Hartman (sports administrator)

Europa. Famous Women

1996 (6 Aug.) One phosphor band (20p) or two phosphor bands (others). Perf 14½.

1935	**1264**	20p dull blue-green, brownish grey and black	30	35	□ □
1936	**1265**	26p dull mauve, brownish grey and black	40	45	□ □
1937	**1266**	31p bronze, brownish grey and black ..	50	55	□ □
1938	**1267**	37p silver, brownish grey and black ..	60	65	□ □
1939	**1268**	43p gold, brownish grey and black ..	65	70	□ □
	Set of 5		2·40	2·75	□ □
	First Day Cover			3·25	□
	Presentation Pack		2·75		□
	PHQ Cards (set of 5)		1·90	5·25	□ □
	Set of 5 Gutter Pairs		5·00		□

Nos. 1936/7 include the "EUROPA" emblem.

1269 *Muffin the Mule*

1270 *Sooty*

1271 *Stingray*

1272 *The Clangers*

1273 *Dangermouse*

50th Anniversary of Children's Television

1996 (3 SEPT.) *One phosphor band* (20p) *or two phosphor bands* (others). *Perf* 14½ × 14

1940	**1269**	20p multicoloured	..	30	35	☐	☐
1941	**1270**	26p multicoloured	..	40	45	☐	☐
1942	**1271**	31p multicoloured	..	50	55	☐	☐
1943	**1272**	37p multicoloured	..	60	65	☐	☐
1944	**1273**	43p multicoloured	..	65	70	☐	☐
		Set of 5	.. .. ..	2·40	2·75	☐	☐
		First Day Cover ..	.. ..		3·25		☐
		Presentation Pack	.. ..	2·75		☐	
		PHQ Cards (*set of 5*)	.. ..	1·90	5·25	☐	☐
		Set of 5 Gutter Pairs	.. ..	5·00		☐	

1274 Triumph TR3

1275 MG TD

1276 Austin-Healey 100

1277 Jaguar XK120

1278 Morgan Plus 4

Classic Sports Cars

1996 (1 OCT.) *One phosphor band* (20p) *or two phosphor bands* (others). *Perf* 14½

1945	**1274**	20p multicoloured	..	30	35	☐	☐
1946	**1275**	26p multicoloured	..	40	45	☐	☐
1947	**1276**	37p multicoloured	..	60	65	☐	☐
1948	**1277**	43p multicoloured	..	65	70	☐	☐
1949	**1278**	63p multicoloured	..	95	1·00	☐	☐
		Set of 5	.. .. ..	3·00	3·25	☐	☐
		First Day Cover ..	.. ..		3·75		☐
		Presentation Pack	.. ..	3·25		☐	
		PHQ Cards (*set of 5*)	.. ..	1·90	5·75	☐	☐
		Set of 5 Gutter Pairs	.. ..	6·25		☐	

1279 The Three Kings

1280 The Annunciation

1281 The Journey to Bethlehem

1282 The Nativity

1283 The Shepherds

Christmas

1996 (28 Oct.) *One phosphor band (2nd class) or two phosphor bands (others)*

1950	**1279**	(2nd) multicoloured	..	30	35	☐	☐
1951	**1280**	(1st) multicoloured	..	40	45	☐	☐
1952	**1281**	31p multicoloured	..	50	55	☐	☐
1953	**1282**	43p multicoloured	..	65	70	☐	☐
1954	**1283**	63p multicoloured	..	95	1·00	☐	☐
	Set of 5	.. ..	..	2·75	3·00	☐	☐
	First Day Cover ..	.. ..	..		3·50		☐
	Presentation Pack	.. ..	..	3·00			☐
	PHQ Cards (set of 5)	..	..	1·90	5·50	☐	☐
	Set of 5 Gutter Pairs	..	..	5·75			☐

Collectors Pack 1996

1996 (28 Oct.) *Comprises Nos.* 1901/4 *and* 1915/54

    Collectors Pack .. .. 25·00   ☐

Post Office Yearbook

1996 (28 Oct.) *Comprises Nos.* 1901/4 *and* 1915/54 *in hardback book with slip case.*

    Yearbook .. .. 35·00   ☐

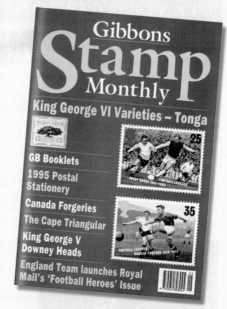

REGIONAL ISSUES

PERFORATION AND WATERMARK. All the following Regional stamps are perforated 15 × 14 and are watermarked Type **179**, unless otherwise stated.

For listing of First Day Covers see pages 122/3.

1 Northern Ireland

N 1   N 2   N 3   N 4

1958–67

NI1	N **1**	3d lilac		20	10	☐ ☐
		p One centre phosphor band		20	15	☐ ☐
NI2		4d blue		20	15	☐ ☐
		p Two phosphor bands		20	15	☐ ☐
NI3	N **2**	6d purple		20	20	☐ ☐
NI4		9d bronze-green (2 phosphor bands)		30	60	☐ ☐
NI5	N **3**	1s 3d green		30	60	☐ ☐
NI6		1s 6d blue (2 phosphor bands)		30	60	☐ ☐

1968–69 One centre phosphor band (Nos. NI8/9) or two phosphor bands (others). No wmk

NI7	N **1**	4d blue		20	15	☐ ☐
NI8		4d sepia		20	15	☐ ☐
NI9		4d vermilion		20	20	☐ ☐
NI10		5d blue		20	20	☐ ☐
NI11	N **3**	1s 6d blue		2·50	3·00	☐ ☐
		Presentation Pack (comprises Nos. NI1p, NI4/6, NI8/10).		3·00		☐

Decimal Currency

1971–91 Type N **4**. No wmk

(a) Printed in photogravure with phosphor bands

NI12	2½p magenta (1 centre band)		80	25	☐ ☐
NI13	3p ultramarine (2 bands)		40	15	☐ ☐
NI14	3p ultramarine (1 centre band)		20	15	☐ ☐
NI15	3½p olive-grey (2 bands)		20	20	☐ ☐
NI16	3½p olive-grey (1 centre band)		20	25	☐ ☐
NI17	4½p grey-blue (2 bands)		25	25	☐ ☐
NI18	5p violet (2 bands)		1·50	1·50	☐ ☐
NI19	5½p violet (2 bands)		20	20	☐ ☐
NI20	5½p violet (1 centre band)		20	20	☐ ☐
NI21	6½p blue (1 centre band)		20	20	☐ ☐
NI22	7p brown (1 centre band)		35	25	☐ ☐
NI23	7½p chestnut (2 bands)		2·00	2·00	☐ ☐

NI24	8p rosine (2 bands)	30	30	☐ ☐
NI25	8½p yellow-green (2 bands)	30	30	☐ ☐
NI26	9p violet (2 bands)	30	30	☐ ☐
NI27	10p orange-brown (2 bands)	35	35	☐ ☐
NI28	10p orange-brown (1 centre band)	35	35	☐ ☐
NI29	10½p blue (2 bands)	40	40	☐ ☐
NI30	11p scarlet (2 bands)	40	40	☐ ☐

(b) Printed in photogravure on phosphorised paper

NI31	12p yellowish green	50	45	☐ ☐
NI32	13½p purple-brown	60	70	☐ ☐
NI33	15p ultramarine	60	60	☐ ☐

(c) Printed in lithography. Perf 14 (11½p, 12½p, 14p (No. NI38), 15½p, 16p, 18p (No. NI45), 19½p, 20½p, 22p (No. NI53), 26p (No. NI60), 28p (No. NI62)) or 15 × 14 (others)

NI34	11½p drab (1 side band)	70	70	☐ ☐
NI35	12p brt emer (1 side band)	70	60	☐ ☐
NI36	12½p light emer (1 side band)	50	50	☐ ☐
	a. Perf 15 × 14	4·00	4·00	☐ ☐
NI37	13p pale chest (1 side band)	1·25	50	☐ ☐
NI38	14p grey-blue (phosphorised paper)	70	50	☐ ☐
NI39	14p dp blue (1 centre band)	55	50	☐ ☐
NI40	15p brt blue (1 centre band)	60	50	☐ ☐
NI41	15½p pale violet (phosphorised paper)	80	65	☐ ☐
NI42	16p drab (phosphorised paper)	1·00	1·00	☐ ☐
	a. Perf 15 × 14	9·00	7·50	☐ ☐
NI43	17p grey-blue (phosphorised paper)	1·00	60	☐ ☐
NI44	17p deep blue (1 centre band)	70	50	☐ ☐
NI45	18p dp violet (phosphorised paper)	90	90	☐ ☐
NI46	18p olive-grey (phosphorised paper)	80	80	☐ ☐
NI47	18p brt grn (1 centre band)	70	70	☐ ☐
	a. Perf 14	90	90	☐ ☐
NI48	18p brt grn (1 side band)	1·00	1·00	☐ ☐
NI49	19p bright orange-red (phosphorised paper)	70	60	☐ ☐
NI50	19½p olive-grey (phosphorised paper)	1·75	2·00	☐ ☐
NI51	20p brownish black (phosphorised paper)	80	60	☐ ☐
NI52	20½p ultramarine (phosphorised paper)	4·00	4·00	☐ ☐
NI53	22p blue (phosphorised paper)	1·00	1·10	☐ ☐
NI54	22p yellow-green (phosphorised paper)	1·00	1·10	☐ ☐
NI55	22p bright orange-red (phosphorised paper)	1·00	70	☐ ☐
NI56	23p bright green (phosphorised paper)	1·00	1·10	☐ ☐
NI57	24p Indian red (phosphorised paper)	1·00	1·10	☐ ☐
NI58	24p chestnut (phosphorised paper)	80	60	☐ ☐
NI59	24p chestnut (2 bands)	1·00	1·00	☐ ☐

NI60	26p rosine (phosphorised paper)	1·00	1·25	☐	☐
	a. Perf 15 × 14	2·00	2·00	☐	☐
NI61	26p drab (phosphorised paper)	1·00	80	☐	☐
NI62	28p deep violet-blue (phosphorised paper)	1·00	1·00	☐	☐
	a. Perf 15 × 14	1·00	1·00	☐	☐
NI63	28p deep bluish grey (phosphorised paper)	1·00	1·00	☐	☐
NI64	31p bright purple (phosphorised paper)	1·25	1·25	☐	☐
NI65	32p greenish blue (phosphorised paper)	1·10	1·10	☐	☐
NI66	34p deep bluish grey (phosphorised paper)	1·25	1·25	☐	☐
NI67	37p rosine (phosphorised paper)	1·25	1·25	☐	☐
NI68	39p bright mauve (phosphorised paper)	1·25	1·25	☐	☐

Presentation Pack (*contains* 2½p (NI12), 3p (NI13), 5p (NI18), 7½p (NI23)) .. .. 4·00 ☐

Presentation Pack (*contains* 3p (NI14), 3½p (NI15), 5½p (NI19), 8p (NI24) *later with* 4½p (NI17) *added*) .. .. 2·25 ☐

Presentation Pack (*contains* 6½p (NI21), 8½p (NI25). 10p (NI27), 11p (NI30)) .. 1·75 ☐

Presentation Pack (*contains* 7p (NI22), 9p (NI26), 10½p (NI29), 11½p (NI34), 12p (NI31), 13½p (NI32), 14p (NI38), 15p (NI33), 18p (NI45), 22p (NI53)) .. .. 7·00 ☐

Presentation Pack (*contains* 10p (NI28), 12½p (NI36), 16p (NI42), 20½p (NI52), 26p (NI60), 28p (NI62)) .. .. 7·00 ☐

Presentation Pack (*contains* 10p (NI28), 13p (NI37), 16p (NI42a), 17p (NI43), 22p (NI54), 26p (NI60), 28p (NI62), 31p (NI64)) .. .. 11·00 ☐

Presentation Pack (*contains* 12p (NI35), 13p (NI37), 17p (NI43), 18p (NI46) 22p (NI54), 26p (NI60a), 28p (NI62a), 31p (NI64)) .. .. 7·00 ☐

Presentation Pack (*contains* 14p, 19p, 23p, 32p *from Northern Ireland, Scotland and Wales* (*Nos.* NI39, NI49, NI56, NI65, S54, S62, S67, S77, W40, W50, W57, W66)) 7·50 ☐

Presentation Pack (*contains* 15p, 20p, 24p, 34p *from Northern Ireland, Scotland and Wales* (*Nos.* NI40, NI51, NI57, NI66, S56, S64, S69, S78, W41, W52, W58, W67)) 7·50 ☐

Presentation Pack (*contains* 17p, 22p, 26p, 37p *from Northern Ireland, Scotland and Wales* (*Nos.* NI44, NI55, NI61, NI67, S58, S66, S73, S79, W45, W56, W62, W68)) 7·50 ☐

Presentation Pack (*contains* 18p, 24p, 28p, 39p *from Northern Ireland, Scotland and Wales* (*Nos.* NI47, NI58, NI63, NI68, S60, S70, S75, S80, W48, W59, W64, W69)) 5·50 ☐

Nos. NI48 and NI59 come from booklets.

1993 (7 Dec.)-**96** *Perf* 15 × 14 (*with one elliptical hole on each vertical side*)

NI69	N 4	19p bistre (1 centre band)	30	35	☐ ☐
NI70c		19p bistre (1 side band)	30	35	☐ ☐
NI71		20p bright green (1 centre band)	30	35	☐ ☐
NI72		25p red (2 bands)	40	45	☐ ☐
NI73		26p red-brown (2 bands)	40	45	☐ ☐
NI74		30p deep olive-grey (2 bands)	45	50	☐ ☐
NI75		37p bright mauve (2 bands)	60	65	☐ ☐
NI76		41p grey-brown (2 bands)	65	70	☐ ☐
NI77		63p light emerald (2 bands)	95	1·00	☐ ☐

Presentation Pack (*contains* 19p, 25p, 30p, 41p *from Northern Ireland, Scotland and Wales* (*Nos.* NI69, NI72, NI74, NI76, S81, S84, S86, S88, W70, W73, W75, W77) 6·00 ☐

Presentation Pack (*contains* 20p, 26p, 37p, 63p *from Northern Ireland, Scotland and Wales* (*Nos.* NI71, NI73, NI75, NI77, S83, S85, S87, S89, W72, W74, W76, W78) 7·00 ☐

No. NI70c was only issued in booklets. It exists with phosphor band at the left or right of the stamp.

2 Scotland

S 1   S 2   S 3   S 4

1958–67

S1	S 1	3d lilac	20	15	☐	☐
		p Two phosphor bands	12·00	1·00	☐	☐
		pa One side band	20	25	☐	☐
		pb One centre band	20	15	☐	☐
S2		4d blue	20	10	☐	☐
		p Two phosphor bands	20	20	☐	☐
S3	S 2	6d purple	20	15	☐	☐
		p Two phosphor bands	20	25	☐	☐
S4		9d bronze-green (2 phosphor bands)	30	30	☐	☐
S5	S 3	1s 3d green	30	30	☐	☐
		p Two phosphor bands	30	30	☐	☐
S6		1s 6d blue (2 phosphor bands)	35	30	☐	☐

No. S1pa exists with the phosphor band at the left or right of the stamp.

1967–70 One centre phosphor band (Nos. S7, S9/10) or two phosphor bands (others) No wmk

S7	S 1	3d lilac	10	15	☐	☐
S8		4d blue	10	15	☐	☐
S9		4d sepia	10	10	☐	☐
S10		4d vermilion	10	10	☐	☐
S11		5d blue	20	10	☐	☐
S12	S 2	9d bronze-green	5·00	6·00	☐	☐
S13	S 3	1s 6d blue	1·40	1·00	☐	☐
		Presentation Pack (containing Nos. S3, S5p, S7, S9/13)	10·00		☐	

Decimal Currency

1971–93 Type S 4. No wmk

(a) Printed in photogravure by Harrison and Sons with phosphor bands. Perf 15 × 14.

S14	2½p magenta (1 centre band)	25	15	☐	☐
S15	3p ultramarine (2 bands)	30	15	☐	☐
S16	3p ultramarine (1 centre band)	15	15	☐	☐
S17	3½p olive-grey (2 bands)	20	20	☐	☐
S18	3½p ol-grey (1 centre band)	20	20	☐	☐
S19	4½p grey-blue (2 bands)	25	20	☐	☐
S20	5p violet (2 bands)	1·00	1·00	☐	☐
S21	5½p violet (2 bands)	20	20	☐	☐
S22	5½p violet (1 centre band)	20	20	☐	☐
S23	6½p blue (1 centre band)	20	20	☐	☐

S24	7p brown (1 centre band)	25	25	☐ ☐
S25	7½p chestnut (2 bands)	1·25	1·25	☐ ☐
S26	8p rosine (2 bands)	30	40	☐ ☐
S27	8½p yellow-green (2 bands)	30	30	☐ ☐
S28	9p violet (2 bands)	30	30	☐ ☐
S29	10p orange-brown (2 bands)	35	30	☐ ☐
S30	10p orange-brown (1 centre band)	35	35	☐ ☐
S31	10½p blue (2 bands)	45	35	☐ ☐
S32	11p scarlet (2 bands)	45	35	☐ ☐

(b) Printed in photogravure by Harrison and Sons on phosphorised paper. Perf 15 × 14.

S33	12p yellowish green	50	30	☐ ☐
S34	13½p purple-brown	70	65	☐ ☐
S35	15p ultramarine	60	45	☐ ☐

(c) Printed in lithography by John Waddington. One side phosphor band (11½p, 12p, 12½p, 13p) or phosphorised paper (others). Perf 14

S36	11½p drab	80	60	☐ ☐
S37	12p bright emerald	1·50	1·25	☐ ☐
S38	12½p light emerald	60	40	☐ ☐
S39	13p pale chestnut	70	40	☐ ☐
S40	14p grey-blue	60	50	☐ ☐
S41	15½p pale violet	70	65	☐ ☐
S42	16p drab	70	45	☐ ☐
S43	17p grey-blue	3·25	2·00	☐ ☐
S44	18p deep violet	80	80	☐ ☐
S45	19½p olive-grey	1·75	1·75	☐ ☐
S46	20½p ultramarine	4·00	4·00	☐ ☐
S47	22p blue	80	1·10	☐ ☐
S48	22p yellow-green	2·25	1·75	☐ ☐
S49	26p rosine	1·00	1·25	☐ ☐
S50	28p deep violet-blue	1·00	1·00	☐ ☐
S51	31p bright purple	1·75	1·50	☐ ☐

(d) Printed in lithography by Questa. Perf 15 × 14

S52	12p brt emer (1 side band)	1·75	1·50	☐ ☐
S53	13p pale chest (1 side band)	70	40	☐ ☐
S54	14p dp blue (1 centre band)	40	40	☐ ☐
S55	14p deep blue (1 side band)	80	1·00	☐ ☐
S56	15p bright blue (1 centre band)	70	40	☐ ☐
S57	17p grey-blue (phosphorised paper)	4·25	2·75	☐ ☐
S58	17p dp blue (1 centre band)	60	50	☐ ☐
S59	18p olive-grey (phosphorised paper)	80	80	☐ ☐
S60	18p brt green (1 centre band)	70	55	☐ ☐
	a. Perf 14	70	60	☐ ☐
S61	18p brt grn (1 side band)	1·00	1·00	☐ ☐
S62	19p bright orange-red (phosphorised paper)	70	55	☐ ☐
S63	19p brt orange-red (2 bands)	1·50	1·50	☐ ☐
S64	20p brownish black (phosphorised paper)	70	50	☐ ☐
S65	22p yell-grn (phosphorised paper)	80	80	☐ ☐
S66	22p bright orange-red (phosphorised paper)	1·00	50	☐ ☐
S67	23p brt green (phosphorised paper)	1·00	1·10	☐ ☐
S68	23p bright green (2 bands)	11·00	12·00	☐ ☐

S69	24p Indian red (phosphorised paper)	85	85	□ □
S70	24p chestnut (phosphorised paper)	75	75	□ □
	a Perf 14	1·25	1·00	□ □
S71	24p chestnut (2 bands)	1·00	1·00	□ □
S72	26p rosine (phosphorised paper)	2·00	2·25	□ □
S73	26p drab (phosphorised paper)	90	90	□ □
S74	28p deep violet-blue (phosphorised paper)	1·00	1·00	□ □
S75	28p deep bluish grey (phosphorised paper)	1·00	1·00	□ □
	a. Perf 14	1·25	1·25	□ □
S76	31p bright purple (phosphorised paper)	1·50	1·50	□ □
S77	32p greenish blue (phosphorised paper)	1·10	1·00	□ □
S78	34p deep bluish grey (phosphorised paper)	1·25	1·25	□ □
S79	37p rosine (phosphorised paper)	1·25	1·25	□ □
S80	39p bright mauve (phosphorised paper)	1·25	1·25	□ □
	a. Perf 14	2·00	1·75	□ □

Presentation Pack (contains 2½p (S14), 3p (S15), 5p (S20), 7½p (S25))	4·00		□
Presentation Pack (contains 3p (S16), 3½p (S17), 5½p (S21), 8p (S26) later with 4½p (S19) added)	2·25		□
Presentation Pack (contains 6½p (S23), 8½p (S27), 10p (S29), 11p (S32))	1·75		□
Presentation Pack (contains 7p (S24), 9p (S28), 10½p (S31), 11½p (S36), 12p (S33), 13½p (S34), 14p (S40), 15p (S35), 18p (S44), 22p (S47))	7·00		□
Presentation Pack (contains 10p (S30), 12½p (S38), 16p (S42), 20½p (S46), 26p (S49), 28p (S50))	7·50		□
Presentation Pack (contains 10p (S30), 13p (S39), 16p (S42), 17p (S43), 22p (S48), 26p (S49), 28p (S50), 31p (S51))	9·50		□
Presentation Pack (contains 12p (S52), 13p (S53), 17p (S57), 18p (S59), 22p (S65), 26p (S72), 28p (S74), 31p (S76))	7·00		□

Nos. S55, S61, S63, S68 and S71 come from booklets.
For combined packs containing values from all three Regions see under Northern Ireland.

1993 (7 Dec)–**96** *Perf* 15 × 14 (*with one elliptical hole on each vertical side*)

S81	S 4	19p bistre (1 centre band)	30	35	□ □
S82		19p bistre (1 side band)	1·25	1·25	□ □
S83		20p brt green (1 centre band)	30	35	□ □
S84		25p red (2 bands)	40	45	□ □
S85		26p red-brn (2 bands)	40	45	□ □
S86		30p deep olive-grey (2 bands)	45	50	□ □
S87		37p bright mauve (2 bands)	60	65	□ □
S88		41p grey-brown (2 bands)	65	70	□ □
S89		63p light emerald (2 bands)	95	1·00	□ □

No. S82 was only issued in booklets.
For combined presentation packs for all three Regions, see under Northern Ireland.

3 Wales and Monmouthshire

W 1	W 2	W 3	W 4

1958–67

W1	W 1	3d	lilac	20	10		
		p.	One centre phosphor band	20	15		
W2		4d	blue	20	15		
		p.	Two phosphor bands	20	15		
W3	W 2	6d	purple	40	20		
W4		9d	bronze-green (2 phosphor bands)	30	35		
W5	W 3	1s 3d	green	30	30		
W6		1s 6d	blue (2 phosphor bands)	35	40		

1967–69 One centre phosphor band (Nos. W7, W9/10) or two phosphor bands (others). No wmk

W7	W 1	3d	lilac	20	10	□	□
W8		4d	blue	20	10	□	□
W9		4d	sepia	20	10	□	□
W10		4d	vermilion	20	20	□	□
W11		5d	blue	20	10	□	□
W12	W 3	1s 6d	blue	3·00	3·50	□	□
			Presentation Pack (comprises Nos. W4, W6/7, W9/11)	3·50		□	

Decimal Currency

1971–92 Type W 4. No wmk

(a) Printed in photogravure with phosphor bands

W13	2½p magenta (1 centre band)	20	15	□	□
W14	3p ultramarine (2 bands)	25	15	□	□
W15	3p ultramarine (1 centre band)	20	20	□	□
W16	3½p olive-grey (2 bands)	20	25	□	□
W17	3½p olive-grey (1 centre band)	20	25	□	□
W18	4½p grey-blue (2 bands)	25	20	□	□
W19	5p violet (2 bands)	1·00	1·00	□	□
W20	5½p violet (2 bands)	20	25	□	□
W21	5½p violet (1 centre band)	20	25	□	□
W22	6½p blue (1 centre band)	20	20	□	□
W23	7p brown (1 centre band)	25	25	□	□
W24	7½p chestnut (2 bands)	1·25	1·50	□	□
W25	8p rosine (2 bands)	30	30	□	□
W26	8½p yellow-green (2 bands)	30	30	□	□
W27	9p violet (2 bands)	30	30	□	□
W28	10p orange-brown (2 bands)	35	30	□	□
W29	10p orange-brown (1 centre band)	35	30	□	□
W30	10½p blue (2 bands)	40	35	□	□
W31	11p scarlet (2 bands)	40	45	□	□

(b) Printed in photogravure on phosphorised paper

W32	12p yellow-green	50	45	□	□
W33	13½p purple-brown	60	70	□	□
W34	15p ultramarine	60	50	□	□

(c) Printed in lithography. Perf 14 (11½p, 12½p, 14p (No. W39), 15½p, 16p, 18p (No. W46), 19½p, 20½p, 22p (No. W54), 26p (No. W61), 28p (No. W63)) or 15 × 14 (others)

W35	11½p drab (1 side band)	85	60	□	□
W36	12p brt emer (1 side band)	1·25	1·10	□	□
W37	12½p light emer (1 side band)	80	60	□	□
	a. Perf 15 × 14	6·00	6·00	□	□
W38	13p pale chest (1 side band)	50	35	□	□
W39	14p grey-blue (phosphorised paper)	65	50	□	□
W40	14p dp blue (1 centre band)	55	50	□	□
W41	15p brt blue (1 centre band)	50	50	□	□
W42	15½p pale violet (phosphorised paper)	80	65	□	□
W43	16p drab (phosphorised paper)	1·50	1·25	□	□
	a. Perf 15 × 14	1·60	1·25	□	□
W44	17p grey-blue (phosphorised paper)	80	55	□	□
W45	17p deep blue (1 centre band)	60	45	□	□
W46	18p deep violet (phosphorised paper)	80	75	□	□
W47	18p olive-grey (phosphorised paper)	80	60	□	□
W48	18p brt grn (1 centre band)	45	45	□	□
	b. Perf 14	1·00	85	□	□
W49	18p brt green (1 side band)	1·00	1·00	□	□
W50	19p bright orange-red (phosphorised paper)	75	45	□	□
W51	19½p olive-grey (phosphorised paper)	2·00	2·00	□	□
W52	20p brownish black (phosphorised paper)	75	75	□	□
W53	20½p ultramarine (phosphorised paper)	4·00	4·00	□	□
W54	22p blue (phosphorised paper)	1·00	1·00	□	□
W55	22p yell-green (phosphorised paper)	80	1·10	□	□
W56	22p bright orange-red (phosphorised paper)	60	50	□	□
W57	23p brt green (phosphorised paper)	80	1·10	□	□
W58	24p Indian red (phosphorised paper)	70	1·10	□	□
W59	24p chestnut (phosphorised paper)	75	75	□	□
	b. Perf 14	1·00	45	□	□
W60	24p chestnut (2 bands)	1·00	1·00	□	□

W61	26p rosine (phosphorised paper)	1·00	1·25	☐	☐
	a. *Perf* 15 × 14	4·50	4·75	☐	☐
W62	26p drab (phosphorised paper)	85	85	☐	☐
W63	28p dp viol-blue (phosphorised paper)	1·00	1·10	☐	☐
	a. *Perf* 15 × 14	1·00	1·00	☐	☐
W64	28p deep bluish grey (phosphorised paper)	1·00	1·00	☐	☐
W65	31p brt purple (phosphorised paper)	1·10	1·10	☐	☐
W66	32p greenish blue (phosphorised paper)	1·10	1·10	☐	☐
W67	34p deep bluish grey (phosphorised paper)	1·00	1·25	☐	☐
W68	37p rosine (phosphorised paper)	1·00	1·25	☐	☐
W69	39p bright mauve (phosphorised paper)	1·00	1·25	☐	☐

Presentation Pack (*contains* 2½p (W13), 3p (W14), 5p (W19), 7½p (W24))	4·00	☐
Presentation Pack (*contains* 3p (W15), 3½p (W16), 5½p (W20), 8p (W25), *later with* 4½p (W18) *added*)	2·25	☐
Presentation Pack (*contains* 6½p (W22), 8½p (W26), 10p (W28), 11p (W31))	1·75	☐
Presentation Pack (*contains* 7p (W23), 9p (W27), 10½p (W30), 11½p (W35), 12p (W32), 13½p (W33), 14p (W39), 15p (W34), 18p (W46), 22p (W53))	7·00	☐
Presentation Pack (*contains* 10p (W29), 12½p (W37), 16p (W43), 20½p (W53), 26p (W61), 28p (W63))	7·50	☐
Presentation Pack (*contains* 10p (W29), 13p (W38), 16p (W43*a*), 17p (W44), 22p (W55), 26p (W61), 28p (W63), 31p (W65))	9·50	☐
Presentation Pack (*contains* 12p (W36), 13p (W38), 17p (W44), 18p (W47), 22p (W55), 26p (W61*a*), 28p (W63*a*), 31p (W65))	9·50	☐

Nos. W49 and W60 come from booklets. The former exists with the phosphor band at the left or the right of the stamp.
For combined packs containing values from all three Regions see under Northern Ireland.

1993 (7 DEC.)–**96** *Perf* 15 × 14 (*with one elliptical hole on each vertical side*)

W70	W 4	19p bistre (1 centre band)	30	35	☐	☐
W71		19p bistre (1 side band)	1·25	1·25	☐	☐
W72		20p brt green (1 centre band)	30	35	☐	☐
W73		25p red (2 bands)	40	45	☐	☐
W74		26p red-brn (2 bands)	40	45	☐	☐
W75		30p deep olive-grey (2 bands)	45	50	☐	☐
W76		37p bright mauve (2 bands)	60	65	☐	☐
W77		41p grey-brown (2 bands)	65	70	☐	☐
W78		63p light emerald (2 bands)	95	1·00	☐	☐

No. W71 was only issued in booklets.
For combined presentation packs for all three Regions see under Northern Ireland.

ISLE OF MAN

Regional Issues

1   2   3

1958–67 *Wmk* **179** *Perf* 15 × 14

1	**1**	2½d red		45	80 ☐ ☐
2	**2**	3d lilac		20	10 ☐ ☐
		p. One centre phosphor band		20	40 ☐ ☐
3		4d blue		1·50	1·10 ☐ ☐
		p. Two phosphor bands		20	25 ☐ ☐

1968–69 *One centre phosphor band (Nos. 5/6) or two phosphor bands (others). No wmk*

4	**2**	4d blue	20	25 ☐ ☐
5		4d sepia	20	30 ☐ ☐
6		4d vermilion	45	60 ☐ ☐
7		5d blue	45	60 ☐ ☐

Decimal Currency

1971 (7 JULY) *One centre phosphor band (2½p) or two phosphor bands (others). No wmk*

8	**3**	2½p magenta	20	15 ☐ ☐
9		3p ultramarine	20	15 ☐ ☐
10		5p violet	40	50 ☐ ☐
11		7½p chestnut	40	65 ☐ ☐
		Presentation Pack	2·00	☐

For comprehensive listings of the Independent Administration issues of the Isle of Man, see Stanley Gibbons *Collect Channel Islands and Isle of Man Stamps.*

CHANNEL ISLANDS
1 General Issue

C 1 Gathering Vraic C 2 Islanders gathering Vraic

Third Anniversary of Liberation

1948 (10 MAY) *Wmk Type* **127** *Perf* 15 × 14

C1	C **1**	1d red		20	20 ☐ ☐
C2	C **2**	2½d blue		30	30 ☐ ☐
		First Day Cover			24·00 ☐

2 Guernsey

(a) War Occupation Issues

Stamps issued under British authority during the German Occupation.

1   2   3

1941–44 *Rouletted.* (a) *White paper. No wmk*

1f	**1**	½d green		2·50	2·25 ☐ ☐
2		1d red		2·00	1·00 ☐ ☐
3		2½d blue		4·00	4·00 ☐ ☐

(b) *Bluish French bank-note paper. Wmk loops*

4	**1**	½d green		18·00	19·00 ☐ ☐
5		1d red		8·50	21·00 ☐ ☐

(b) Regional Issues

1958–67 *Wmk* **179** *Perf* 15 × 14

6	**2**	2½d red		35	40 ☐ ☐
7	**3**	3d lilac		35	30 ☐ ☐
		p. One centre phosphor band		20	20 ☐ ☐
8		4d blue		25	30 ☐ ☐
		p. Two phosphor bands		20	20 ☐ ☐

1968–69 *One centre phosphor band (Nos 10/11) or two phosphor bands (others). No wmk*

9	**3**	4d blue	10	25 ☐ ☐
10		4d sepia	15	20 ☐ ☐
11		4d vermilion	15	30 ☐ ☐
12		5d blue	15	30 ☐ ☐

For comprehensive listings of the Independent Postal Administration issues of Guernsey, see Stanley Gibbons *Collect Channel Islands and Isle of Man Stamps.*

3 Jersey

(a) War Occupation Issues

Stamps issued under British authority during the German Occupation.

1 2 Old Jersey Farm 3 Portelet Bay

4 Corbière Lighthouse

5 Elizabeth Castle

6 Mont Orgueil Castle

7 Gathering Vraic (seaweed)

1941–42 *White paper No wmk   Perf* 11

1	1	½d green	..	3·75	3·00	☐ ☐
2		1d red	..	4·00	3·00	☐ ☐

1943 *No wmk   Perf* 13½

3	2	½d green	..	6·00	5·50	☐ ☐
4	3	1d red	..	1·50	75	☐ ☐
5	4	1½d brown	..	3·00	3·00	☐ ☐
6	5	2d orange	..	4·00	3·00	☐ ☐
7a	6	2½d blue	..	1·00	1·50	☐ ☐
8	7	3d violet	..	1·00	2·75	☐ ☐
		Set of 6	..	15·00	15·00	☐ ☐

(b) Regional Issues

8

9

1958–67 *Wmk* 179   *Perf* 15 × 14

9	8	2½d red	..	35	50	☐ ☐
10	9	3d lilac	..	35	30	☐ ☐
		p One centre phospnor band		20	20	☐ ☐
11		4d blue	..	25	30	☐ ☐
		p Two phosphor bands		20	25	☐ ☐

1968–69 *One centre phosphor band* (4d *values*) *or two phosphor bands* (5d) *No wmk*

12	9	4d sepia	..	20	25	☐ ☐
13		4d vermilion		20	30	☐ ☐
14		5d blue	..	20	40	☐ ☐

For comprehensive listings of the Independent Postal Administration issues of Jersey, see Stanley Gibbons *Collect Channel Islands and Isle of Man Stamps.*

REGIONAL FIRST DAY COVERS

PRICES for First Day Covers listed below are for stamps, as indicated, used on illustrated envelopes and postmarked with operational cancellations (before 1964) or with special First Day of Issue cancellations (1964 onwards). First Day postmarks of 8 June 1964 and 7 February 1966 were of the machine cancellation "envelope" type.

£sd Issues

18 Aug. 1958	*Guernsey 3d (No. 7)*	11·00	☐
	Isle of Man 3d (No. 2) ..	22·00	☐
	Jersey 3d (No. 10) ..	11·00	☐
	Northern Ireland 3d (No. NI1)	22·00	☐
	Scotland 3d (No. S1)	8·00	☐
	Wales 3d (No. W1)	8·00	☐
29 Sept. 1958	*Northern Ireland 6d, 1s 3d (Nos. NI3, NI5)*	28·00	☐
	Scotland 6d, 1s 3d (Nos S3, S5)	16·00	☐
	Wales 6d, 1s 3d (Nos. W3, W5)	16·00	☐
8 June 1964	*Guernsey 2½d (No. 6)*	18·00	☐
	Isle of Man 2½d (No. 1) ..	22·00	☐
	Jersey 2½d (No. 9)	18·00	☐
7 Feb. 1966	*Guernsey 4d (No. 8)*	8·00	☐
	Isle of Man 4d (No. 3) ..	8·00	☐
	Jersey 4d (No. 11)	8·00	☐
	Northern Ireland 4d (No. NI2)	6·00	☐
	Scotland 4d (No. S2)	7·00	☐
	Wales 4d (No. W2)	6·00	☐
1 March 1967	*Northern Ireland 9d, 1s 6d (Nos. NI4, NI6)*	2·00	☐
	Scotland 9d, 1s 6d (Nos. S4, S6)	2·00	☐
	Wales 9d, 1s 6d (Nos. W4, W6)	1·75	☐
4 Sept. 1968	*Guernsey 4d, 5d (Nos. 10, 12)*	1·00	☐
	Isle of Man 4d, 5d (Nos. 5, 7)	2·00	☐
	Jersey 4d, 5d (Nos. 12, 14) ..	1·25	☐
	Northern Ireland 4d, 5d (Nos. NI8, NI10)	1·00	☐
	Scotland 4d, 5d (Nos. S9, S11)	1·00	☐
	Wales 4d, 5d (Nos. W9, W11)	1·00	☐

Decimal Issues

7 July 1971	*Isle of Man 2½p, 3p, 5p, 7½p (Nos. 8/11)*	2·50	☐
	Northern Ireland 2½p, 3p, 5p, 7½p (Nos. NI12/13, NI18, NI23)	2·50	☐
	Scotland 2½p, 3p, 5p, 7½p (Nos. S14/15, S20, S25)	2·50	☐
	Wales 2½p, 3p, 5p, 7½p (Nos. W13/14, W19, W24)	2·50	☐
23 Jan. 1974	*Northern Ireland 3p, 3½p, 5½p, 8p (Nos. NI14/15, NI19, NI24)*	1·50	☐
	Scotland 3p, 3½p, 5½p, 8p (Nos. S16/17, S21, S26)	1·50	☐
	Wales 3p, 3½p, 5½p, 8p (Nos. W15/16, W20, W25)	1·50	☐

6 Nov. 1974	*Northern Ireland* 4½p, (*No.* NI17)	1·00 ☐	
	Scotland 4½p (*No.* S19) ..	1·00 ☐	
	Wales 4½p (*No.* W18) ..	1·00 ☐	
14 Jan. 1976	*Northern Ireland* 6½p, 8½p (*Nos.* NI21, NI25)	70 ☐	
	Scotland 6½p, 8½p (*Nos.* S23, S27)	70 ☐	
	Wales 6½p, 8½p (*Nos.* W22, W26) ..	70 ☐	
20 Oct. 1976	*Northern Ireland* 10p, 11p (*Nos.* NI27, NI30)	1·00 ☐	
	Scotland 10p, 11p (*Nos.* S29, S32)	1·00 ☐	
	Wales 10p, 11p (*Nos.* W28, W31)	1·00 ☐	
18 Jan. 1978	*Northern Ireland* 7p, 9p, 10½p (*Nos.* NI22, NI26, NI29)	1·25 ☐	
	Scotland 7p, 9p, 10½p (*Nos.* S24, S28, S31)	1·25 ☐	
	Wales 7p, 9p, 10½p (*Nos.* W23, W27, W30)	1·25 ☐	
23 July 1980	*Northern Ireland* 12p, 13½p, 15p (*Nos.* NI31/3)	2·00 ☐	
	Scotland 12p, 13½p, 15p (*Nos.* S33/5)	2·00 ☐	
	Wales 12p, 13½p, 15p (*Nos.* W32/4)	2·00 ☐	
8 April 1981	*Northern Ireland* 11½p, 14p, 18p, 22p (*Nos.* NI34, NI38, NI45, NI53) ..	2·00 ☐	
	Scotland 11½p, 14p, 18p, 22p (*Nos.* S36, S40, S44, S47) ..	2·00 ☐	
	Wales 11½p, 14p, 18p, 22p (*Nos.* W35, W39, W46, W54)	2·00 ☐	
24 Feb. 1982	*Northern Ireland* 12½p, 15½p, 19½p, 26p (*Nos.* NI36, NI41, NI50, NI60)	2·50 ☐	
	Scotland 12½p, 15½p, 19½p, 26p (*Nos.* S38, S41, S45, S49)	2·50 ☐	
	Wales 12½p, 15½p, 19½p, 26p (*Nos.* W37, W42, W51, W61)	2·50 ☐	
27 April 1983	*Northern Ireland* 16p, 20½p, 28p (*Nos.* NI42, NI52, NI62)	3·50 ☐	
	Scotland 16p, 20½p, 28p (*Nos.* S42, S46, S50)	3·50 ☐	
	Wales 16p, 20½p, 28p (*Nos.* W43, W53, W63	3·50 ☐	
23 Oct. 1984	*Northern Ireland* 13p, 17p, 22p, 31p (*Nos.* NI37, NI43, NI54, NI64)	2·50 ☐	
	Scotland 13p, 17p, 22p, 31p (*Nos.* S39, S43, S48, S51) ..	2·50 ☐	
	Wales 13p, 17p, 22p, 31p (*Nos.* W38, W44, W55, W65)	2·50 ☐	
7 Jan. 1986	*Northern Ireland* 12p (*No.* NI35)	1·25 ☐	
	Scotland 12p (*No.* S37) ..	1·25 ☐	
	Wales 12p (*No.* W36)	1·25 ☐	
6 Jan. 1987	*Northern Ireland* 18p (*No.* NI46)	1·50 ☐	
	Scotland 18p (*No.* S59)	1·50 ☐	
	Wales 18p (*No.* W47)	1·50 ☐	
8 Nov. 1988	*Northern Ireland* 14p, 19p, 23p, 32p (*Nos.* NI39, NI49, NI56, NI65)	1·75 ☐	
	Scotland 14p, 19p, 23p, 32p (*Nos.* S54, S62, S67, S77)	1·75 ☐	
	Wales 14p, 19p, 23p, 32p (*Nos.* W40, W50, W57, W66)	1·75 ☐	
28 Nov. 1989	*Northern Ireland* 15p, 20p, 24p, 34p (*Nos.* NI40, NI51, NI57, NI66)	2·25 ☐	
	Scotland 15p, 20p, 24p, 34p (*Nos.* S56, S64, S69, S78)	2·25 ☐	
	Wales 15p, 20p, 24p, 34p (*Nos.* W41, W52, W58, W67)	2·25 ☐	
4 Dec. 1990	*Northern Ireland* 17p, 22p, 26p, 37p (*Nos.* NI44, NI55, NI61, NI67)	3·25 ☐	
	Scotland 17p, 22p, 26p, 37p (*Nos.* S58, S66, S73, S79)	3·25 ☐	
	Wales 17p, 22p, 26p, 37p (*Nos.* W45, W56, W62, W68)	3·25 ☐	
3 Dec. 1991	*Northern Ireland* 18p, 24p, 28p, 39p (*Nos.* NI47, NI58, NI63, NI68)	3·25 ☐	
	Scotland 18p, 24p, 28p, 39p (*Nos.* S60, S70, S75, S80)	3·25 ☐	
	Wales 18p, 24p, 28p, 39p (*Nos.* W48, W59, W64, W69)	3·25 ☐	
7 Dec. 1993	*Northern Ireland* 19p, 25p, 30p, 41p (*Nos.* NI69, NI72, NI74, NI76	2·50 ☐	
	Scotland 19p, 25p, 30p, 41p (*Nos.* S81, S84, S86, S88) ..	2·50 ☐	
	Wales 19p, 25p, 30p, 41p (*Nos.* W70, W73, W75, W77)	2·50 ☐	
23 July 1996	*Northern Ireland* 20p, 26p, 37p, 63p (*Nos.* NI71, NI73, NI75, NI77)	3·25 ☐	
	Scotland 20p, 26p, 37p, 63p (*Nos.* S83, S85, S87, S89) ..	3·25 ☐	
	Wales 20p, 26p, 37p, 63p (*Nos.* W72, W74, W76, W78)	3·25 ☐	

POSTAGE DUE STAMPS

PERFORATION. All postage due stamps are perf 14 × 15

D 1   D 2

1914–22 *Wmk Type* **96** (*Royal Cypher* (*'Simple'*)) *sideway*

D1	D 1	½d green	..	..	50	50	□
D2		1d red ..	..	..	50	50	□
D3		1½d brown	..	..	40·00	18·00	□
D4		2d black	..	..	50	70	□
D5		3d violet	..	..	2·50	1·00	□
D6		4d green	..		25·00	4·00	□
D7		5d brown	..	..	5·00	3·25	□
D8		1s blue	..	..	28·00	3·75	□
	Set of 8	..	..	..	90·00	28·00	□

1924–31 *Wmk Type* **107** (*Block* G v R) *sideways*

D10	D 1	½d green	..	..	90	75	□
D11		1d red ..	..	..	60	60	□
D12		1½d brown	..	..	40·00	18·00	□
D13		2d black	..	..	1·00	40	□
D14		3d violet	..	..	1·50	40	□
D15		4d green	..	..	13·00	3·00	□
D16		5d brown	..	..	29·00	24·00	□
D17		1s blue	..	.	8·50	75	□
D18	D 2	2s 6d purple/*yellow*	..		40·00	2·00	□
	Set of 9 ..	..	..	..	£120	45·00	□

1936–37 *Wmk Type* **125** (E 8 R) *sideways*

D19	D 1	½d green	..	..	7·50	7·00	□
D20		1d red ..	..	..	1·50	1·50	□
D21		2d black	..	..	7·00	9·00	□
D22		3d violet	..	..	1·50	1·60	□
D23		4d green	..	..	23·00	23·00	□
D24a		5d brown	..	..	16·00	21·00	□
D25		1s blue	..	..	11·00	7·00	□
D26	D 2	2s 6d purple/*yellow*	..		£250	8·00	□
	Set of 8 ..	..	..	..	£300	70·00	□

1937–38 *Wmk Type* **127** (G vi R) *sideways*

D27	D 1	½d green	..	..	8·00	4·50	□
D28		1d red ..	..	..	2·50	50	□
D29		2d black	..	..	2·50	50	□
D30		3d violet	..	..	12·00	90	□
D31		4d green	..	..	65·00	10·00	□
D32		5d brown	..	..	12·00	1·50	□
D33		1s blue	..	..	60·00	1·50	□
D34	D 2	2s 6d purple/*yellow*	..		60·00	2·50	□
	Set of 8 ..	..		..	£200	19·00	□

1951–52 *Colours changed and new value* (1½d) *Wmk Ty*
127 (G vi R) *sideways*

D35	D 1	½d orange	..	..	1·00	2·50	□
D36		1d blue	..	..	1·50	1·25	□
D37		1½d green	..	..	1·75	2·50	□
D38		4d blue	..	..	35·00	13·00	□
D39		1s brown	..	..	28·00	5·50	□
	Set of 5 ..	..	..	..	60·00	22·00	□

1954–55 Wmk Type 153 (Mult. Tudor Crown and E 2 R) sideways

D40	D 1	½d	orange	6·00	4·50 □
D41		2d	black	4·00	4·00 □
D42		3d	violet	50·00	32·00 □
D43		4d	blue	18·00	19·00 □
D44		5d	brown	25·00	9·00 □
D45	D 2	2s 6d	purple/*yellow*	£110	3·50 □
		Set of 6		£190	65·00 □

1955–57 Wmk Type 165 (Mult. St Edward's Crown and E 2 R) sideways

D46	D 1	½d	orange	1·25	2·25 □
D47		1d	blue	5·50	1·50 □
D48		1½d	green	5·50	5·00 □
D49		2d	black	40·00	3·25 □
D50		3d	violet	6·00	1·25 □
D51		4d	blue	21·00	3·75 □
D52		5d	brown	32·00	2·00 □
D53		1s	brown	70·00	2·00 □
D54	D 2	2s 6d	purple/*yellow*	£160	8·00 □
D55		5s	red/*yellow*	90·00	25·00 □
		Set of 10		£375	48·00 □

1959–63 Wmk Type 179 (Mult St Edward's Crown) sideways

D56	D 1	½d	orange	10	1·00 □
D57		1d	blue	10	50 □
D58		1½d	green	90	2·75 □
D59		2d	black	1·25	50 □
D60		3d	violet	40	30 □
D61		4d	blue	40	30 □
D62		5d	brown	45	75 □
D63		6d	purple	60	30 □
D64		1s	brown	1·40	30 □
D65	D 2	2s 6d	purple/*yellow*	4·25	45 □
D66		5s	red/*yellow*	8·00	1·00 □
D67		10s	blue/*yellow*	10·00	5·00 □
D68		£1	black/*yellow*	45·00	8·00 □
		Set of 13		65·00	19·00 □

1968–69 Design size 22½ × 19 mm No wmk

D69	D 1	2d	black	20	60 □
D70		3d	violet	25	60 □
D71		4d	blue	25	60 □
D72		5d	orange-brown	4·50	6·00 □
D73		6d	purple	60	90 □
D74		1s	brown	2·00	1·40 □
		Set of 6		7·00	9·00 □

1968–69 Design size 21½ × 17½ mm No wmk

D75	D 1	4d	blue	5·00	5·00 □
D76		8d	red	1·00	1·00 □

Decimal Currency

1970–77 No wmk

D77	D 3	½p	turquoise-blue	10	20 □ □
D78		1p	reddish purple	10	15 □ □
D79		2p	myrtle-green	10	15 □ □
D80		3p	ultramarine	15	15 □ □
D81		4p	yellow-brown	15	15 □ □
D82		5p	violet	20	20 □ □
D83		7p	red-brown	35	45 □ □
D84	D 4	10p	red	30	20 □ □
D85		11p	green	60	60 □ □
D86		20p	brown	60	50 □ □
D87		50p	ultramarine	1·50	50 □ □
D88		£1	black	3·50	75 □ □
D89		£5	orange-yellow and black	35·00	2·00 □ □
		Set of 13		38·00	5·00 □ □

D77/82, D84, D86/8 *Presentation Pack* 11·00 □
D77/88 *Presentation Pack* 6·00 □

1982 No wmk

D 90	D 5	1p	lake	10	10 □ □
D 91		2p	bright blue	20	10 □ □
D 92		3p	deep mauve	10	15 □ □
D 93		4p	deep blue	10	20 □ □
D 94		5p	sepia	20	20 □ □
D 95	D 6	10p	light brown	20	25 □ □
D 96		20p	olive-green	40	30 □ □
D 97		25p	deep greenish blue	50	70 □ □
D 98		50p	grey-black	1·00	75 □ □
D 99		£1	red	2·00	50 □ □
D100		£2	turquoise-blue	4·50	50 □ □
D101		£5	dull orange	12·00	50 □ □
		Set of 12		19·00	3·75 □ □
		Set of 12 *Gutter Pairs*		40·00	□
		Presentation Pack		20·00	□

D 5   D 6   D 7

1994 (15 Feb.) Perf 15 × 14 (with one elliptical hole on each vertical side)

D102	D 7	1p.	red, yellow and black	10	10 □ □
D103		2p.	magenta, purple and black	10	10 □ □
D104		5p.	yellow, red-brown and black	10	10 □ □
D105		10p.	yellow, emerald and black	15	20 □ □

D 4

D106	D 7	20p.	blue-green, violet and black	30	35	☐	☐
D107		25p.	cerise, rosine and black	40	45	☐	☐
D108		£1	violet, magenta and black	1·50	1·60	☐	☐
D109		£1.20	greenish blue, blue-green and black	1·75	1·90	☐	☐
D110		£5	greenish black, blue-green and black	7·50	7·75	☐	☐
		Set of 9		11·50	12·50	☐	☐
		Presentation Pack		12·50		☐	

ROYAL MAIL POSTAGE LABELS

These imperforate labels were issued as an experiment by the Post Office. Special microprocessor controlled machines were installed at post offices in Cambridge, London, Shirley (Southampton) and Windsor to provide an after-hours sales service to the public. The machines printed and dispensed the labels according to the coins inserted and the buttons operated by the customer. Values were initially available in $\frac{1}{2}$p steps to 16p and in addition, the labels were sold at philatelic counters in two packs containing either 3 values ($3\frac{1}{2}$, $12\frac{1}{2}$, 16p) or 32 values ($\frac{1}{2}$p to 16p).

From 28 August 1984 the machines were adjusted to provide values up to 17p. After 31 December 1984 labels including $\frac{1}{2}$p values were withdrawn. The machines were taken out of service on 30 April 1985.

Machine postage-paid impression in red on phosphorised paper with grey-green background design. No watermark. Imperforate.

1984 (1 May - 28 Aug)

Set of 32 ($\frac{1}{2}$p to 16p)		17·00	25·00	☐ ☐
Set of 3 ($3\frac{1}{2}$p, $12\frac{1}{2}$p, 16p)		3·00	3·50	☐ ☐
Set of 3 on First Day Cover (1 May)			6·50	☐
Set of 2 ($16\frac{1}{2}$p, 17p) (28 August)		4·50	4·50	☐ ☐

OFFICIAL STAMPS

Various Stamps of Queen Victoria and King Edward VII Overprinted in Black.

I.R. OFFICIAL (O 1)	I. R. OFFICIAL (O 2)	O.W. OFFICIAL (O 3)
ARMY OFFICIAL (O 4)	ARMY OFFICIAL (O 5)	GOVᵀ PARCELS (O 7)
BOARD OF EDUCATION (O 8)	R.H. OFFICIAL (O 9)	ADMIRALTY OFFICIAL (O 10)

1 Inland Revenue

Overprinted with Types O 1 or O 2 (5s, 10s, £1)

1882–1901 *Queen Victoria*

O 1	52	$\frac{1}{2}$d	green ..	12·00	3·00	☐	☐
O 5		$\frac{1}{2}$d	blue ..	25·00	15·00	☐	☐
O13	67	$\frac{1}{2}$d	vermilion ..	1·50	50	☐	☐
O17		$\frac{1}{2}$d	green	4·00	3·00	☐	☐
O 3	57	1d	lilac (Die II)	1·50	65	☐	☐
O 6	64	$2\frac{1}{2}$d	lilac	£120	40·00	☐	☐
O14	70	$2\frac{1}{2}$d	purple on blue	50·00	4·00	☐	☐
O 4	43	6d	grey (Plate 18)	75·00	20·00	☐	☐
O18	75	6d	purple on red	£100	22·00	☐	☐
O 7	65	1s	green ..	£2500	£450	☐	☐
O15	78	1s	green ..	£225	25·00	☐	☐
O19		1s	green and red ..	£800	£175	☐	☐
O 9	59	5s	red ..	£1300	£400	☐	☐
O10	60	10s	blue ..	£2500	£525	☐	☐
O11	61	£1	brown (Wmk Crowns)	£20000		☐	☐
O12		£1	brown (Wmk Orbs)	£27500		☐	☐
O16		£1	green	£3750	£500	☐	☐

O20	79	½d blue-green	17·00	1·50	☐ ☐
O21		1d red	10·00	70	☐ ☐
O22	82	2½d blue	£450	90·00	☐ ☐
O23	79	6d purple	£85000	£65000	☐ ☐
O24	89	1s green and red	£550	95·00	☐ ☐
O25	91	5s red	£4000	£1500	☐ ☐
O26	92	10s blue	£15000	£9500	☐ ☐
O27	93	£1 green	£12000	£7000	☐ ☐

2 Office of Works

Overprinted with Type O 3

1896–1902 *Queen Victoria*

O31	67	½d vermilion	90·00	40·00	☐ ☐
O32		½d green	£150	75·00	☐ ☐
O33	57	1d lilac (Die II)	£150	40·00	☐ ☐
O34	74	5d dull pur & bl	£800	£175	☐ ☐
O35	77	10d dull pur & red	£1400	£275	☐ ☐

1902–03 *King Edward VII*

O36	79	½d blue-green	£350	80·00	☐ ☐
O37		1d red	£350	80·00	☐ ☐
O38	81	2d green and red	£600	80·00	☐ ☐
O39	82	2½d blue	£700	£250	☐ ☐
O40	88	10d purple and red	£5000	£1500	☐ ☐

3 Army

Overprinted with Types O 4 (½d, 1d) or O 5 (2½d, 6d)

1896–1901 *Queen Victoria*

O41	67	½d vermilion	1·50	75	☐ ☐
O42		½d green	1·75	4·00	☐ ☐
O43	57	1d lilac (Die II)	1·50	75	☐ ☐
O44	70	2½d purple on blue	4·00	3·00	☐ ☐
O45	75	6d purple on red	16·00	10·00	☐ ☐

Overprinted with Type O 4

1902 *King Edward VII*

O48	79	½d blue-green	2·00	65	☐ ☐
O49		1d red	1·50	55	☐ ☐
O50		6d purple	70·00	32·00	☐ ☐

4 Government Parcels

Overprinted with Type O 7

1883–1900 *Queen Victoria*

O69	57	1d lilac (Die II)	28·00	8·00	☐ ☐
O61	62	1½d lilac	£100	25·00	☐ ☐
O65	68	1½d purple and green	14·00	2·00	☐ ☐
O70	69	2d green and red	45·00	7·00	☐ ☐
O71	73	4½d green and red	£100	75·00	☐ ☐
O62	63	6d green	£800	£275	☐ ☐
O66	75	6d purple on red	28·00	10·00	☐ ☐
O63	64	9d green	£650	£180	☐ ☐
O67	76	9d purple and blue	55·00	15·00	☐ ☐
O64	44	1s brown (Plate 13)	£425	70·00	☐ ☐
O64c		1s brown (Plate 14)	£750	£110	☐ ☐
O68	78	1s green	£120	70·00	☐ ☐
O72		1s green and red	£160	50·00	☐ ☐

1902 *King Edward VII*

O74	79	1d red	17·00	6·00	☐ ☐
O75	81	2d green and red	65·00	18·00	☐ ☐
O76	79	6d purple	£100	18·00	☐ ☐
O77	87	9d purple and blue	£225	50·00	☐ ☐
O78	89	1s green and red	£350	85·00	☐ ☐

5 Board of Education

Overprinted with Type O 8

1902 *Queen Victoria*

O81	74	5d dull pur & bl	£575	£120	☐ ☐
O82	78	1s green and red	£1000	£400	☐ ☐

1902–04 *King Edward VII*

O83	79	½d blue-green	20·00	8·00	☐ ☐
O84		1d red	20·00	7·00	☐ ☐
O85	82	2½d blue	£550	60·00	☐ ☐
O86	85	5d purple and blue	£2250	£1000	☐ ☐
O87	89	1s green and red	£40000	£30000	☐ ☐

6 Royal Household

Overprinted with Type O 9

1902 *King Edward VII*

O91	79	½d blue-green	£150	95·00	☐ ☐
O92		1d red	£130	85·00	☐ ☐

7 Admiralty

Overprinted with Type O 10

1903 *King Edward VII*

O107	79	½d blue-green	9·00	5·00	☐ ☐
O102		1d red	5·00	2·50	☐ ☐
O103	80	1½d purple and green	60·00	45·00	☐ ☐
O104	81	2d green and red	£110	55·00	☐ ☐
O105	82	2½d blue	£130	45·00	☐ ☐
O106	83	3d purple on yellow	£110	40·00	☐ ☐

Minimum Price. The minimum price quoted is 10p. This represents a handling charge rather than a basis for valuing common stamps. Where the actual value of a stamp is less than 10p this may be apparent when set prices are shown, particularly for sets including a number of 10p stamps. It therefore follows that in valuing common stamps the 10p catalogue price should not be reckoned automatically since it covers a variation in real scarcity.

YES OR NO

PLEASE ANSWER

WHICH DO YOU PREFER?

1. SEE STAMPS YOU WANT BEFORE YOU BUY? — YES ☐ NO ☐
2. PERUSING WITHOUT PRESSURE? — YES ☐ NO ☐
3. IN THE COMFORT OF YOUR OWN HOME? — YES ☐ NO ☐
4. WITHOUT OBLIGATION, INTIMIDATION OR EMBARRASSMENT? — YES ☐ NO ☐
5. SERVICE WITH DISCOUNTS OFF CATALOGUE? — YES ☐ NO ☐
6. STOP SERVICE ANYTIME? — YES ☐ NO ☐
7. DISSATISFIED WITH YOUR CURRENT APPROVAL DEALER? — YES ☐ NO ☐

ANSWER YES TO ANY OF THE ABOVE QUESTIONS THEN YOU ARE SUITED TO OUR APPROVAL SERVICE!

SEE FOR YOURSELF WHY OVER 1000 COLLECTORS NOW TAKE AVON APPROVALS

COMPLETE THE COUPON NOW!

APPLICATION FORM ✂

PLUS! UNIQUE £200

It's NEW! £200 Loyalty Bonus Program!

LOYALTY BONUS PROGRAM

OK I'M INTERESTED IN YOUR £200 LOYALTY BONUS PROGRAM. PLEASE SEND ME A SELECTION WITHOUT OBLIGATION TO PURCHASE. I CAN CANCEL ANYTIME.

I COLLECT COUNTRIES/SUBJECTS:

1 ....
2 ....
3 ....
4 ....
5 ....

I COLLECT MINT ☐ & OR USED ☐

IMPORTANT – PLEASE INDICATE ABOVE
I am a serious adult collector willing to spend an average of £12+ per selection. **REFERENCE (or CREDIT CARD NUMBER FOR REF. ONLY):**

....
Expiry Date ....

I will return those stamps not required and pay for the rest within 12 days of receipt

USUAL
SIGNATURE...

Who have you had approvals from

before? ....
FULL INSTRUCTIONS AND STANDARD CONDITIONS SENT WITH EACH SELECTION

NAME: ....

ADDRESS: ....
....
....
.... POSTCODE: ....

TELEPHONE NO: .... CBS

(Access/Visa/Mastercard/Eurocard)

AVON Approvals

MAIL TO: AVON APPROVALS P.O. BOX 29, STROUD, GLOS GL6 6RW

YOU SAVE IN ADDITION TO CATALOGUE DISCOUNTS:
SPEND £16 – SEND £12
SPEND £20 – SEND £15
SPEND £40 – SEND £30 ETC.

EXISTING CLIENTS ENTERED AUTOMATICALLY – THEREFORE PLEASE DO NOT RE-APPLY

AVON STAMPS ADDED VALUE – WE LEAD: OTHERS FOLLOW

ALL THIS* FOR JUST £1

To introduce you to our approvals

* Unmounted mint BE stamps FACE value **£25**
* In single G.B. stamps, catalogue value **£25**
* European top values, catalogue value **£25**
* Stamps of your choice, value **£25**

TOTAL	(You work it out)	**£**

THE R. WARREN APPROVALS SERVICE

The Stamp Shop in your letterbox!

THE R. WARREN APPROVALS SERVICE. The stamp shop that comes through your letterbox! build your collection from the comfort of your own home. **View before your buy.**

£100 VALUE FOR JUST £1.00 P&P. Offer open to everyone - **no obligation to purchase.** What's the catch? Simply that we're confident that you'll want to deal with us again and again

CHECK OUT THE DIFFERENCE. Deal with one of the major approval houses in the world. Founded in the 70's and still in original hands. PTS, ASDA and UDPA members in good standing. Original, reliable, personal service. Differences you'll happily appreciate.

WORLDWIDE STOCKS. Well over 500.000 (yes, five hundred thousand) *individually* priced sets, short sets and singles. We stock it all! Consistently updated with fresh material every week - even your stamps in exchange. Our commitment to philately is long term.

COMPETITIVE PRICES AND GENEROUS DISCOUNTS. Internationally competitive prices *with up to 25% off!* Stay with us for 12 months (nearly everyone does) and we give you a BONUS DISCOUNT up to an extra 5% of *EVERYTHING* you've spent. (Something we've done for years). Naturally, we welcome ALL major cards (probably the first UK approval company to do so). Larger purchases may be spread without charge (we're not without our imitators here either!). It all adds up to *real*, not imaginary value. Can you really afford not to try us?

EVERYONE WELCOME. We can help you - *Whatever your budget*. Young and old. Beginner and specialist. Delivery as quickly (or as slowly!) as you like - with written confirmation. *We don't just "cherry-pick" the best.* Join the countless hundreds of satisfied clients who already know when they are on to a good thing.

TOTAL SERVICE GUARANTEE. Inspect, consider, choose what you buy *BEFORE* you buy it . In the privacy of your own home. Fully computerised service guarantees prompt delivery and accurate accounting - no fiddly credit notes! Knowledgeable staff and 24-hour telephone and fax availability. We've mailed hundreds of thousands of selections. *Benefit NOW from our wealth of expertise.* We aim to deal with you more than once.

All offers subject to stock. If sold out we will substitute with equal or greater value.
Credit vouchers given for stamps of your choice. This offer valid until April 1998.

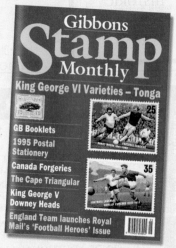

THE GREATEST RANGE OF GREAT BRITAIN ALBUMS

We offer probably the world's largest range of high quality albums to both display and protect your stamps. A very special range of tailor-made albums have been developed for today's discerning GB collector with supplements produced each January to keep you right up to date.

GB LUXURY HINGELESS ALBUMS

The very ultimate in quality, convenience and style.

- Three detailed volumes.
- Navy blue leatherette hingeless binders.
- Embossed with the national crest.
- Expertly arranged leaves containing illustrations.
- Clear protective mounts affixed in place.
- Features Issue dates, face values and colours.
- Each album housed in a neat matching slipcase.

Complete 3 volume GB Set

5284	Volume 1 (1840-1970)	£89.95
5285	Volume 2 (1970-1989)	£109.95
5290	Volume 3 (1990-1995)	£64.95
5284(SO)	Special Set Offer	£219.95

Special 2 volume QEII set

5546	Volume 1 (1952-1989)	£119.95
5581	Volume 2 (1990-1995)	£64.95
5546(SO)	Special Set Offer	£159.95

GB STANDARD ALBUM

The best value album currently available.

- Houses an entire collection in a single volume.
- Navy blue peg fitting binder with attractive cover design.
- Large page size and high capacity.
- Luxury slipcase.
- Selected stamp illustrations.
- Extra pages for popular phosphor band variations.

5284STSG	GB Standard (1840-1995)	£39.95
5285STB	Volume 2 Binder	£24.95

FREE 1996 SUPPLEMENT

– With all these albums